Between the Rivers

A History of Early Calaveras County, California

SECOND EDITION

O. Henry Mace

Paul Groh Press
Murphys, California

Second edition, second printing, 2002 by
Paul Groh Press
P.O. Box 303, Murphys, CA 95247
Telephone (209) 728-9207
Additonal copies available from the publisher.

ISBN 0-9720502-0-5

Originally published as a feature in the
Calaveras Enterprise
San Andreas, California

Cover: Produced by an unknown artist, and very much resembling
the Calaveras countryside, this woodcut
illustration entitled "To Him Who in the Love of Nature, "
accompanied the poem "Thanatospsis," by William Cullen Bryant
in Gems for the Fireside; O. H. Tiffany, editor; A. W. Mills, publisher; Tecumseh, Michigan; 1884.

This book is dedicated to those who have dedicated a portion of their lives to the history of Calaveras County, including:

Judge J. A. Smith, 1880 - 1962
Archie Stevenot, 1882 - 1968
Emmett P. Joy, 1902-1971
Richard Coke Wood, 1905 - 1979
Ray Garamendi, 1917 - 1991
and Willard P. Fuller, Jr.

Contents

List of Maps   **vi**

Foreword   **vii**

Preface   **viii**

1. The 48ers and Before Early explorers and settlers.   **1**

2. Government on the Move State capitols and county seats.   **4**

3. The Sad Legacy of the Gold Rush (Part I) Native Indians of the Mother Lode.   **7**

4. The Sad Legacy of the Gold Rush (Part II) The Me-wuk Indians of Calaveras.   **10**

5. Law & Disorder, Pride & Prejudice   Lynch law and the foreign element.   **13**

6. Fact and Fiction in the Mother Lode (Part I) The legend of Joaquin Murietta.   **16**

7. Fact and Fiction in the Mother Lode (Part II) The saga of Black Bart.   **19**

8. Fact and Fiction in the Mother Lode (Part III) Bret Hart on the Stanislaus.   **22**

9. Fact and Fiction in the Mother Lode (Part IV) Mark Twain in Angels Camp.   **25**

10. No Thanks Given Hard times and lonely holidays in camp.   **28**

11. Choose Your Poison Crossing the ithsmus.   **31**

12. A Most Perilous Journey (Part I) Westward by wagon train.   **34**

13. A Most Perilous Journey (Part II) Crossing the Sierra Nevada.   **37**

14. The Carriers (Part I)   The birth of the express business.   **40**

15. The Carriers (Part II) Wells Fargo takes command.   **43**

16. For a Pinch or a Dollar The camp store.   **45**

17. A Pleasant Success Commerce in Pleasant Springs.   **48**

18. The Phoenix of Oregon Gulch The ups and downs of Campo Seco.   **51**

19. They Came Too The women of the Gold Rush.   **54**

20. Watery Ghosts of the Mok Camps and crossings of the lower Mokelumne River.   **57**

21. High Expectations West Point, Mosquito Gulch, and surrounds.   **60**

22. Down the River of Skulls Early camps of the Calaveras River.   **63**

23. She's No Lady Jenny Lind and surrounds.   **66**

24. Mines, Miners, Mining & the Mother Lode (Part I) Placer mining.   **69**

25. Mines, Miners, Mining & the Mother Lode (Part II) The advent of modern mining methods.   **73**

26. Of Iron Rust & Iron Horses (Part I) The birth of Copperopolis.   **76**

27. Of Iron Rust & Iron Horses (Part II) Railroads and railroad towns come to Calaveras.   **80**

28. El Rio Guadalupe Laquisimes Appelamminy Estanislao The Stanislaus river and ferries.   **84**

29. The Crossing at Slumgullion Robinson's Ferry and Melones.   **87**

30. Beside Valley Trails Mines, roads, and ranches of the Salt Spring Valley.   **91**

31. Lodes of Business The hard facts of hard rock mining.   **95**

32. The Mother Lode's Fourth Estate Early newspapers of California and Calaveras.   **99**

33. From Saintly Beginnings San Andreas camp and town.   **102**

34. Tall Tales & a Golden Ledge (Part I) Henry Angel's creek and camp. **106**

35. Tall Tales & a Golden Ledge (Part II) Angels and Altaville. **109**

36. Fevers, Quacks, and Healers Medicine men and charlatans. **112**

37. Out of the Silent Wood The Murphy brothers leave their mark. **115**

38. The Hill A melting pot above the Mokelumne. **119**

39. Stars of the Stage The stagecoach and coachmen. **123**

40. The Mountain Mines Sheepranch, Mountain Ranch, and surrounds. **127**

41. Creekside Camps (Part I) Calaveritas, Fourth Crossing, and Dogtown. **130**

42. Creekside Camps (Part II) San Antone, San Domingo, and Cave City. **133**

43. The Producers (Part I) Calaveras County's major mining districts. **136**

44. The Producers (Part II) More money-making mines. **139**

45. Giants Along the High Trail (Part I) The Big Tree resort. **142**

46. Giants Along the High Trail (Part II) Roadside stops on the Big Tree Road. **145**

47. All the World in a Single Room Calaveras' one-room schools. **148**

Bibliography **152**

Index **154**

Maps

California Indian Tribe Locator **7**

Locations of Black Bart Robberies **21**

49er Routes across Panama **33**

49er Routes into California (Good general map of Gold Rush area of California) **38**

Upper and Lower Rich Gulch areas including Angier's Store at Pleasant Springs **50**

Gold Camps of the Lower Mokelumne area including Camanche, Campo Seco, etc. **58**

Glencoe, Railroad Flat, West Point, and surrounding area **62**

Gold camps of the lower Calaveras River - Jenny Lind to San Andreas **67**

Mother Lode locator showing other major Gold Belts of Calaveras County **70**

Southwest Calaveras County including Milton, Telegraph City, Copperopolis **78**

Stanislaus River camps and ferries **86**

Robinson's Ferry, Melones, Carson Hill, and surrounding area **88**

Salt Spring Valley - Peach Orchard to Hodson **92**

San Andreas and surrounds - North Branch to Third Crossing **103**

Angels Camp and surrounds including Cherokee and Albany Flat **111**

Angels Camp showing streets and mining claims **106**

Murphys and surrounds including Vallecito and Douglas Flat **118**

Mokelumne Hill and surrounding rivers, camps, and gulches **121**

Sheep Ranch, Mountain Ranch, and surrounding creeks, camps, and gulches **129**

Calaveritas, Fourth Crossing, Dogtown and surrounds **131**

Fricot City, San Antone, San Domingo, and surrounds **134**

Foreword to the Second Printing

Although a decade has past since this work was first published, it remains among only a handful of significant books on the subject of Calaveras County history. Sadly, much of the history between our rivers remains outside the general public's reach, as was the case for the years this volume was out of print. Considering the scope and quality of our historical inheritance, the unavailability of such works are a great loss to those of us who pursue knowledge of the people and events that came before us. That is why I have chosen to make *Between the Rivers* again available to the public.

If you think, as you read these pages, that our past is far more extraordinary than our present -- you're right. We will never have the chance to step into a world or onto a stage set with the myriad of opportunities and resources that were available to the native inhabitants and pioneers of Calaveras County whose stories are found herein.

Paul Groh, Publisher
Murphys, California
2002

Author's Preface

Many years ago (they're passing too quickly to count now), as a child, watching the movie version of H. G. Well's, "Time Traveler", I decided that when I grew up I wanted to be someone who traveled back in time to visit all the famous people, places, and events of the past. As I leafed through stacks of *Science* and *Mechanic's Illustrated* that predicted atomic powered cars by 1970 and personal space shuttles to moon-based condos by 1990, I felt sure that I would be dashing about the centuries by my 30th birthday. But with maturity came the sad realization that time travel was not only unlikely, but inherently illogical as well, so I chose the next best option -- I collected old photographs and prints, and I studied history.

Perhaps it was my interest in photography that drew me to concentrate my studies on 19th century America. Invented in the 1830s, the photographic process itself is very much a form of time machine. The photographs found throughout this book give the reader a chance to see people and places that have long since ceased to exist. The birth of America's political system, westward expansion, the industrial revolution, a devastating war with Mexico, and a terrible civil war can still be viewed today through photographs -- as can the Gold Rush.

With the obvious exception of the Civil War, no single event had a greater impact on 19th century America than the California Gold Rush. Knowing the impact of gold on today's society, imagine its effects in a time when every monetary denomination above 50¢ was represented by a gold coin. For most of America, a single $20 gold piece, called a Double Eagle, represented a month's work, and an ounce of raw gold sold for about $12. Believing that California streams were filled with tons of the precious metal, it is no wonder that men and women endured untold hardships in a mass exodus to that distant El Dorado.

Nowhere is the history of California's Gold Rush more thoroughly presented than in the history of Calaveras County. Evidence indicates that gold was mined there even before Marshall's discovery, and history records that the area was mined early and extensively by all methods. For the thousands of emigrants who made the arduous journey, the divergent wilderness landscape that would become Calaveras County provided riches for some, a new home for others, and a final resting place for many.

When I first approached the Calaveras Enterprise with the idea of a weekly column on the history of Calaveras County, they were skeptically receptive. Previous articles on people and events from the county's past had always been well-received, but the Enterprise is, after all, a newspaper, and old news is no longer news. But my intention was not so much to inform, as to entertain and enlighten, and, judging from my mail and from requests for back issues of the column, I must have succeeded to some degree. But as the work progressed, and as I scampered up and down highways 49 and 16 in search of Calaveras' roots, I began to see the necessity for a truly accurate and objective county history. The subjects became more specific and the pursuit for facts more determined.

Presented here in book form, the 47 installments of "Between the Rivers" represent the most accurate and thorough history of Calaveras County published to date -- to which I quickly add that it is a history far from complete, which no doubt contains a few minor inaccuracies. Regardless, I am confident that this chronicle of Calaveras' "golden years" is, and will remain both a valuable resource for historians and an entertaining, enjoyable addition to any library.

So many people provided invaluable assistance in the writing of these articles that I hesitate to attempt to acknowledge them for fear of leaving someone out. Should that happen, I can only assure that individual that their name is brightly highlighted somewhere in my erratic mental Rolodex.

Nearly every *Enterprise* employee (some of which have moved on to other callings), has provided friendly assistance in some form. Special thanks go to former editors **Sandie Cuneo**, who saw merit in my methods, and **Carol Cook**, whose support was invaluable and who always made me feel appreciated (writers cherish back-pats). **Craig Koscho** was also helpful and accommodating in regard to this and other ongoing projects.

My thanks to publishers **Lois and Harold Truett** for providing access to *Enterprise* files essential to the production of this book. Also, I have no doubt that **Deborah Mullen**'s wonderful layouts of my original articles did much to enhance their reader appeal.

Producing a different historical essay each week required quick access to well-organized and accurate archival records. This book would never have been possible without the assistance of **Dee Tipton** and the files of the **Calaveras Historical Society**, and **Lorraine Kennedy** and the files of the **Calaveras County Archives**. Amador County archivist and author **Larry Cenotto** provided valuable details about Calaveras County's early years, as well as access to related documents in the Amador archives. My sincere appreciation to **Bill Fuller** for reviewing and correcting mining-related material. Mr. Fuller's previously published articles and essays were a superb resource as well.

Special thanks go to **Judith Marvin** at Foothill Resource Associates for allowing me access to her extensive historical files, for permitting me to regularly interrupt her work day to quiz her on names and locations, for guiding me to historic sites, for editing this book, and for her friendship.

A big thank you goes to my wife Kathryn, who spent endless hours in front of the computer screen formatting and manipulating text and photos originally intended for a newspaper format so that they would fit comfortably into a book.

Finally, thank you to my readers, whose appreciativeness and support are my greatest reward.
    O.H.M.

1
The 48ers and Before

OOK at a map of the Central Mother Lode, and you'll notice that the north and south boundaries of the various counties are determined by their most obvious geographical features, the rivers. It is highly fitting that these waterways are used to indicate those boundaries, since they were the first "trails" and landmarks used by the Indians, and they guided the first white explorers of the region, perhaps as early as 1806. In that year, the Spanish military officer Gabriel Moraga began a series of explorations (more properly called "campaigns", as we shall see) into California's Central Valley and the Sierra Foothills.

Until the 1800s, the area of California settled by Spaniards was generally limited to that section of the coast running from San Diego to San Francisco. The most easterly settlement was Soledad, southeast of Monterey some 35 miles and still only about 25 miles from the Pacific. There had been a few expeditions into the interior, primarily through the Mojave Desert, and only as far north as the Kern river. The vast and fertile interior valley which lay between the coastal mountains and the Sierra Foothills was designated on maps of the period as "tierra incognita" -- unknown land.

As the 19th century began, there were only some two dozen private ranchos in California, many of which were near Monterey. As farms and pueblos began to spring up farther inland, they fell prey to bands of marauding Indian tribes who ranged far from their villages along the San Joaquin River and its tributaries. Gabriel Moraga organized over forty-five separate campaigns against these Indians during the period 1806 to 1811, several of which took him into the foothills of the Sierra Nevada. Moraga quickly learned that the Indians found their way back and forth simply by following the vast network of rivers and streams. The major rivers of this system -- the Kings, Merced, Tuolumne, Stanislaus, Calaveras, Mokelumne, Cosumnes, American, and Feather -- as well as Mariposa Creek, were all explored by Moraga. According to his diaries, the names bestowed on these rivers were the Kings, Merced, Dolores, Guadalupe, San Francisco (1806), Le Pasión, San Francisco (1808), Las Llagas, and Sacramento, respectively.

While Moraga has been called "the best soldier of his time", and a "ruthless indian fighter", it appears that some of his explorations were purely expeditionary -- searching for mission sites and mapping the locations of Indian villages. Regardless of the reason for his travels, he deserves credit for opening California's Central Valley, and until proven otherwise, it must be assumed that he was the first white man to visit what is now the Mother Lode region. It would be nearly 20 years before another would venture there.

[Note should be made at this point that, in this writer's opinion, "Mother Lode" refers to the area containing a gold-bearing geological formation which extends from Mariposa in the South, to Georgetown in the North. The Mother Lode "region" therefore, encompasses El Dorado, Amador, Calaveras, Tuolumne, and Mariposa Counties. Other counties may consider themselves part of Gold Country, but they are not part of the Mother Lode.]

When Mexico declared its independence in 1821, it marked a major change for the future of California. Liberal policies of the new Mexican Republic brought a massive increase in the number of land grants, making large parcels of California land available to all Mexicans of "good character". (Many of today's California land titles are based upon these early grants and often retain the original names.) At the same time, to the dismay of the Mexican government, Americans were finding their way to California, both by ship and from the great western plains through treacherous Sierra passes.

In 1826, trapper Jedediah Strong Smith led an expedition from northern Utah into southern California where he was arrested then expelled by Governor Echeandia. Smith gave the pretense of leaving by crossing over the Cahon Pass, then proceeded northward into the Central Valley. There, he organized a permanent camp from which he and his men conducted trapping expeditions along the Stanislaus river, which Smith called the Appelamminy. When he decided to leave California in May of 1827, this first American to set foot in the Mother Lode region also became the first white man to cross the Sierra Mountains. The arduous trip took over a month, but Smith rested only ten days before returning to Californian via his original southern route.

Except for a few skirmishes between Indians and the Spanish military, the Sierra and its foothills would see little more of the white man until the

The Middle Bar bridge, completed in 1852, was the second of several at that location on the Mokelumne River to be destroyed by floods. (Amador County Archives)

1840's. Beginning with the Bidwell-Bartleson party in 1841, a number of American emigrants entered California through the dangerous snow-covered passes of the High Sierra, then headed westward toward Sutter's Fort. Sutter had established his compound in what is now the city of Sacramento in 1840. The fort quickly became an entry point for overland immigrants and a supply station for trappers and explorers headed into the mountains or foothills. A number of trappers worked the rivers of the Mother Lode area prior to the discovery of gold, however, there is no specific documentation of these visitations. It is known that Sutter and a band of his Indian workers sawed lumber on a stream located in today's Amador County, inspiring the name Sutter Creek.

The rivers of the Sierra foothills run West, but the flood of 1848 had a decidedly eastern flow. It was a torrent of would-be millionaires who had heard that California rivers were lined with gold. Like most floods, it began as a trickle.

Two months after James Marshall picked up that first nugget from the American River at Sutter's Mill, Captain Charles Weber sent a party from Tuleberg (Stockton) to prospect the Sierra Foothills. They discovered gold on the Mokelumne and nearly every ravine northward to the American River. Later, some of Weber's men returned to the Mokelumne and established a camp in an area which now probably lies beneath the waters of the Camanche Reservoir. Still others continued southward to leave their names forever etched in the history of Calaveras County.

The earliest Calaveras County prospectors were undoubtedly Mexican, and the first of these appear to have been Don Antonio Coronel and Benito Perez of Los Angeles. They arrived on the Stanislaus in the spring of 1848, and found a large area of placer gold by secretly watching the local Indians prying nuggets from crevices in the rocks along the river bottom. Coronel, Perez, and the rest of their party pulled several thousand dollars worth of gold from the spot with only a few day's work. The gold nuggets, being the size of melon seeds, inspired the Mexicans to call the place Melones.

Late that same summer, a large group of miners left their slow-paying claim near Hangtown and headed southward, mining all of the streams along

This rusty metal span is all that is left to mark the once booming town of Middle Bar. Like the town and its many previous bridges, this landmark will soon be lost forever to the ravages of time.

the way with moderate success. At a point some five miles north of the Stanislaus River, the various members of the group went their separate ways. George and Henry Angel, John and Dan Murphy, and James Carson established mining camps along the streams which now bear their names.

At about the same time, on the Mokelumne River, Colonel Jonathan Stevenson and about 100 of his men had begun mining at Middle Bar. Part of this group would continue up the river to establish other camps along the "Mok" and its tributaries. The wide, but shallow Middle Bar soon became a favorite river crossing for northbound travelers, and with the later construction of a graded road and bridge, the town of Middle Bar grew to considerable size and importance. The town and many of its bridges have since been washed away in floods.

The 48ers were generally a well-behaved lot. They were mostly resident Californians who had left their regular jobs to make their riches in the gold-filled gulches of the Sierra Foothills. They worked side by side, friend or stranger, with seldom a disagreement or quarrel. There was gold enough for all, and it belonged to whoever plucked it from

where it lay. But that was 1848 -- the Gold Rush of '49 would quickly change all that.

By the Winter of 1848, the area that would be called the Mother Lode was taking shape. California now belonged to the United States and in two short years the republic would be divided into counties. El Dorado County would take its name from the Spanish legend of a golden land supposed to lie somewhere on the North American continent. Mariposa County used the name given by Moraga when he saw the abundant colorful butterflies of the area. The central counties would take the names of the rivers that gave them birth: the Calaveras and Tuolumne. Despite being cut in half by the controversial formation of Amador County in 1854, Calaveras would still become one of the largest gold producing counties in the state. And, with the help of a visitor from Missouri, it would also become one of the most famous tourist attractions in the Mother Lode. Then and now, Calaveras is a unique and independent part of Gold Country. One cannot help but attribute that independence to its location -- between the rivers.

2
Government on the Move

N May 12, 1846, the United States went to war against Mexico. American aggression in California was only one of many causes of that war, but when the Treaty of Guadalupe Hidalgo was signed in May of 1848, California became the property of the United States. The distant government in Washington made no plans for organizing the newly acquired territory, and California remained under military rule until the Constitutional Convention of September 1849. Among the many decisions made at that convention was the appointment of Peter H. Burnett as Governor and the locating of the territorial capital at San Jose. It was there that the first California legislature met, in a disorganized session that was later dubbed "The Legislature of a Thousand Drinks".

While San Jose provided more than enough libation for the varied assortment of district representatives (most of whom were store owners and businessmen), the pueblo was sorely lacking in lodging and shortly after that notorious first session the search for a new capital was on. There was no shortage of applicants (nearly every California city of any size was considered), but the long-time Californian General Mariano Vallejo suggested that a new city be built specifically for the purpose. In June of 1851, some nine months after California was admitted to the Union, a site was chosen on the Carquinez Straits between San Francisco and Sacramento, and the town of Vallejo became the new state capital.

Vallejo proved even less suitable as a government center than San Jose. There were no appropriate existing buildings to house either the state archives or the legislature, and no money in the fledgling state treasury to build them. Even so, the legislature did meet there and it was February of 1853 before a bill was passed making the town of Benicia the third ill-fated capital of California. Sitting on the mud flats of the Sacramento River just seven miles from Vallejo, Benicia offered a two-story brick building to house the government, but otherwise little more than the previous locations.

The 1854 legislature met up-river in Sacramento, now one of the largest cities in the state. They were greeted by a friendly but noisy procession of residents intent on making their city the final site of the state capital. The California law-makers were

Could this be the "Pleasant Valley" designated by the 1850 Legislature as Calaveras' first county seat? Probably not, but it was the site of Calaveras's first courthouse at Double Springs.

duly impressed, and the state archives made one last trip -- up the Sacramento River to its new and permanent home.

Meanwhile, the county of Calaveras was having similar problems, and probably for the same reason -- politics. Why would the state government keep moving the capital to unsuitable locations? The state government would make and enforce the rules and regulations that controlled mining and commerce, and the city that hosted that government would have their finger on the pulse of California. Also, a great deal of commerce would be created by the execution of state business.

In January of 1850, the California legislature was in heavy debate over the formation of county governments. When a bill to create those counties

The building that houses Mokelumne Hill's Hotel Leger was the home of Calaveras County Government during the middle part of the nineteenth century.

passed the Senate, it included a proposal for the county of Calaveras, lying between the Cosumnes and Stanislaus Rivers and stretching from the Costal Mountains east of San Francisco Bay to the Nevada border. The county seat would be Stockton.

State legislators had been in session since December of 1849, and were eager to conclude this important but tedious chore. So the territorial assembly quickly took up the Senate bill in mid-February. There were numerous proposed amendments by representatives intent on giving their districts the best possible advantage, and several of these centered around the formation of Calaveras County. Assemblyman Drury Baldwin, one of the few representatives of the mining district, introduced an amendment reducing Calaveras in size, and creating the additional county of San Joaquin. It also designated the county seat for Calaveras as Pleasant Valley, a small mining camp once located near today's Jenny Lind.

Why would Baldwin have designated this obscure camp as the county seat? From all appearances, he had only hours to draft his proposal securing a separate county for the mining district. It seems likely that, unable to decide which town would be best suited for the position, and afraid of alienating certain of his constituents, he simply chose the first name which entered his head. It would be easy enough to change the county seat after legislation

passed and he had time to choose a proper location. In fact, this is exactly what he did on April 15, 1850, when he introduced legislation changing the county seat to Double Springs, an equally obscure camp that had been the site of the first county meeting just two weeks earlier. To insure that no questions were asked, deeds relating to the sale of property in Double Springs included the words "or Pleasant Valley". There is no evidence that Double Springs was called Pleasant Valley before passage of the legislation designating that town as the Calaveras County Seat. Even so, as a result of this political manipulation, Double Springs inherited the county government.

There has been speculation that Baldwin meant to make Pleasant Springs, the county seat. This mining community northeast of Mokelumne Hill was discussed in the celebrated diary of John Doble who visited Pleasant Springs in February of 1852, two years after Calaveras County was created. The community was centered around a store, built in the fall of 1849 by Carl Grunsky, and taken over by D. L. Angier late in 1850. Exactly when the area came to be called Pleasant Springs is unknown, but it is highly unlikely that it would have been considered for the county seat prior to Angier's arrival.

Like California's first capital, Calaveras' first county seat did not even have time to settle-in before larger and more active communities, notably

Jackson and Mokelumne Hill, were vying to steal it away. In a controversial (and often highly romanticized) action, the county government was "shanghaied" to Jackson in 1851, only to be removed to Mokelumne Hill some nine months later by legislative action. Although Jackson took revenge by forming their own county in 1854, the Calaveras County Seat would remain at Mok Hill until 1866.

Even though an 1863 election resulted in the designation of San Andreas as county seat, it was not until a Supreme Court ruling of October 1866 that the county government was actually transferred to that city. Mok Hill had refused to recognize the results of the vote, citing that the returns were fraudulent and that San Andreas did not have the suitable buildings required by law. Even though county officials were forced to relocate their offices to the new seat of government, it was another year before a courthouse was completed in San Andreas.

Despite being born of political manipulation and built on early political deception, the state and county have fared well. Today, Sacramento and San Andreas seem to have settled in nicely as the final choice between four state capitals, and five county seats -- between the rivers.

Calaveras County's brick courthouse, its facade now hidden by the Hall of Records, was built in 1866 and restored in 1976. The rock wall shown here was built in the 1880's to enclose a prison for the county jail.

3
The Sad Legacy of the Gold Rush
Part One

I T was not gold that brought the first white man to the Mother Lode region -- it was the Indian. It was the Indian that brought friars who opened the missions; it was the Indian that brought the military to protect the missions; and, it was Indian raids on inland ranchos that brought that same military up the tributaries of the San Joaquin River into the foothills of the Sierra mountains. When California was discovered by Spain in the 1500s, it already had a population of over one quarter of a million people. One eighth of the total native population of the area now belonging to the United States lived in an area which comprised only one-twentieth of the country's land mass. That area is now the state of California.

The natives of California were not typical of other American Indians. They were generally peaceful, and led very basic lifestyles. For food, they collected acorns, hunted and fished. The home of a typical California Indian was tepee shaped, and covered in reeds, tule mats, or wooden strips instead of the skins typically used by familiar Plains Indians. The average village, with a population of 75 to 100, had a chief and a shaman (witch doctor). Three or four of these villages, lying close to one another, made up a tribelet. The villages of the tribelet were friendly and cooperative within themselves, but may or may not have been friendly with neighboring tribelets.

It has been estimated that over 125 different dialects were spoken among the Indians of California. In many cases, tribelets within walking distance of each other spoke languages so different that communication was nearly impossible. Those groups who shared a common language are often called "tribes", although they are not tribes in the sense of familiar Indian nations such as Sioux, Comanche, or Navaho. Interaction between local tribelets was rare, and even though they may have been part of the same linguistic group, their regional dialects may have had major differences. Most of those early languages have been lost forever to time, but many of the words remain as California place names. For example, the counties of Yolo, Yuba, Colusa, Modoc, Tehema, Tuolumne, Mono, Shasta, and Napa, all took their names from local Indian dialects

Many rivers, lakes, mountains, and other geographic features also owe their names to Indian languages.

When the first Spanish explorers traveled up the California coast, they were met at each stop by friendly, helpful natives who presented them with gifts of food and trinkets. The white man was greeted with outstretched hand and without fear or malice. But the Spanish saw only the savage in need of civilization. Had it been possible for these Indians to foresee the future, there is no doubt that they would have used every means available to drive the white man back into the sea.

It is interesting that the story of the near-obliteration of the California Indian began with such an unlikely group as the Franciscan Friars. In 1768, Spain's active monarch, Charles III, expelled the Jesuit priests from New Spain (Mexico) and replaced them with fourteen friars under the leadership of Father Junipero Serra. Their objective was to convert the friendly natives of Upper California and establish five missions. In fact, by 1823 there were 21 missions stretching from San Diego to Sonoma and the primary source of labor on those missions was the California Indian.

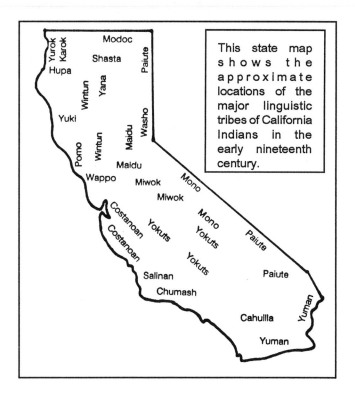

This state map shows the approximate locations of the major linguistic tribes of California Indians in the early nineteenth century.

The first true California Indians to be converted were the Diegueno (including the dialectic sub-groups, Ipai and Tipai), who lived in the area around the Mission San Diego de Alcala, established in 1769 by Father Serra. The Dieguenos did not convert easily, however, and in fact, the mission was attacked by natives just one month after it was opened. In 1775, the Dieguenos ransacked and burned the mission, killing Father Luis Jayme. Even so, this bold tribe was highly susceptible to "bribery", and with gifts of blankets, clothing, and trinkets, the friars eventually won out. By the 1800s, the Dieguenos had become servants of the mission and the Spanish military.

As the missionaries moved northward this trend continued and initial resistance by the local natives was soon neutralized by material enticements or military force. Many of the Indians then went to work for the mission or in the presidios, pueblos, and ranchos that soon sprang up around it. In reality, the Indian men were little more than slaves and the native women became playthings for the Spanish soldiers.

In addition to these abuses, the California Indian had been introduced to white man's diseases. A smallpox epidemic ran rampant through the mission Indians in 1829, and in 1838 the disease wiped out an estimated 60,000+ natives in the area north of San Francisco. Throughout the early 19th century,

the mortality rate was so high that only one out of ten Indian children could be expected to survive to adulthood. But the worst plight of the California Indian was yet to come--the Gold Rush of 1849.

In the mid-19th century, three dialectic groups ("tribes") of Indians occupied the area we now call the Mother Lode--the Maidu, who lived along the upper American and Cosumnes rivers; the Yokut (sometimes called Mariposan), who occupied the entire Central Valley, including the area around Stockton and the lower Calaveras and Tuolumne Rivers; and the Me-wuk, who resided along the entire western slope of the Sierra Nevada to the base of the foothills, from the southern San Joaquin River to the Cosumnes River in the North. Although these tribes and their various tribelets spoke district dialects, they were all members of the Penuitian linguistic family. While there were similarities in lifestyles, their individual cultures were unique.

It was probably a band of Yokut that Moraga followed into the Sierra foothills in the early 1800s. The "converted" Chumash Indians often ran away from the missions and sought refuge with the valley Yokuts. The aggressive Yokuts would also raid ranchos as far south as Santa Barbara, stealing cattle and horses. Moraga was sent to put and end to these raids and to locate Yokut villages so that the missionaries could attempt to convert the neophytes and recover runaway Chumash workers.

Most tribes of California indians relied heavily on acorn meal as their primary food staple. Acorns were crushed in a mortar, as shown here, or on community grinding rocks.

California Indians built typically shaped tee-pees but used reeds, tule mats or planks as a covering instead of animal skins. (Chaw'se State Park)

During the years prior to the gold rush, the Sierra Foothill region may have been visited infrequently by Spanish soldiers and American trappers who had a tendency to shoot any Indian on sight. But when gold-seekers began to invade the Mother Lode region early in the summer of 1848, they quickly learned, like the missionaries, that Indians could be put to good use. Indians knew where gold could be found, they knew where the best hunting grounds were, and, they knew their way around the unfamiliar foothill terrain. For the most part, the Indians confronted by the miners were Me-wuk, living in what is now Amador, Calaveras, Tuolumne and Mariposa counties. Peaceful and non-aggressive, the Me-wuk reluctantly accepted the arrival of the white man, unaware that his presence would eventually mean the near-annihilation of their tribe.

4
The Sad Legacy of
the Gold Rush
Part Two

OLD was discovered at Sutter's Mill in January, 1848. By May, additional gold discoveries had been made in nearby areas, and by June, over two thousand men were digging for gold. A month later, that figure had doubled. By the end of that year, there were so many men working the rivers and tributaries of the Sierra Foothills that the first year's gold yield was estimated at over ten million dollars. Then, on December 5, 1848, President Polk mentioned California gold in his presidential message. The rush was on!

When the year 1849 began, the estimated population of the California territory (exclusive of Indians) was 26,000. By July it had nearly doubled to 50,000. By the end of the year, there were an estimated 80,000 new arrivals, with the total population now topping 100,000 plus. Most of these people were then residing on lands that had belonged to California Indians for many centuries. Without notification of any kind to those rightful owners, the government of Mexico had turned over ownership of that land to the United States on February 2, 1848. In the eyes of both the Spanish and Americans, "savages" had no right to land ownership.

In the third issue of *Harper's Monthly Magazine*, dated August 1850, there is an article on the death of President Taylor, news of a cholera epidemic in Mexico, and this small item:

From California we have intelligence to the 17th of June. Difficulties had arisen with the Indians in different sections of the country, and several severe battles between them and detachments of U.S. troops had been fought. They grew mainly out of the hostile disposition of the Indians which is often excited and encouraged by the lawless conduct of the whites. Measures were in progress which, it was hoped, would restore quiet and security.

Just what these measures were is unknown, but they apparently had little effect, for in the March 1851 issue we find this entry:

From California our advices are to the 15th of January. Renewed difficulties have occurred with the Indians, and the general impression seemed to be that no friendly arrangement could be made with them. They demand the free use of their old hunt-ing grounds, and will listen to no proposition which involves their surrender. The settlers suffer grievously from their marauding incursions, and have been compelled to raise and arm companies to repel them. A serious and protracted war is apprehended.

Unfortunately for the Indian race, the "battles" and "incursions" referred to in these articles were generally sporadic and ineffective raids by small tribal groups. Longstanding differences between the various tribes as well as difficulty in communication kept them from taking a united stand. In California, as in other parts of the American West, the white man demanded that the Indian accept his invasion of their domain and change their way of life to his requirements. While a few aggressive tribes, such as Northern California's Modocs, continued to fight against white oppression throughout the 19th century, most California Indians were non-aggressive by nature and simply tried their best to avoid or accept the American presence. Among these were the Me-wuk of the Sierra Foothills.

It is estimated that before the gold rush period there were nearly twenty thousand Me-wuk living in the Mother Lode area. Like all Indians, they lived off the land. They gathered acorns, hunted for small game, and fished in nearby rivers. Their houses (called o'chum or u'mucha) were tepee shaped, consisting of a frame of poles covered with several layers of cedar strips or planks. They dressed in typical skin coverings which hung from the waist. The Me-wuk were well known for their use of soaproot, which could be found in abundance near most villages. Used for a variety of purposes, soaproot and other Me-wuk items were traded to neighboring Indians (primarily the Monos and Washoe) for salt, pumice, and skins not native to the Me-wuk area.

As with most California Indians, individual Mewuk villages were quite independent, though they did interact to a minor degree with neighboring clans of their tribelet, which usually consisted of no more than four villages. Village chiefs occasionally invited their neighbors to join in ritual ceremonies which often lasted three or four days. Primary among these events was the "Ceremony of the Dead", a mourning ritual for those village members who had passed away during the previous year.

This Me-wuk roundhouse, called a hung'e, is built over a large circular dugout used for ceremonies and large gatherings. (Chaw'se State Park)

Since most Me-wuk chiefs wielded little power, hosting these events was probably the highlight of their reign.

Ceremonies were held in the village roundhouse (hung'e), built by excavating a large round depression and covering it with a circular plank roof. Both men and women participated in these rites which often included screams and wailings that were described by the whites as "the most frightening sound ever heard".

The Me-wuk generally made every attempt to live with the ever-increasing white population. While they did occasionally trade gold for beef and whiskey, they tried their best to ignore the white man and continue with their traditional way of life. However, in his famous diary, prospector John Doble describes the Me-wuk participating in a ceremony at the village near Angier's store in 1852 as, "dressed in all manners of way from a shirt above to a full fine cloth dress with calf boots and high top beaver [hat] with a belt and revolver". It appears that, only four years after the first American settlers came to the Mother Lode region, some Indians were already dressing in white man's clothing. Doble also describes visiting a Me-wuk grinding rock (chaw'se) to watch the squaws crush and cook acorn meal, and attending a ceremony at the roundhouse where other Americans were coming and going apparently without any resistance from the Indians.

A large number of the Me-wuk who had this type of close contact with whites were soon overcome by white man's diseases, including cholera, measles, smallpox, and syphilis, among others. Shoved off of their hunting grounds and ever-tempted by

The Me-wuks were known for their superb basket making which, during the early years of white rule, provided many of them with their only means of support. (Amador County Archives)

the abundance of the white man's food and liquor, many Indians were shot or hung for stealing. Others were shot on sight by those who saw the Indians as little more than wild animals. Of the quarter-million Indians who roamed California before the arrival of the white man, an estimated 20,000 were members of the Me-wuk tribe. By 1856, there were only about 50,000 Indians remaining in the entire state, and just 3000 of those were Me-wuk.

It seems incredible that in just a few short decades the entire native population of a region as large as California could be virtually destroyed. The pathos of this tragedy is only accentuated by the continued plight of those remaining Indians who were herded onto poorly run reservations or given worthless lands as restitution for their mistreatment. It is due primarily to Indian pride and resourcefulness that tribal life is now seeing a resurgence in California and Indian children are being taught to understand and respect the ways of their ancestors. It is equally important, however, that the non-Indian population of California also learn understanding and respect for the proud race which once lived a simple life -- between the rivers.

5
Law & Disorder,
Pride & Prejudice

HILE the first gold-seekers who came to the Sierra Foothills in 1848 were primarily resident Californians, the 49ers generally were not. They were a mixed bag who came from the four corners of the Earth -- Missourians, Georgians, New Yorkers, Irish, Scotch, Australians, Chileans, Mexicans, and Chinese, to name just a few. When California became a state in 1850, three quarters of the population lived in the area from the Central Valley to the Nevada border. Over ninety percent of these people were new residents, and one-quarter of those were from foreign countries. Many came not only to seek their fortunes in the gold fields, but to escape from legal problems back home. It was a mixed bag that was about to explode.

When California entered the Union, it provided for local government and local law enforcement. But early elections, often marked by overt corruption, were little more than popularity contests. County sheriffs and justices of the peace seldom had any knowledge of the law, and in most cases didn't care to learn. In the gold camps, the miners themselves set down the laws and acted as judge, jury, and executioner. Although abuses were wide spread, the regulations that each camp made and enforced were a practical alternative to anarchy, and the penalties of ear cropping, branding, whipping, and hangings were certainly an effective crime deterrent.

The majority of miners, while they may have been Irish, Australian, or otherwise, considered themselves "free, white Americans" and made no attempt to hide their prejudices -- primarily against Mexicans (among whom Chileans, Peruvians, and other Spanish speaking immigrants were included), Indians, and the Chinese. A white man who raped an Indian maiden or Spanish señorita was more likely to receive congratulations than punishment. Even if he was brought to trial, most camps had instituted laws which disallowed the testimony of Chinese, Indians, or blacks. Despite the fact that thousands of Indian children were kidnapped and sold into slavery, there is little evidence that any of the white men who perpetrated these crimes were ever brought to justice.

When crimes were committed against whites, the nearest Indian, Chinaman, or Hispanic was the first suspect. If they were lucky enough to receive a trial, it might allow time for a legitimate suspect and motive to be found. Otherwise, they would most certainly receive the maximum penalty for the crime. It was not unusual for a Mexican to have his ears cut off and his head shaved for stealing, only to find out later that the real culprit was someone else. There would be no apologies or restitution. After all, he was only a "greaser" (just one of many derogatory terms which owe their origin to 19th century bigotry and racism).

In the early 1850s, some 50,000-plus Chinese came to California, primarily as cheap "indentured" labor for Chinese-owned placer mining companies. When the placer gold began to run out, these workers were in direct competition with displaced American miners for the few jobs provided by hydraulic and deep-rock mining. Nearly every mining town of size had a "Chinatown", and there were two noticeably large settlements, one in Weaverville, Trinity County, and another called Chinese Camp in Tuolumne County. Many Chinamen were members of a "tong", sort of a fraternal organization with its roots in Chinese political history. Rival tongs occasionally came to blows, to the delight and entertainment of the white miners. This occurred in Weaverville on July 15, 1852, and at Chinese Camp on September 26, 1856. While history calls them California's "Chinese Wars", neither lasted more than a few hours and casualties were few. Typifying the prejudices of the miners, a journalist for the *San Francisco Bulletin* wrote, "It was a very bad battle as so few were killed."

The Chinese were viewed as an "inferior race" -- unclean, heathenish, and generally sub-human. They smoked opium, and seemed addicted to gambling and prostitution. Their pigtails (called "cues"), an important social and religious symbol, became the source of much amusement for miners and torment for the Chinamen. Some towns even passed laws requiring them to be cut off, knowing that the Chinamen would rather leave than comply with such a law.

No one seemed to notice or care that the Chinese were the most resourceful people in the camps. Their businesses were well organized and run with an obvious pride for work well done. They successfully worked claims deserted by white miners, squeezing out every last flake of gold. Despite the fact that the Chinese were overcharged for everything they

In this early illustration from the gold fields, a store owner dashes in to protect his property when a fight breaks out between miners and gamblers. (From a 19th Century Harper's Magazine)

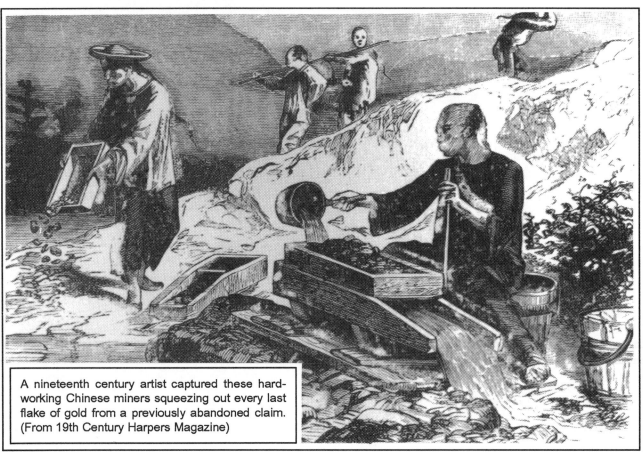

A nineteenth century artist captured these hard-working Chinese miners squeezing out every last flake of gold from a previously abandoned claim. (From 19th Century Harpers Magazine)

purchased, they survived, moderately prospered, and were responsible for nearly 25% of the state's tax revenues during the Gold Rush period. In Calaveras County, the 1860 census showed that 23% of the county was Chinese -- compared to 16% statewide.

Wherever there is money, there are crooks and the Mother Lode had its fair share. Cheats, con men, thieves, and a variety of scoundrels quickly invaded every camp, town, and settlement. Lured by the stories of quick riches, honest men who failed to realize their dreams in the gold fields turned to the bottle -- then to crime. In most camps, the crime of theft was punishable by whipping -- 40 lashes. Theft of more than $100 was punishable by death. Miner John Bucroft of Murphys Camp wrote a short but now famous letter which read:

I take the opportunity of writing these few lines to you, hoping to find you in good health. Me and Charley is sentenced to be hung today at 5 o'clock for a robbery. Goodbye. Give my best to Frank and Sam and Church.

Nearly every settlement in the Mother Lode had a store, and nearly every store had a monte dealer. Despite the fact that the odds in this card game were overwhelmingly in favor of the house, most miners were easily induced to play. Often the dealer would take in more gold dust in one night then an average miner could pan in a week. The store also served as hotel and saloon. If the camp were especially lucky, a "lady of delights" might also reside there. Although both gambling and prostitution were legal, a drunk or unwary miner was easy prey for cheats and hustlers. Many "floozies" were quite adept at acquiring a miner's entire fortune without ever performing the expected service. When caught, her punishment, if any, would be light, for a single woman in Gold Country was as valuable as gold itself.

There were, of course, legitimate gamblers who were as practiced at their profession as any miner, storekeeper, or prostitute. They relied heavily upon a knowledge of mathematics and the odds of the game. The best gamblers, like the best miners, were those with vast experience. Unlike the miner, the gambler dressed in the finest "duds", with a satin vest and crisp, blocked hat. His hands were uncallused, and his manners were generally that of a gentleman. While there were exceptions, the typical professional gambler was honest. Confident in his own abilities and armed with favorable odds, he had no reason to be otherwise.

The perpetrators of organized thievery, if continuously successful, soon became the basis for legend (an intermingling of fact and fiction, with little of the former and much of the latter). And there were those who discovered that there was gold in Mother Lode legend as well as in Mother Lode streams. In the next few chapters, we'll take a look at Murietta and Bart...Twain and Harte, dealers in fact and fiction -- between the rivers.

6
Fact and Fiction in the Mother Lode
Part One

 NE of the major problems a historian must overcome is the tendency of people to believe wide-spread and long-standing legends as fact. And nowhere is this a greater problem than in the history of America's western frontier, starting with Davy Crockett and Daniel Boone and continuing through Wyatt Earp and Billy the Kid. A fictional character is just that, the product of someone's imagination. But a real person who is fictionalized is still a real person and many people believe that if the person is real than so are the stories that are written about them. Numerous supposedly historical figures were created by writers who specialized in this type of sensational fiction popularized by the notorious "dime novel". Many of these "legends" tried hard to live up to the readers' expectations—others tried hard to live it down.

A historian, when researching and writing about a particular historical figure, must take all stories into account, then either prove or disprove them, culling out only the "facts". In many cases, the facts are few. When writing about these individuals the historian may include the various unproven accounts, taking great care to indicate that they are unsubstantiated. When a noted historian fails to do this, he or she is simply fueling the fire of legend. Such is the case with the story of the Mother Lode's legendary bandit, Joaquin Murietta.

On May 11, 1853, California Governor John Bigler signed a legislative act authorizing the organization of a band of California Rangers under the command of Captain Harry Love. Their purpose, to capture or kill a "party or gang of robbers commanded by the five Joaquins", specified as Joaquin Botellier, Joaquin Carrillo, Joaquin Murieta, Joaquin Ocomorenia, and Joaquin Valenzuela. These men were believed to be responsible for the majority of all cattle rustling, robberies, and murders perpetrated in the Mother Lode region since 1850.

In July of 1853, a group of Love's rangers came across a group of Mexican men near Panoche Pass in San Benito County. (This pass lies some 50 miles from Monterey, in the Costal Mountains – over 100 miles from the Mother Lode area.) A confrontation

occurred, and two of the Mexicans were killed. The rangers cut off the hand of one and the head of the other, and later placed them in jars of alcohol to preserve them. They claimed the badly mutilated hand to be that of the notorious "Three-fingered Jack", and the head to be that of Joaquin Murieta.

Despite the fact that no positive identification of the detached appendages could be made–and despite the fact that only one Joaquin was alleged to have been killed, the governor paid a reward of $1000 to Captain Love, and the matter was considered settled. (Later, apparently for no logical reason, the legislature approved an additional $5000 bonus.) Those, are the facts.

In 1854, a San Francisco journalist who wrote under the pen-name "Yellow Bird", published a sensational and highly fictional account of the life of Joaquin Murieta. It tells of a handsome young Mexican whose wife is raped by miners, and whose brother is hung for a crime he didn't commit. As a result of these atrocities, the young Joaquin swears vengeance on all Americans, forms a band of "cutthroats", and proceeds to rain havoc on the hated "Yankees". At least until he is captured and decapitated by Love's rangers. That, is the legend.

The alleged head of Joaquin began a tour of California, being displayed at only the finest establishments specializing in the showing of dismembered limbs. Many viewing the pickled part nodded knowingly, "Yes, that's Joaquin, I worked next to him in the mines." A young señorita, claiming to be Murieta's sister, denied that the head was that of her famous brother bandito. That, was the sideshow.

Throughout Gold Country, the Murieta legend grew and flourished. It seems that the dashing Joaquin stayed in every hotel, drank in every bar, and robbed every town from Grass Valley to Mariposa and beyond–sometimes all in the same day. Even the author of Amador's county history, J.D. Mason, got into the act when he wrote in 1881, "This renowned bandit commenced his career in this county." He then proceeds to give accounts of Joaquin stealing a horse and killing the owner of a "public house" in 1852.

In Calaveras County, the Joaquin legend was represented by the one and only photograph ever

A jar containing the alleged head of Joaquin was displayed at various locations throughout California

taken of the bandit. Frequently published over the years, the original image now rests in a display case at the Old Timer's Museum in Murphys. The story goes that the picture is a daguerreotype given to Constable Ben Marshall who came to Murieta's aid during a run-in with whites at a gambling tent in Murphys. It is true that in 1850, when this incident supposedly occurred, portraits were taken by the daguerreotype process, a method that produced a distinctive image on a silver-coated copper plate. The picture in question, unfortunately, is not a daguerreotype (assuming that the one on display in Murphys is the original). It is either an ambrotype or tintype, two similar processes that were invented in 1854 and 1856, respectively. If it could be proven that this image was actually Joaquin Murieta, photographed a year or more after his alleged demise, it would also be proof that Captain Love received an unjust reward. As for the Marshall story, it is not unlikely that the future sheriff of Calaveras County met and befriended a man who called himself Joaquin or even Murieta. Whether or not this was *the* Joaquin Murieta we will never know.

It is a fact that California's Mexican population was generally badly mistreated by Americans and as a result of this mistreatment, many of them turned to a life of often vicious crime. It is a fact that many of these criminals bore the name Joaquin and

it is likely that many more took that name as the Murieta legend grew. When the "Five Joaquins" act passed the state legislature in 1853, the appointed rangers were cautioned that there were numerous "respectable citizens" who bore the same names, including a Judge Joaquin Carrillo. Was there, then, a real Joaquin Murieta? Probably. Was he the "legendary" Murieta? Probably not. While the legend has basis in fact, it has been proven to be mostly fiction.

Such is not the case with one of the Mother Lode's later legendary figures.

On a cool November afternoon in 1883, two men were introduced to each other near a tobacco shop on Bush Street in San Francisco. One was introduced as Charles Bolton, the other as Mr. Hamilton. The latter gentleman's real name was Harry Morse, special detective for Wells Fargo and Company. It was his belief that the gentleman to whom he had just been introduced was not a mine owner, as his near acquaintances believed, but an accomplished stage robber. Morse later described Bolton:

"He was elegantly dressed, carrying a little cane. He wore a natty little derby hat, a diamond pin, a large diamond ring on his little finger, and a heavy gold watch and chain. He was about five feet eight inches in height, straight as an arrow, broad-shouldered, with deep-sunken bright blue eyes, high

Joaquin's second in command was the viciously ruthless caballero called "Three-Fingered Jack"

cheekbones, and a large handsome grey moustache and imperial, the rest clean shaven. One would have taken him for a gentleman who had made a fortune and was enjoying it."

Morse's final observation in that statement would prove to be overwhelmingly accurate.

Evidence at the scene of a stage coach robbery in Calaveras County had led Detective Morse to suspect Bolton of the theft. The bandit had made off with 228 ounces of gold amalgam -- the finished product of the gold recovery process for deep rock mines that looks much like a golden sponge. During those years, the gold amalgam was shipped to San Francisco for sale to the U.S. Mint. This particular shipment came from the Patterson Mine in Tuolumne County. Even if the amount of the theft had not been so large, Morse would have been called in, for he was not after just any bandit -- he was specifically hired to track down the legendary Black Bart!

WILL BE EXHIBITED
FOR ONE DAY ONLY!

AT THE STOCKTON HOUSE!
THIS DAY, AUG 12, 9 A.M., UNTIL 6 P.M.

THE HEAD
Of the renowned Bandit!

JOAQUIN!
—— AND THE ——
HAND OF THREE FINGERED JACK!
THE NOTORIOUS ROBBER AND MURDERER.

"JOAQUIN" and "THREE-FINGERED JACK" were captured by the *State Rangers*, under the command of Capt. Harry Love, at the Arroya Cantina, July 24th. No reasonable doubt can be entertained in regard to the identification of the head now on exhibition, as being that of the notorious robber, Joaquin Murietta, as it has been recognized by hundreds of persons who have formerly seen him.

7
Fact and Fiction in the Mother Lode
Part Two

HE saga of the legendary Black Bart has considerable basis in fact, unlike many other notable outlaws of the Old West. These facts come from the well-kept files of Wells Fargo, and from contemporary eyewitness accounts. Still, there are many important details that are seldom published, and many popular accounts of the "gentleman bandit" are highly sensationalized. Of course, without sensationalism there would be no legends.

Here are the facts, according to Wells Fargo: On November 3, 1883, the stage from Sonora to Milton was robbed by a bandit wearing a flour sack mask. Due to being fired upon by the stage driver and/or a young passenger, the bandit left behind a number of clues in his haste, one of which was a handkerchief with a laundry mark. By tracing this mark, investigators determined that a San Francisco resident named Charles Bolton was responsible for the crime. He was arrested in that city about two weeks after the robbery. After a long period of questioning, and upon being presented with the overwhelming evidence of his guilt, Mr. Bolton confessed to the crime. Despite the fact that Bolton also admitted to having committed 27 other robberies, he pleaded guilty to only the 28th and last. On November 17th, 1883, he was sentenced by a Superior Court Judge at San Andreas to six years in San Quentin State Prison. No additional charges were brought.

The fourth robbery to which Bolton had confessed, but for which he was never tried, occurred August 3rd, 1877. The stage was in route from Point Arena (see map) to Duncan Mills. It was at this robbery that Bolton decided to leave his now famous poem signed "Black Bart, the PO-8". An extended version was left at his next robbery on July 25th of the following year. It is printed here for those few who may not have yet had the privilege (Where have you been?) of reading its hackneyed, doggerel lines:

Here I lay me down to sleep
To wait the coming morrow,
Perhaps success, perhaps defeat,
And everlasting sorrow.

I've looked long and hard for bread,
For honor and for riches;
But on my toes too long you've tred,
You fine-haired sons of bitches.

Let come what will, I'll try it on,
My condition can't be worse;
And if there's money in that box
'Tis munny in my purse.

Although poems were left only at these two robberies, there were other trademarks of a Black Bart heist -- the unusual flour sack mask, and the robber's distinctive deep voice which almost always commanded, "Throw down the box." He also made every attempt to avoid violence or injury to his victims and always treated any ladies who were present with utmost courtesy.

From these facts it is easy to see how the Black Bart legend was born. In the eyes of the press, however, Bolton did not live up to Bart. It was discovered that the real man behind the legend was

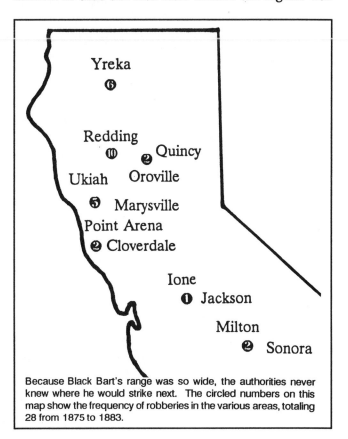

Because Black Bart's range was so wide, the authorities never knew where he would strike next. The circled numbers on this map show the frequency of robberies in the various areas, totaling 28 from 1875 to 1883.

Bart carefully chose the locations of his robberies so that the stage driver had no option but to stop and meet his demands. (From 19th Century Harpers Magazine)

Charles E. Boles, a former Sergeant in the Illinois Volunteer Infantry with a wife and children in Hannibal, Missouri. He had established the Bolton alias, in part, to protect his family should he be caught. The newspapers printed a variety of stories, based primarily on unsubstantiated speculation. Among the most widely related is the theory that Wells Fargo made a deal with Bolton to the effect that if he would plead guilty to the final robbery, return the stolen property from that robbery, and promise not to rob any more of their stages, they would file no further charges and even pay him a yearly pension.

In light of the overwhelming evidence against Bolton -- his handkerchief found at the scene, witnesses who identified him as having been in the area, and his lack of an alibi -- it seems likely that he would have jumped at the deal. But why would Wells Fargo make such an offer? If there really was such a bargain, one can only speculate that their investigators were simply satisfied with having Black Bart behind bars and wanted the affair brought to a quick and clean finish. As for the pension, there is no evidence that Bolton (Boles continued to use this alias during and after his incarceration) ever received any payments from Wells Fargo. Company officials flatly denied that such a deal was ever made. In fact, the company had Bolton watched following his release from San Quentin, and after losing track of him, issued a warning to their agents that Black Bart might again be back in business.

Whatever happened to Charles Boles? There are many theories, and few facts. He was released from San Quentin prison on January 21, 1888. Met by a barrage of reporters, he said little, only that he would commit no further crimes. He wrote to his wife that he would not be returning home, although he someday wished to. He stayed in San Francisco for a few days, then headed South. Wells Fargo agents reported sighting him in Modesto, Merced, and Madera. On February 28, 1888, Boles checked into a hotel in Visalia under the name M. Moore. He left his bag with the hotel clerk, but never returned for it. The bag was sent to Wells Fargo. Among its contents was a pair of shirt cuffs bearing Bolton's now familiar laundry mark. Although there were numerous reports and stories of the further exploits of Black Bart, there is no solid evidence that he was ever seen again. The 1892 city directory for Hannibal, Missouri contains the listing: *Mrs. Mary Boles, Widow of Charles E. Boles.* At least in the eyes of his wife -- Black Bart was dead.

In the years that followed Charles Bolton's arrest, many highly fictitious accounts of his long and distinguished career were written. Many of these stories are repeated today as truth. But let's look at the facts: Black Bart never fired a shot in his entire career as a bandit. He robbed only Wells Fargo stages, but never stole from passengers -- taking only the strong box and possibly the mail bags. He operated over a wide area of the state of California, carefully studying the lay of the land and planning both the robbery and his escape to the last detail. The man behind the alias was a quiet, dapper gentleman with a mysterious background and a flair for humor and irony. With facts like these, who needs fiction?

Just as fiction is drawn from fact, so can fact be drawn from fiction. It is from the writings of California's early journalists and authors that we get the most vivid picture of life in the land of 49ers. Many of these men and women did not come to the gold fields as writers. Their change of occupation may have come as the result of a need to express to others the sights and sounds of their adventure, or simply as a last attempt at survival in a land where their hopes and dreams seemed to have quickly been dashed.

Alias Black Bart - Newspapers ran this etching of Charles Bolton in 1883. It was based on a photograph ordered by Wells Fargo shortly after his arrest. (Courtesy of Calaveras County Historical Society)

In 1854, a young New Yorker arrived in San Francisco to join his mother, who had married an Oakland politician. He was 17 years old, overly well-dressed, and somewhat effeminate in his actions -- not at all the type of person one would expect to survive in the land of outlaws and argonauts. But for four years, the young lad stumbled his way along in a variety of jobs, and while he was never particularly successful at anything he attempted, he did manage to survive until 1858, when he was hired as a printer's "devil" (errand boy). He began writing poetry and small articles and soon it seemed he had found his niche in California as writer and junior editor for the Northern Californian, a weekly newspaper published on Humboldt Bay. But in 1860, the young man wrote an article that could have put an end to his career and his life -- and the world would never have known the name Bret Harte.

8
Fact and Fiction in the Mother Lode
Part Three

RANCIS B. Hart was born in 1836, the second son of a New York school teacher. During the early part of his life, he was a frail child who made few friends and was always considered mature for his age. He learned to read at the age of four and it became his favorite pastime. While he did not do especially well in school, his love for reading afforded him an extensive self-education. When his father changed the spelling of the family's last name to put an end to mix-ups with another Hart family, he began signing his name, Frank B. Harte. The "B" stood for Brett, his grandmother's maiden name.

[At this point the reader should be made aware that Bret Harte has been this writer's hero and idol since childhood. It is with that acknowledgement, but without apology, that this wholly factual but obviously "slanted" biography is presented. OHM]

Frank Harte began writing poetry at age 10, shortly after his father's untimely death. At age 11, one of his poems, "Autumn Musings", was printed in the *Sunday Morning Atlas* newspaper. While it would be many years before he would again see his name in print, he never forgot the thrill of being "published" for the first time.

When the California Gold Rush began, Frank Harte was only 12 years old. He understood the excitement -- he and his older brother, Henry, liked to hang around the docks, watching the ships prepare to sail for San Francisco. But when Henry himself left for the gold fields in 1850, young Frank was content to stay behind, working as a clerk and reading his books. By age 15, he had outgrown his sickliness and was becoming well-known in social circles as a "dapper" dresser. He seldom missed attending lectures by the great orators of the day, including Ralph Waldo Emerson.

It was at this time that his mother made the acquaintance of an Oakland businessman named Colonel Williams. Within a few months they were married and on their way to California. Frank and his sister were to follow after she had completed her term at school. They began their journey in February, 1854. While it would be 14 years before the name of Bret Harte would receive world-wide recognition as the chief storyteller of pioneer California, the early travels and experiences of young Frank Harte would play a major role in creating that fame. Ironically, his adventures began when he and his sister boarded a steamship named "The Star of the West".

The Star took them as far as Nicaragua, where they crossed over to the Pacific Ocean via river boat, wagon, and mule--a spectacular journey for two youngsters who had never been outside the city. On the western coast, they stayed overnight in a rat-infested hotel before boarding an overcrowded ship called the "Brother Jonathan", bound for San Francisco. The ship broke down several times along the way, once in sight of a Mexican town in which a revolution was being fought, and the ship arrived so late in San Francisco that it had already been feared lost.

During his first few months in California, Frank befriended a young Mexican vaquero and learned about life on a Spanish rancho. He visited a gambling hall and due to inexperience, won and lost $300 in only a few minutes. Once, he had breakfast with a professional gambler who was on his way to a duel which, Frank found out later, he did not survive. Without knowing it, he was already collecting a cast of characters and story lines for the future Bret Harte. He was also unaware that his greatest adventure was just around the corner.

Frank had tried a number of jobs in the San Francisco area, including working as a clerk in a drug store where he accidently gave out the wrong prescription and almost killed someone. It seemed he just couldn't find his niche. Late in 1854, Colonel Williams told Frank about a teaching job that was available at a small mining camp in the foothills. He applied for the position, and despite his lack of teaching credentials, Frank was hired to instruct thirty-two pupils for a salary of $48 per month.

Everything went well through the winter, but in May of 1855 the placer claims began to play out and attendance at the school was down to nine pupils. Since Frank was paid "per student" it was no longer worth his while to stay.

While in San Francisco, Frank had met a miner from Robinson's Ferry on the Stanislaus River in

Calaveras County. He decided that this might be a good time to look the gentleman up and perhaps try his own luck at prospecting for gold. Having spent most of his salary on clothes, it was necessary to make the 40-mile trip on foot. Still a "dapper" dresser, Frank had only tight-fitting patent leather shoes in which to make the journey. By the time he reached his destination, he had a much greater appreciation for the miner's "functional" attire.

While the little town in which Frank Harte taught has never been positively identified, it can be determined from his personal accounts of the journey that the town lay approximately 40 miles south/southeast of Robinson's Ferry, in the lower elevations of the foothills. The town of La Grange, in the corner of Stanislaus County has been mentioned as a possibility, and both the history of the town and its surrounding terrain fit Harte's description. Whatever the town was called, Harte drew from it many of the characters for his stories, including "M'liss", "Cressy", and "A Tale of Three Truants". He also frequently used the name "Red Mountain" -- for whatever conjecture may be drawn from it, there is a Red Mountain near La Grange. Perhaps most notably, one of his more obscure stories was titled "Guardians of La Grange".

After two and one-half days of walking over rough countryside, Frank Harte arrived on a cliff overlooking the Stanislaus River and the town of Robinson's Ferry on the other side. Those who have seen this area of the Stanislaus (east of the highway 49 crossing) prior to its inundation by the New Melones Reservoir, can better visualize Harte's description of what lay before him:

"*. . . . the canyon of the Stanislaus River, which roared over its boulders and ledges at the bottom. Beyond it and on a bench or shelf a hundred feet or so above it, there lay a clutter of white tents, with a few frame shacks in the midst of what passed for a business center.*"

The miner that Frank had met in San Francisco was gone, but his easy-going former partners offered a share of their claim to Harte, who cautiously accepted it and worked it with some success over the next few months. At the Gum Tree Claim in Calaveras County, Frank Harte learned all about gold mining and the life of a miner. Through visits to local mining towns, he discovered the variety of people who gave the mining camps their color. Frank never gained any great wealth from his claim, but he did gain a wealth of material for his future life's work. Without ever knowing it, Frank Harte had struck it rich in Calaveras County.

Known in youth for his stylish attire and colorful neckties, Bret Harte's tastes began to mellow in his older years as this portrait shows.

In the Winter of 1855, the partnership was dissolved and the Gum Tree abandoned. While his former partners moved northward to richer diggings, Frank returned to San Francisco. Although he spent only one year in Gold Country, from his later stories one would have thought that he had lived a lifetime there.

Over the next two years Frank worked again as a druggist (being much more careful this time), taught school again (this time as a private tutor), and rode shotgun for Wells Fargo (two months after he was fired, his replacement was shot by a bandit). He began to write regularly, and in 1857, his short poem entitled "The Valentine" was published in San Francisco by the *Golden Era*. Not yet sure he wanted the readers to know who he was, he signed it simply "Bret".

Frank Harte got his first big break in the Winter of 1858 when he was hired by the newly opened *Northern Californian*, a four-page weekly paper in Union, California, near Eureka. Though he began as an errand boy and typesetter, he quickly rose to the title of junior editor and was often left in charge of the paper in the absence of the editor.

Although this 1875 school house in LaGrange was built long after Bret Harte taught in the area, its adobe predecessor may have been where he first taught school.

This was the case in February of 1860, when Frank received word that a group of whites had attacked and killed sixty nearby peaceful Indians, mostly women and children. Outraged by the news, Frank wrote and published a scorching article condemning the massacre and calling the perpetrators "butchers". Unfortunately, this was not the opinion of the majority of the town. In fear of his life, and to save the newspaper from losing all of its advertisers, Frank departed again for San Francisco.

At was at this time that things began to change for the better. He was quickly hired as a typesetter by the *Golden Era* and began writing both poetry and prose under the pen name Bret Harte. One of these articles was read by the wife of the famous western explorer John C. Fremont, who was so impressed by it that she actually went to the offices of the paper to meet its author. From that day, the Fremonts and others of their social circle were both fans and mentors of Bret Harte. Over the next few years, with their help, he would write for the *Atlantic Monthly*, the *San Francisco Bulletin*, the *Alta California*, and eventually become associate editor of the *Californian*.

By 1867, Harte had enough good work to produce two bound volumes, one poetry and the other prose. He accepted editorship of a new paper called the *Overland Monthly*, and for its premier issue wrote the story that would bring him world-wide fame, "The Luck of Roaring Camp." In 1869, he followed with his equally successful "Outcasts of Poker Flat." Both of these stories were based on people and places he visited while mining in Calaveras County. His trip to the gold fields had yielded little gold -- now, nearly 15 years later, the experience was yielding nuggets.

From 1855 until his death in 1902, Bret Harte produced eight novels, fifteen novelettes, two hundred short stories, and more than one thousand poems and lesser works. His stories were read and praised around the world as "the most original American writings of the century". Then and now, Harte's stories take us into the heart of early California. Through his unsurpassed descriptive style, we see the best and the worst that people can be -- and its not always a happy sight. In fact, Harte's stories almost never have a happy ending -- and *there*, is the real truth in his fiction.

9
Fact and Fiction in
the Mother Lode
Conclusion

HEN the American Civil War began, the state of Missouri was probably the most split state in the Union. Generally speaking, people south of the Missouri River sided with the Confederacy, those north of the river mostly sided with the Federals. Even though the town of Hannibal lay on the Mississippi River well north of its intersection with the Missouri, a number of its young men joined the Southern cause. Among them was 25 year old riverboat pilot Samuel Clemens.

During the early years of the war, many Confederate units were completely self-organized and operated entirely independent of the Confederate government. Such was the case with Marion's Rangers, in which Clemens was elected Second Lieutenant despite having absolutely no military experience. It didn't take long for him to realize that he wasn't cut out for the job. He resigned his commission after only a few weeks, and to avoid further involvement in a war for which he had no stomach, Sam set out for the Nevada Territory with his brother, Orion.

Over the next three years, Sam worked (and lounged) at various positions, eventually settling as a writer for the *Territorial Enterprise* in Virginia City. He frequented a bar there, called the Old Corner Saloon, where he would order a drink for himself and a friend by asking the bartender to "mark twain," meaning to make two marks on the blackboard back of the bar. This was how the proprietor kept their tab for the evening. Clemens first picked up the term while working on the riverboat, where it indicated two fathoms of water beneath the keel. It quickly became his nickname in the bar, and later his "nom de plume."

In 1864, then editor Twain's free-wheeling, highly slanted, and not always entirely factual writing got him into considerable trouble with both the citizens of Carson City and the editor of a rival paper, the latter going so far as to challenge Sam to a duel. Having even less a propensity for dueling than for soldiering (and knowing that dueling was illegal in Nevada), Clemens resigned his editorship and caught a stage for San Francisco.

Sam's first job in California was as a reporter for San Francisco's *Morning Call.* Unimpressed by both the work and his employer, he sought new outlets for his writing. One of these outlets was Bret Harte's newspaper, the *Californian.* In later years, Twain would credit Harte with having guided him towards his successful career by helping him to polish his rough "backwoods" style of writing. It seems only logical to assume that Harte also told Twain about his earlier adventures in the Mother Lode, and that many of the ideas for his own stories came from his experiences in the gold camps. Although there is no specific evidence that such a conversation took place, it seems highly coincidental that only three months after they met, Twain was on his way to Jackass Hill–just across the river from Harte's old Gum Tree claim.

It is true that there were other inducements for his leaving San Francisco, most of them involving money. He had lost his job with the *Call* and was now quite heavily in debt. Among those debts was $500 which he owed a bail bondsman for his friend Steve Gillis, who had been arrested on charges of attempted murder after a fracas with a bartender. Shortly after Twain arranged for his bail, Steve "skipped" to Nevada, leaving Sam holding the bag. It was Steve's brother Jim who enticed Twain to escape from his troubles and return with him to his claim on Jackass Hill. Tired of city hassles and ready to get back to the "easy life," he and Jim left for Tuolumne County in December of 1864. By late February 1865, Twain was back in San Francisco, unaware that his three cold, rainy months "pocket prospecting" in the Mother Lode would soon bring him fame and fortune.

The following notation is from Mark Twain's Notebook #4, made in February 1865, just a few days before he left for San Francisco:

Coleman with his jumping frog--bet stranger $50–stranger had no frog & C got him one–in the meantime stranger filled C's frog full of shot & he couldn't jump–the stranger's frog won

The story he noted was related to him by the bartender at the Angel's Hotel in Angel's Camp.

The Angels Hotel, much as it appeared when Mark Twain stayed there in 1865. (Calaveras County Historical Society)

Twain kept a diary throughout most of his travels in the West, various notations from which were used as basis for later fictional characters and stories. This entry would, of course, later become "Jim Smiley and His Jumping Frog," now known as "The Celebrated Jumping Frog of Calaveras County."

It was not the content of the frog story that would make Twain famous (he was not the first to hear it, nor the first to publish it), it was the style in which he told it. Twain later said that when Ben Coon first told the story in the barroom, not one listener laughed or even smiled. Twain himself was perplexed by its success, calling it a "villainous backwoods sketch," and believing it to be among the lesser of his writings to that date. Even so, it appeared, as a result of error and without Twain's knowledge, in the *New York Saturday Press* of November 18, 1865. As was the custom of the day, it was reprinted by magazines and newspapers around the world.

Back in San Francisco, Twain continued to write for the *Californian*, and in March, 1866, left for Hawaii as correspondent for the *Sacramento Union*.

With his fame as a humorist growing more widespread each day he began lecturing and in December of 1866, sailed for New York. He would return to California only once, on a business trip in the spring and summer of 1868, but that state would never again be his home.

It is interesting to note the parallels between Mark Twain and Bret Harte, two men from very different backgrounds and with very different views of life. Neither came west to seek their fortune, the reasons for their relocation were purely inconsequential. Both more or less "fell into" the writing profession after trying their hand at various and sometimes unlikely jobs. Both got into trouble by championing the cause of minorities (Harte for the Indians and Twain for the Chinese). Both received their greatest notoriety while working for San Francisco newspapers through stories inspired by a short but adventurous visit to the gold fields. It is also interesting that although Twain began writing later and received tutelage from Harte, his world-wide fame came first. Except for their first meeting, Harte and Twain never really like each other personally and in fact, when asked if he knew Bret Harte, Twain once answered, "Yes, I know the son-of-a-bitch."

California in the gold rush era was a treasure chest for storytellers. Few, like Harte and Twain, had the talent to put those tales down on paper with the style and literary quality to bring them to the masses. For the most part, the best "tall tales" never made it past the swinging doors of a smokey barroom. Even so, much of this whiskey-inspired fiction was repeated so often that, by the twentieth century, it had been recorded as fact. Whether it be Joaquin's exploits in Murphys or the "Calaveras Constrictor" hissing its way along the road to Mok Hill, a story must be taken for what it is – a story. It is not history. Pure history is based on fact. Yet these stories are all a part of history and in their way they take us deeper into the lives of California's pioneers than any history book ever could.

So here's to Harte and Twain, purveyors of Mother Lode fiction – here's to Joaquin, a product of legend and fact – and here's to Bart, a factual legend – for they and their tales are forever a part of history – between the rivers.

On a lifelong journey that started in Hannibal, Missouri, and ended in Hartford, Connecticut, Samuel Clemens made a three month stop in the Mother Lode that helped transform him into the world famous Mark Twain.

10
No Thanks Given

HE following letter, dated November 23, 1851, was written by miner Jack Ingram to his wife Sallie:

Been in diggins three months now. Of the 100 men who was here when I arrived, only about 40 remain. We are all averaging about $10 a day, but provisions is very high and going up. Paid $1 for loaf of hard bread and $2.50 for a pound of cheese. Quit buying pork when it went to $5. Was presented with bill from Morgans for $28 for tools and tents. He can wait or take back whats left.

Youll be proud to know I attended a preachin last Sunday under a live oak by Rev Orly Fitzgerald a Methodist. Wernt but 10 men attended but the preacher put on a wailer. Got talkin with him after and went to his camp for coffee. Best I had since I got here with sweet bread his wife sent along. He told me about some of the things he seen in some of the camps. Made my skin crawl. Missed a day of work but felt the need for friendly talk.

Rained hard all day yesterday and got so cold last night I thought it might snow. Makes for easier diggin till a freeze comes but cant keep a fire going. Glad to have my skins but want sorely for a cabin. Wolves stole some meat from a neighbors tent just inches from his head. Ben Prices cabin now has ten men living in it. Ain't but one room bout 15 foot square but keeps the warm in and wolves out. Williams and me talked about cuttin some logs to start our own place but would put us behind in our work too much right now.

My shoulders still sore from the fall but dont notice it when I work. Looking at the condition of some of the men I cant greatly complain. I dont espect older ones lasting out the cold and wet. By winter I fear the camp will get much smaller.

The beans is about cooked so I will close. Tell Momma Lizzy I said hello. Will send some money in the next letter if I can.

In noting the date of this letter, one might wonder why there is no mention of the upcoming Thanksgiving and Christmas holidays. Assuming that his wife lived in the East, the letter would probably not be received for four to six weeks and both parties were certainly aware of that. There are a number of reasons why no mention was made. First and foremost was money. Jack had no doubt set out for California expecting to strike it rich, probably even with the intention of being home before Christmas, his pockets lined with gold dust. He makes a point of mentioning the high cost of living and the low daily "take" from his claim. (Of course he does not mention the cost of whiskey, tobacco, and gambling which were also part of the monthly expenditures for most miners.)

Thanksgiving was not as widely observed in 1851 as it was after the Civil War. Journalist Sarah Hale began campaigning to make it a permanent holiday in 1827, but generally the day was observed or ignored according to the whims of individual state governments and local churches. The California miner had many more important things on his mind, and even if he were aware of a holiday it was unlikely that he would observe it. Many miners did not even observe the Sabbath, although the day was often set aside to provide time for washing, mending, building, and buying provisions.

As the winter approached, tents were traded for lean-tos or makeshift shacks to keep out the icy winds and snow. Ten or twelve miners might crowd into these one room dwellings. (From a 19th century Harpers Magazine)

Even if a miner survived the rigors of life in the wilderness, he might not survive the wrath of an angered neighbor, as this contemporary cartoon depicts. (From a 19th century Harpers Magazine)

The typical miner's dinner consisted of boiled beans, stale bread and coffee. Sharing with your fellows was essential to survival. (From a 19th Century Harpers Magazine)

The average miner of 1851 spent every daylight hour working his claim. His income from seven days work was about $50 to $75. His weekly costs for food, tools, and supplies were around $50. If he was lucky enough to have a good week, the extra money would be spent on new clothes or perhaps lumber, canvas, and nails to build a makeshift cabin. Log cabins were occasionally built, but as Jack says in his letter, there just wasn't time. For the most part, extra money from a good week was used to pay off bills that had accumulated during bad weeks.

Most mining camps had some sort of a trading post or general store. The storekeeper was usually a former miner who was smart enough to see that there was more money to be made in provisions than in prospecting. In addition to stocking food, clothing, and tools, the store also served as tavern, hotel, and community center. When local governments were established, the store owner often became the "alcalde" (a term held over from the Spanish indicating the equivalent of a mayor), or legislative representative. Credit was available to camp members with productive claims, and an account was considered in good standing as long as regular payments were made. If an account reached the point where it was approaching the estimated value of the claim (and they frequently did) the store proprietor might call in the debt, requiring the miner to either sell out or turn over ownership.

Store owners were often quite ruthless. Knowing that they had the "only game in town", they set prices at the maximum amount they could get away with and frequently charged less to friends and more to newcomers or strangers. As stacks of gold dust began to back up at the mint in San Francisco, prices began to skyrocket. Prices of goods being shipped from the East were already inflated as they left port. By the time charges were added for shipping fees, storage, and transportation to the mines, even wholesale costs were outrageous. The following is taken from a store ledger dated September 1852:

Account of John Geiger

Bread . . . $ 2	Coffee . . . . $ 5
Coffee . . . $ 5	Potatoes . . . $ 6
Candles . . $ 1	Bread . . . . $ 5
Molasses . $ 2	Goods . . . . $ 3
Boots . . . . $ 20	Freight . . . $ 15
Pork . . . . $ 10	Total . . . $ 89
Bread . . . $ 3	Bal. For . $ 23
Salt . . . . . $ 1	Total . . . $112
Nails . . . . $ 5	Paid . . . $ 60
Pck Handle $ 6	Bal. Due $ 52

It is not difficult to see that the primary sustenance for a miner was bread and coffee. One can only hope that the "freight" bill at the bottom was for shipment of gold dust to San Francisco. More likely it is for simple mail which could often cost in excess of $5 per letter.

The average miner spent several months in route to California across the Western Plains or by ship to and from an arduous crossing of Central America. By the time he finally reached gold country he was well worn and likely quite broke. If he was lucky enough to find a claim that produced any gold at all, he worked it seven days a week and maybe made enough to pay his bills. In the summer, the creeks often dried up and he either had to pay for water or use a less productive method called dry panning. In the winter, he would work for days on end in the pouring rain, and sometimes an entire camp would be washed away in a flash flood. In short, the average California miner was overworked, overcharged, and underpaid.

So why did they stay? Gold mining is like gambling -- every small payoff is a promise of the big jackpot to come. And the Mother Lode did produce some jackpots. There were those who made several million dollars the first month. There were some who found single nuggets worth thousands. There were even some who worked years at their meager claims and then finally hit a rich strike. And of course these stories quickly made their way (usually in exaggerated form) to the other mining camps both near and far, encouraging luckless miners to stay their cause.

As for Jack Ingram, we have another letter which closes the last chapter of his California adventure, like that of many of his fellow miners:

San Francisco
February 6, 1852

My Dearest Sallie,

Booked passage by way of Panama Route for February 22. Took all I had so I will have to find work here in San Francisco for the next two weeks. My board is paid to the tenth. . . . This will be my last letter as I will be there before another would arrive.

Yours as always, Jack

We can only hope that sometime in late March of 1852, Jack and Sallie celebrated their own personal Thanksgiving, and put behind them a tortuous and fruitless search for Lady Luck -- between the rivers.

11
Choose Your Poison

T the beginning of 1849 there were, exclusive of Indians, about 26,000 persons living in California. By the middle of the summer, that number had doubled -- and by the end of the year, it had jumped to 115,000 plus. Around 80% of that population was made up of American males, over half of whom were engaged in mining as a profession. The little bay-side village of Yerba Buena grew from 812 citizens in 1848 to 5000 by the summer of 1849, changed its name to San Francisco, and by 1850 was a full fledged city of 25,000 people. The greatest percentage of these individuals had made their way to California from the eastern United States.

To say that traveling coast to coast was difficult in the early 1850s is a major understatement. It was, at the least, perilous -- and at its worst, deadly. The prospective prospector did have a choice of routes, however. Prior to the discovery of gold, California bound travelers usually either made their way across the western plains in a covered wagon or caught a sailing ship around South America's Cape Horn. Barring delays, the plains route took about three and a half months and the ship route six to nine. A third, faster route was also available, but it required crossing Mexico, a country in which Americans were not particularly welcome.

All of these routes were used to some degree during the gold rush years, but two new shorter routes quickly became popular. These required the taking of a steam or sailing ship by way of the Atlantic Ocean to Central America, then crossing over to the Pacific side to board a second ship for San Francisco. Crossings were made through Panama from 1848, and also through Nicaragua after 1850. Of the thousands who used these routes during the 1850s, few knew in advance of the hardships that such a trip would entail. Owners of steamship companies advertised that their ships were the fastest and safest. Of course, none of the ads even hinted at the dangers of the voyage, nor the enormous difficulties the traveler would encounter upon arrival in Central America.

As passengers boarded a steamer in one of the many eastern harbors, they were generally more excited than concerned. Many were taking their first ocean voyage, and most were looking forward to an adventure of unfamiliar sights and sounds. For the

most part, this excitement and anticipation lasted about as long as it took for the ship to break into open waters. As it reached the Atlantic, the ship began to roll and toss, leaving most of its passengers groaning in their berths. It would be skirting the coast of Florida before a few pale and languid passengers would begin to venture on deck or show up to pick at their food in the dining room.

As the vessel slipped along through tropical waters, the seas were generally calmer and the weather more pleasant so that by the time it reached Greytown in Nicaragua or Chagres in Panama, the passengers were just beginning to return to good spirits. Upon disembarking in Central America, their excitement again quickly turned to concern. A contemporary traveler described the city of Chagres in 1850:

The village itself is merely a collection of huts and is situated in the midst of what appears to be a swamp. Logs of wood are laid along the center of the streets to enable passengers to avoid the deep mud which is always to be found there.

Its climate is, without doubt the most pestiferous for whites in the whole world. The thermometer ranges from 78 to 85 all the year, and it rains every day. Bilious, remittent, and congestive fevers, in their most malignant forms, seem to hover over Chagres, ever ready to pounce down on the stranger.

Due to the miserable state of the little town, and its general lack of accommodations, the traveler usually made arrangements to embark on the crossing of the isthmus as soon as possible. This journey began on the Chagres River, where a boatman was hired to carry passengers and luggage upstream to the town of Gorgona, from which the remainder of the crossing would be by mule or on foot. The large, dugout-type canoes, usually overcrowded with passengers and luggage, were propelled by pole and/or paddle for the entire 50 or so miles. The stream was dark and muddy, and in some areas quite narrow and rapid. Thick forests lined the banks, and it would not be unusual for the traveler to get his or her first glimpse of monkeys, large snakes, alligators, and jungle cats. The air was filled with swarms of disease-carrying mosquitos and if the traveler did not bring his own food and drink, there was none to be had along the way. (Even if there were, the partaking of local food or drink

Throughout the Gold Rush years, eastern seaports were overflowing with would-be argonauts arriving from almost every town and city to board steamers and sailing ships bound for "Californy". (From a 19th Century Harpers Magazine)

San Francisco Bay was littered with ships abandoned by their crews - off to the foothills in search of the Mother Lode's daughter - Lady Luck. (Calaveras Historical Society)

was a sure-fire way to catch cholera or dysentery.) If all went as planned the village of Gorgona would be reached in twelve to fifteen hours.

Gorgona offered little more in the way of accommodations than Chagres, and those who were not lucky enough to rent a cot in the local hotel-hut were forced to sleep on the ground. Many simply chose to stay awake and await the next day's journey to Panama City.

The road from Gorgona to Panama was little more that a beaten path with numerous potholes and swampy crossings. Rarely would enough mules be available to carry both luggage and passengers, leaving the traveler to walk the full 25 miles. Hopefully he or she had brought proper footwear for the trek. (Wherever possible, ladies were provided with a mule or, on rare and lucky occasions, a rickety wagon.) Within eight to ten hours, the then weary travelers would catch sight of the towering white spires of the Cathedral of Panama. Again their spirits were raised by the false hope that their torturous journey would soon be over. Still, the worst was yet to come.

Once in Panama City, the travelers found themselves surrounded by throngs of Americans, many who had been waiting weeks for a chance to board one of the few ships headed for San Francisco. The few hotels, little more than barns with rows of cots, would already be overflowing. Within a few days, the provisions brought along would run out (if they were not stolen first), and the travelers would be forced to partake of local fare – primarily boiled beans, fat pork swimming in grease, and hardtack. Cockroaches crawled across the tables and disputed possession of food morsels. Flies swarmed around every fleshy animal (human or otherwise) in the daytime, and mosquitos feasted at night.

If a traveler were lucky enough to find available space on an outbound ship, it would no doubt be as rickety, overcrowded, and pest infested as the Panama hotels. Ships designed to carry 500 passengers seldom left a Central American port with less than 1000 on board. The vessel would no doubt break down several times along the way, and it

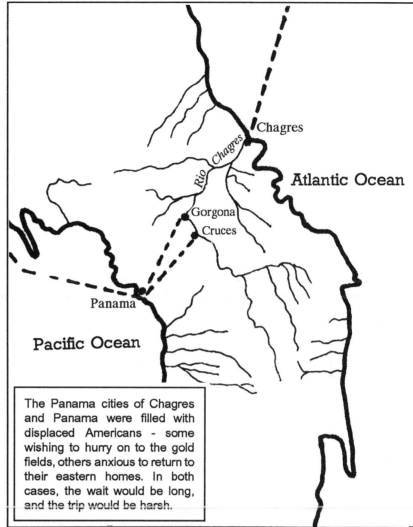

The Panama cities of Chagres and Panama were filled with displaced Americans - some wishing to hurry on to the gold fields, others anxious to return to their eastern homes. In both cases, the wait would be long, and the trip would be harsh.

would be unusual not to come across several storms and/or gales that would toss the creaky ship and its passengers and cargo to and fro. During the voyage twenty or more unlucky souls would be buried at sea, mostly due to cholera. It was the final leg of the journey--and it was the worst of it.

If the ship were a steamer, the voyage from Panama to San Francisco would take from 30 to 50 days. A sailing ship might take three times that. It is likely that, by the time he reached San Francisco, the traveler had expended all the funds he had brought along. Exorbitant travel costs in Central America, plus the additional food and accommodations needed during delays would quickly eat away at the argonaut's "stake". And in California, he would find that everything was twice the price it was in the east. With luck, he might find a job or trade all he owned for a pick and a pan. Then, weary and disheartened, he set out to for his final destination – between the rivers.

33

12
A Most Perilous Journey
Part One

I N 1849, the United States consisted of some 30 states stretching from the Atlantic Ocean to a line formed by the western borders of Minnesota, Iowa, Missouri, Arkansas, and Louisiana. The various territories which lay to the west of that line were, for the most part, unexplored and unsettled. Those adventurers who were brave (or foolhardy) enough to travel to the west usually stuck to a few trails which had been established by the early explorers. The best known of these western routes were the Sante Fe Trail, established in 1821; the Old Spanish Trail of 1829; the Oregon Trail of 1841; and the Central Trail, also known as the Emigrant Trail and the 49er Trail. In 1849 alone, over 20,000 easterners made their way to California by way of the Emigrant Trail.

When setting out for California, the forty-niner first had to reach one of the staging areas; primarily Independence or St. Joseph, Missouri; or Council Bluffs (Omaha), Nebraska. These were reached by well established trails along the Ohio, Mississippi, and Missouri Rivers; or by traveling through the Great Lakes and down the Illinois River. Whether the traveler brought his own wagon and provisions from home, or simply arrived with a "stake" intended for purchasing these items, there was a considerable amount of preparation required before setting out on the perilous western trek.

In the spring of 1849, there were over 10,000 emigrants in the bustling little Missouri town of St. Joseph. Wagons were being reinforced and secured, canvas covers attached and weatherproofed, while food, guns, and other supplies were stocked. Horses were traded for hardier mules or oxen, many specially bred and trained to handle the rigors of a long overland pull. An 1850 emigrant "guide book" (of which there were many) suggests the following supply list for a party of four men:

5 oxen with yokes, chain, and shoes; 1 wagon, light and strong; 2 good rifles; 8 heavy Mackinaw blankets; 800 lbs. Flour and Meal; 200 lbs. Hardtack; 300 lbs. Bacon sides; 100 lbs. Dried Apples; 100 lbs. Sugar; 40 lbs. Coffee; 50 lbs. Rice; 10 lbs. Fine Salt; also, tea kettle, coffee pot, 2 camp kettles-one tin & one sheet iron, frying pan, water barrel, milk can, tin plates and cups, knives and forks, etc.

The estimated weight of the supplies listed was 1705 pounds–the cost of the entire outfit, $522.16.

If they weren't already part of an established "company," individuals and families would ban together to form a wagon train. This would necessitate the hiring of a wagon master and a scout or guide. During the many weeks along the trail, the master served as mayor, sheriff, judge, preacher, doctor, and negotiator for the mobile community.

Many emigrant companies were organized in the large cities of the northeast with such colorful names as the Buckeye Rovers or the Helltown Greasers. Some were formed with the intention of remaining organized even after reaching the California gold fields. These were given names like Union Mining and Trading Company, Boston and the California Joint Mining Company, and the Columbus Industrial Association.

Unfortunately, many companies were designed to fleece unsuspecting travelers. It might be suggested that the group "pool" their resources and allow the organizers to purchase the necessary equipment and supplies -- at a substantially reduced rate, of course. After the money was collected and turned over to the alleged benefactors, that was the last anyone would see of them.

Rarely, if ever, did a complete company or train make it all the way to California without losing a number of their group. Due to the hardships of the trail, many people turned back. Others settled in or near the few towns or forts that were passed along the way, or upon reaching the treacherous Rockies or Sierra Nevada, split off and took the somewhat easier route to Oregon. All had been warned of the ordeals they would face, but few really understood until they actually began to experience adversity.

The initial portion of the Emigrant Trail followed the Platte River through what would later become the state of Nebraska. This river ran just south of Council Bluffs, and was reached from St. Joseph by a cross-country trek of about 300 miles. A well established road could be followed along the banks of the river, passing by Fort Kearney, the Roubidoux Trading Post at Scott's Bluff, and Fort Laramie; finally arriving at Independence Rock. (The names of many early emigrants can still be seen carved or painted on this famous landmark, southwest of Casper, Wyoming.) At this point, the

Literally thousands of streams would be crossed in the 2000 mile journey to California. Fortunately, by 1850, ferries were in operation at most rivers that were either too deep or had currents too swift to allow fording by wagon. (Harpers Magazine)

As emigrant trains set out across the Kansas plains, few of the travelers were truly aware of the devastating hardships to come. (From a 19th century Harpers Magazine)

travelers left the Platte River and continued along the road running parallel to Sweetwater Creek.

By now, the typical wagon train would have been involved in several skirmishes with Indians, forded several swollen streams, and fought off one or more outbreaks of cholera. There would have been numerous breakdowns on the potholed and boulder-strewn roads, and many travelers were forced to leave behind treasured cargo to lessen the load on weary mules or oxen. Now, nearly one thousand miles and some seventy-five days from their starting point, emotions were strained and tempers were wearing thin. Here came the test of a true wagon master--for the worst was yet to come.

At South Pass, 7550 feet up slopes of the Continental Divide, a decision was made whether to take the Sublette Route to the west or the Salt Lake route (Mormon Trail) to the south. The two routes would intersect again, 182 miles west of Salt Lake City. The southern route was longer, but allowed the emigrants their first contact with civilization since Fort Laramie. If supplies were low, there would be no choice--the Salt Lake route must be taken.

The trail now followed Pacific Creek down the western slope of the divide to the ferry at Green River, and on to the trading post at Fort Bridger on Black's Fork. From this point, the road became extremely rough and in many places almost non-existent. The hills were long and steep and the trail crooked. The many creeks and rivers were often swollen from mountain rains and their banks thick with deep mud. Some rivers could only be crossed by ferry, and these (generally run by the Mormons) could only be used during low water, when the current was least rapid. The train was now making only a few miles each day and the 225 miles from the Great Divide to Salt Lake City must have seemed like a lifetime.

Finally, after crossing the same stream (appropriately called Last Creek) seventeen times in five miles, the company climbed a gentle hill and were met with a grand view of the Great Salt Lake and the nearby settlement of the same name. At Salt Lake City, the travelers meet friendly new faces for the first time in three months. They were now 1128 miles into their journey, with nearly a thousand miles to go. Supplies were stocked, repairs were made, and the trek began anew.

Now the train backtracked somewhat, northward along the Bear River. To continue westward, the company must first circumvent the Great Salt Lake and the southern route would have taken them across 100 miles of salt desert. But the roads were better now, and soon they would reach the western junction of the Sublette Road. From here to the Humbolt River in Nevada, the trail was generally easier going, although the water from this river, often called the "Humbug" by 49ers, was putrid and highly alkaline. The road which paralleled the Humbolt was wide and flat for nearly 400 miles. Then came the Humbolt Sink, and thirty-five miles of treacherous desert.

Once again, a decision had to be made. There were several recommended routes across the desert, but two were the most used -- a northern route, which connected with the Truckee river and took the traveler through the Sierra mountains via Truckee Pass; or southwest to the Carson River and Kit Carson Pass. Most chose the Carson route, but whatever the choice, this desert would be only the first of two obstacles which stood between them and their final destination. For those who survived the deadly desert, a seemingly impassible wall of mountains awaited, guarding the gold which lay beyond.

13
A Most Perilous Journey
Conclusion

HE length of the 49er Trail from Missouri to the edge of the Humbolt Sink in Nevada was approximately 1750 miles. By the time the average emigrant train reached this point, it had been reduced to fifty percent of its original size. Many of the travelers had turned back, some had settled along the trail, and perhaps as many as 15 percent of the members had died in route. The trail was littered with thousands of dead oxen and mules, as well as tools, furniture, and other heavy items discarded to ease the load on overworked teams. By this time, every member of the company had been ill at least once and many had been sick throughout the trip. Now, weak and discouraged, they were told to prepare for the worst – 35 miles of desert, then the crossing of the Sierra Mountains.

In traveling overland to California, timing was of great importance. The train needed to leave Missouri late enough in the spring to avoid the rainy season and rivers swollen by the runoff from mountain snows. Still, they had to leave early enough to assure a crossing of the mountains before the snows began to fall. This meant a departure time from mid-April to mid-May, which, barring lengthy delays, would put their arrival at the Humbolt Sink in late August or early September. At this time of year, the temperature in the Nevada desert reached an average of 120 degrees during the day. Therefor, most of the traveling would be done at night, when the temperature cooled to 95°.

From this stifling heat the caravan would climb the eastern slope of the mountains to an elevation of about 8000 feet, where nighttime temperatures were well below freezing. In the 15 to 20 days it took to travel from the Humbolt Sink to Carson Pass, the travelers saw the dramatic change in weather that Northern California was already known for. The hot, dry summer was quickly becoming a cold, wet fall. As clouds gathered over the distant mountain peaks, the traveler's thoughts no doubt turned to a grizzly story they had once heard -- about a train of emigrants called the Donner Party.

Prior to the gold rush migration of 1849, only a few bands of travelers had attempted to cross into California through the Sierra Nevada range. Most of these followed the trails established by early

trappers such as Jedediah Smith, James Pattie, and Ewing Young; or explorers such as Kit Carson and John C. Fremont. The first emigrant train for California was organized in 1841 by John Bidwell. The caravan left Missouri in June of that year, but difficulties along the trail put them in the Sierra Mountains in late September, after a heavy snow storm. Having long since abandoned their wagons, the party trudged along far south of the established trail, and primarily by luck, came across the Stanislaus River which they then followed down into the San Joaquin Valley.

Probably the most daring (or foolhardy) crossing of the Sierra range was made by John Fremont in late January of 1844 -- the dead of winter. Led by Kit Carson and John Fitzpatrick, Fremont's troop barely endured the crossing, surviving primarily by butchering their horses for food as they fell from exhaustion. While Fremont chose an easier southern route for his return crossing, the river, trail, and pass (all given the name "Carson") which they had followed into California would become one of the most popular routes of the 49ers.

Many of California's early settlers did their best to aid emigrant travelers, often sending food and supplies to companies who would otherwise never have made it past the mountains. In October 1846, John Sutter sent two Indian guides, seven mules, and some food, across the mountains to a group led by George and Jacob Donner. In January, a handful of battered men stumbled down from the snow covered hills to report that the entire train had become snowbound and the emigrants, including some women and children, were starving.

By the time rescue parties reached the group in late February, Sutter's two Indians along with 38 men, women, and children had perished. But amazingly, 45 had survived. They had subsisted on boiled shoe leather, tree bark, pine needle tea, and reportedly, the flesh of their fallen comrades. The lake and the pass where the incident occurred (on the Truckee branch of the Emigrant Trail) has since borne the Donner name.

When members of an emigrant train were informed that they had finally reached the summit of the Sierra Mountains they were elated to know that they were at last in California. But when their eyes searched the western horizon for signs of the

The Emigrant Trail was littered with abandoned wagons, tools and furniture, as well as the carcasses of dead oxen and mules driven beyond their limits. (Harpers Magazine)

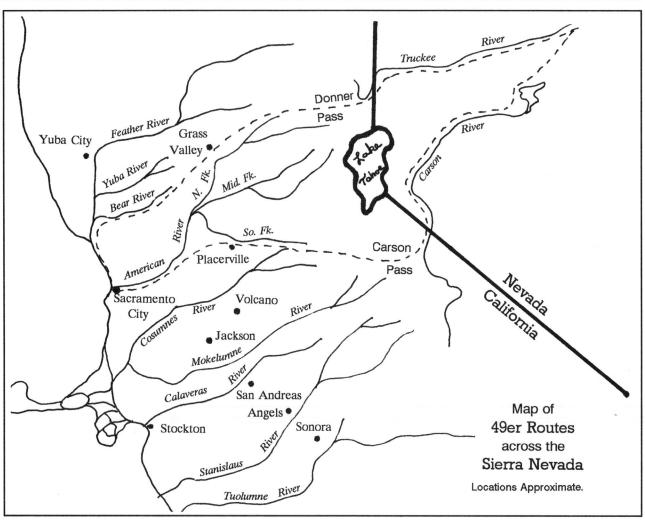

Map of
49er Routes
across the
Sierra Nevada

Locations Approximate.

fertile San Joaquin Valley and saw only miles and miles of pine covered hills, their joy quickly turned to dismay. They were in California, but the nearest settlement was still nearly one hundred miles distant, down a boulder strewn trail that crossed dozens of washed out creeks and wound its way through the ragged terrain.

An 1850 "emigrant guide" describes the descent from the summit:

You will now have thirty miles of the worst road you have seen. It is enclosed on both sides by high rocky cliffs. The stream has an extremely rapid current that comes rushing down from the mountains, roaring like a cataract. It is bridged at all the crossings, though each bridge should be carefully inspected before it is used. The road is very rocky, that it is difficult, in many places, to get along with a wagon. Near the summit, there are immense banks of snow, and an overcoat is not uncomfortable in July or August. After we get thirty miles west of the summit, we encounter no more serious hills to Sacramento City. Watch your stock well in these mountains; for the Indians, or somebody else, have a fashion of driving them off.

From the same guide, there is this footnote concerning the Sierra Mountains:

There is no chance to get around the Sierra Nevada. All who go to California overland have them to cross; and for some forty miles, the difficulties to encounter are great, there being many steep and rocky hills to ascend and descend, and some of them are very lengthy.

Throughout the cross-country journey, water was always a problem for emigrant travelers. When one wanted a drink, there was never enough. When one wanted to cross a stream, there was always too much. The few streams that weren't highly alkaline were often polluted from the debris and wastes of earlier travelers. In crossing the Nevada desert the caravans prayed for rain. Upon reaching the Sierras they prayed for blue skies – a mountain storm meant either impassible streams or drifting snow.

As they made their way along the final miles of the Emigrant Trail, the emotions of those early travelers must have been highly mixed. No one who had not already made the trip could have imagined the hardships they would endure. Few arrived at the mines with more than the clothes they were wearing. A startling 75% of the animals (oxen, mules, and cattle) died in route, or were butchered for food. 65% of the wagons were damaged beyond repair or had to be abandoned – either to save the

The dashing and handsome Kit Carson led Fremont on a winter crossing of the Sierra along a river and through a pass which has since borne his name.

lives of a valuable team or because the team had already died. 80 to 90 percent of all personal property was discarded along the trail as each item quickly became more of a burden than a necessity. Greater than the thrill of arriving was the simple satisfaction of knowing you had survived the journey – for many did not.

Regardless of the route taken or the perils encountered, when the emigrant gold miners reached California they had only one choice left--to make the best of the situation. There was no turning back. After a short rest and a good meal, they set out on a new journey. It would not be nearly as long, but it might be just as perilous – and it would certainly be as adventurous. Their destinations: Muletown, Misery Flat, Jackass Gulch, Slabtown, Scorpion Gulch, Average, Dogtown, Hawkeye, Hicks, and a thousand other camps with similar names, where former doctors, lawyers, farmers, and school-teachers dug for treasure in the rocky ravines – between the rivers.

14
The Carriers
Part One

HETHER immigrant travelers came to California by way of the Panama Route or overland across the mountains and plains, the trip would have taken its toll. By the time they reached the mines they had already been away from their families for several months. They could only hope that the few letters sent by way of eastbound strangers they had met along the route would reach their loved one's hands. In some cases, six to eight months would pass before a wife would hear from her beloved argonaut. But she would certainly hear of cholera epidemics and Indian attacks and wonder if her man had survived. On the overland trail emigrants could mail letters at the few military installations along the way, or perhaps put their trust in a traveler who had decided to turn back.

Those who chose a Central American route had few opportunities to send correspondence. Again it required placing trust in someone traveling the same route in the opposite direction. It is truly remarkable that, according to contemporary accounts, very few of these letters failed to reach their destination.

The first California territorial post office was established in San Francisco late in 1848. For nearly one full year this was the only post office in the state, and there were no provisions for pick-up and delivery from nearby towns. This meant that whether you lived 15 miles or 50 miles away, you had to travel to San Francisco to get your mail. It was not unusual for that office to receive a letter simply addressed in the manner of: John Doe, Somewhere in the Mines, c/o San Francisco.

By the fall of 1849, nearly every foothill stream and river was dotted with red-shirted miners digging, panning, and sluicing. Areas containing more than a few workers were called "camps." Some camps would quickly become towns, others would just as quickly disappear without a trace. But in every town and camp there were three things the miners held in reverence, for these were the things they wanted most and had the least of: gold, women, and mail from home. But the post office in San Francisco was many miles away, across the wide San Joaquin Valley.

The primary transportation routes to the mines were the Sacramento and the San Joaquin rivers, with the cities of Sacramento and Stockton as their eastern terminals. These cities were still miles from foothill gold camps, over rough and often poorly marked trails. No one would make the trip to San Francisco just for mail -- or would they?

In the summer of 1849, Alexander Todd, who had unsuccessfully tried his hand at gold mining, was looking for a new money-making venture. In the bustling town of Jacksonville he struck upon an idea. For a fee of one dollar each, he would record the names of the miners and act as their agent to carry and retrieve mail from the post office in San Francisco. In addition to the registration fee, Todd would charge one ounce of gold dust for each letter delivered. Few complained of the price.

Within a few weeks, Todd was doing a booming business, with clients in Sonora, Columbia, Mokelumne Hill, and many other towns and camps. Soon he was being asked to carry gold dust out and to bring food and provisions back to the camps. Alexander Todd was now in the express business.

While Todd was not the first express carrier in California, he was one of the first in the mines and he was certainly one of the most successful. But as the 1850s began, competition became fierce. As towns boomed and roads were improved, more and more enterprising souls set out to make their fortunes in the transportation of mail and supplies. Newspapers were filled with ads for express companies who operated under a variety of names, such as: Freeman & Co; Elliott's Accommodation Express; Everts, Davis and Company; and the California Penny Post Company. The following ad, which ran in the Daily Alta California in 1851, shows the variety of routes and services provided by Calaveras County's premier express company:

EXPRESS TO STOCKTON AND
THE SOUTHERN MINES

We have made arrangements to run a daily express through to San Francisco from Stockton and all parts of the Southern Mines and vice versa. Gold Dust, Letters and Packages, received by us in Stockton and all parts of the Southern Mines, and shipped to all parts of the United States and Europe through Adams and Company or any house parties may desire. Drafts purchased in sums to suit, payable in all parts of the United States and

The town of Sonora in Tuolumne County grew quickly &, due primarily to its close proximity to the active mines at Columbia & Jamestown, was one of the first Mother Lode communities to have regular express service. (Calaveras Historical Society)

Europe. We have a daily line of stages running between Stockton and Sonora, carrying our Express. Also, a Daily Express between Stockton, Double Springs, Mokelumne, Carsons Creek, and Angels. Collections made in San Francisco and all places as above. Orders, letters, and packages left at Burgess, Gilbert & Stills Book Store, on the Plaza, or at our office with Mr. J. W. Gregory, Montgomery street.

REYNOLDS & CO. San Francisco, June 14th, 1851.

Adams and Company, mentioned above, was organized in 1840 as the New York and Boston Express Company, by Alvin Adams and P. B. Burke. When the partnership was dissolved the following year, Adams continued on his own with great success and eventually took on a new partner, Daniel Haskell. It was Haskell who arrived in San Francisco on October 31, 1849, to organize the West Coast branch of Adams and Company. In a very short time, Haskell had formed agreements with many of the smaller express companies (including Todd and Reynolds) for shipments to the east, and had put many others out of business.

By 1851, Adams and Company was recognized as the leading shipper in California. They were the only express company offering a speedy "pony express" to some of the more important mining communities; the only one to include a "special messenger" to protect gold shipments; and they were the first express company to branch out into the banking business.

Meanwhile, back at the mines, nearly every camp of any size had an express office, usually situated in the general store. By the summer of 1851, only 25 of the now hundreds of camps had a post office and even there the locals would probably be more likely to rely upon the hard working, hard riding express carrier rather than entrusting their mail to the U.S. Government.

A letter sent to New York from Mokelumne Hill by way of Adams and Company would reach San Francisco in about two and a half days. There, it would be placed on the next steamer for Nicaragua, then make a short overland haul to the Atlantic and another steamer to New York. Packages and mail sent through Adams were accompanied by an expressman who made sure the items were kept safe from harm and assured that they were not delayed in any way. While most passengers needed four months for the journey, a Mok Hill letter would make the trip from San Francisco to New York in two months or less.

The cargo entrusted to the expressman on his return trip might include a miner's wife and/or

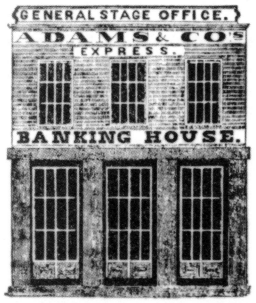

family. Because of the hardships involved in traveling to California, few women tried to make the trip alone. But in the experienced hands of an Adams & Company expressman, the journey would be as quick and uneventful as possible. (In 1854, a young Bret Harte and his little sister made their way via Panama to San Francisco in the care of an expressman who had been hired by Harte's stepfather.) During one year, an expressman of this type might spend as many as eight months aboard various steamships.

Despite the fact that Adams and Company so dominated those early years of the California express business, another group would soon be organized whose name would overshadow all existing express agencies of the time. On March 18, 1852, a group of New York businessmen met to make final preparations for a new express venture that would, like Adams and Company, include a banking division. Among the company officers elected that day were Johnston Livingston, James McKay, Edwin Morgan, Henry Wells, and William George Fargo.

15
The Carriers
Conclusion

N May, 1852 the newly formed Wells Fargo and Company sent Samuel Carter and Ruben Washburn to open a California branch of its express forwarding and banking concerns. Like Adams & Company, who had come to California in 1849 and was already well established, Wells Fargo was formed in the East and most of the major stock holders still resided there. Unlike Adams and Company, Wells Fargo was backed by big-money bankers and wealthy businessmen. Within six months of its arrival in San Francisco, the company had established offices in every major city and mining town in Northern California and were already forwarding freight and mail for many of Adams' former clients.

In November of 1852 Wells Fargo bought out Gregory and Company Express, one of the larger inland express companies. This was followed in 1853 by the purchase of Todd and Company, one of the oldest express agencies in California. In 1854 Wells Fargo extended their territory to include Los Angeles and Southern California, then bought out Hunter and Company in the Northern Mines. Wells-Fargo was now the largest express company in California, and Adams and Company was -- quite literally -- on the run.

Adams had only one chance to survive -- by proving that they were faster and more efficient. Several "unspoken" challenges were made, and the competition began. Probably the most famous race between the two rivals came in December of 1853 when pony express riders from both companies vied to be the first to arrive in Portland, Oregon with a Presidential message that had come to San Francisco by steamer. The two express men rode day and night, through rivers and mountains, in rain and snow. Adams and Company won the race - but they were soon to loose the battle.

Despite indications of an oncoming financial depression, Wells-Fargo continued to expand and prosper. Unfortunately, their competitor was not so solvent. During the winter of 1854, rumors of a depression in the east reached California. Meanwhile, in the gold fields, mining operations were greatly hampered by a lack of rain, causing a noticeable reduction in gold shipments and deposits. In the resulting panic, several banks were forced to close their doors -- among them was Adams and Company.

Regardless of efforts by the company and local newspapers to disconnect Adams banking from Adams express in the eyes of the public, the fate of both concerns were sealed. A petition of insolvency, filed on February 27, 1855, marked the end of Adams and Company and the beginning of Well Fargo's domination in California and the West.

Wells Fargo's extensive assets allowed their bank to stand the withdrawal runs that had closed Adams & Company and others. As a result of weathering this crisis, confidence in the company was high and its future secured. By the end of 1855, California had fifty-five Wells-Fargo express offices, with extended pony express and stage lines. By 1860, the company had expanded into the Pacific Northwest, and had 147 offices throughout the west. (While it is difficult enough to follow the proliferation of California express companies and their assimilation by Well Fargo, it should be noted that Henry Wells was also president of American Express, which was expanding and merging at an equally impressive rate in the east.)

Almost every Mother Lode town of size had a Wells Fargo office. (If one were to believe the many historical plaques placed by various well-intending groups, nearly every building in every town was used as a Wells Fargo office at one time or another.) During the early years, the express man might arrive by horse, with or without a pack mule. Express wagons became more common as roads improved and eventually both express mail and passengers were carried by stagecoach. It was convenient, therefore, if the express office was located in or near a hotel or, at least, in the town's most active section.

In addition to transporting packages and mail the express office also offered services connected with its banking division. (Sort of an early "branch office.") Money or gold could be sent for deposit, checks could be cashed, or "drafts" could be purchased and sent. One method of sending money to the Eastern United States or even overseas, was the "First of Exchange." Each exchange note was filled out in triplicate, and each copy was then sent by different forms of mail. Wells Fargo's receiving branch would then pay the first copy to arrive and cancel those that followed, providing triple insurance that important payments would arrive at their destination.

A Wells Fargo "First Draft" provided triple security for payments sent by mail. *(Courtesy of Smalldon's Americana)*

Miners were at first quite pleased with the mail services they were receiving. After all, four-month-old mail was better than no mail at all. But eventually it was determined that communication between California and the east had to be expedited, and in 1857 Congress passed a bill authorizing an overland mail system. The contract was awarded to Butterfield & Company, a joint stock association made up primarily of men who also had interests in Adams & Company, National Express, Wells Fargo, and American Express.

The first overland stage (actually a large covered wagon) left San Francisco on September 14, 1858. Its eastern counterpart picked up the mail bags at Tipton, Missouri, the western terminus of the railroad, on the 17th. There was only one west bound passenger, a newspaper correspondent for the New York Herald. The Postmaster General had determined that a southern route would be best (the fact that he was a Southerner himself likely influenced that decision), and the two stages met on the dusty trail near El Paso, Texas just twelve days later. Despite this lengthy route which took the stage first to California's southern border, the mail arrived in San Francisco just 24 days after leaving St. Louis. For the first time, homesick miners would receive letters within a month of their writing. By 1860, the bulk of all California mail was being handled by Butterfield Overland Express.

As the Civil War approached the overland mail was switched to a more northerly route, numerous new express companies became involved, and the Pony Express was formed. Wells Fargo continued to operate the Overland Mail Company and took over the western leg of the Pony Express in 1861.

When the transcontinental telegraph was completed in October of 1861, California at last became one with the nation. News of the war was transmitted by wire in only a few minutes, and San Francisco newspapers printed accounts of major Civil War battles within just a few days of their occurrence. By then, most Mother Lode towns had a post office and regular mail delivery.

While the miner still relied on the Overland Express to keep him in touch with home, letters now took only a couple of weeks to reach their destination. The old timers no doubt remembered, with no great fondness, a time when a letter took four to six months to arrive and then was retrieved from the San Francisco post office for an ounce of gold by an enterprising young carrier who took it upon himself to become the one reliable link between the outside world and the lonely miner who toiled for riches -- between the rivers.

16
For a Pinch or a Dollar

URING the early years of the Gold Rush, a miner who set up camp by himself in Calaveras County did not have to worry about being alone for long. Within months of its establishment a successful gold claim generated a camp and the camp soon became a town. More often than not, the first permanent structure in that camp would be the camp store.

In 1848 and during the early part of 1849, few who came to the Calaveras foothills in search of gold were disappointed. But as the full force of the rush was felt, placer gold was quickly depleted and gold mining soon became a gamble. Those who were not successful often went looking for other methods to make their fortune. Those who had been moderately successful might go looking for something to invest in. Because every camp needed supplies, the logical alternative to mining was store keeping.

The camp store was more than just a place to buy food and tools. When a newcomer arrived in camp, he went directly to the store to learn about available claims and local mining laws. In bad weather the store became a hotel for those who did not yet have a roof to sleep under and the storekeeper often served meals until campfires could be relit. A passerby could also find food and lodging for a fair price, although the accommodations might be nothing more than a blanket on the floor and the food a rusty pan of boiled beans.

Because liquor was usually dispensed here by the bottle or by the drink, the camp store quickly became a gathering place for the miners. Accordingly, it also served as a sort of "town hall" where laws were set down and lawbreakers were tried.

While it could be said that storekeepers were generally honest, pleasant, and helpful, they were in business to make money and some were not above a little price gouging or "creative" bookkeeping. The following quote comes from an 1850 guide book to the California mines, under a section called "Mercantile and Trading Operations":

The people of California are, like they are in every other part of the civilized world, after the profits. Everyone makes as much off the man he is trading with as he can. Some of the keenest, sharpest traders in the world are to be found there. The exorbitant rents, and other corresponding expenses most of the merchants have heretofore been subject to, have tended more to keep up the prices of groceries and provisions than any other cause, and has enabled those who were doing business on a more independent basis to realize enormous profits.

In most towns, the store owner extended credit to almost every permanent resident of the camp. Even though some ran their bills into the thousands of dollars, surprisingly few ever ran out on their debt. During the early years of the Gold Rush the town of Sonora in Tuolumne County was the major business center for the Southern Mines. What follows is a sampling of the debts owed Sonoran store owner John McGuire in 1849 (spelling and diction have been corrected for easy reading):

Red, that lives with Dancing Bill . . . . . . *$ 30.50*
Dancing Bill -
*   needles, thread, shoes, stockings* . . . . . . *$ 18.00*
The man that's in his tent - pants, shoes . *$ 26.00*
Martin, that has the woman . . . . *$ 10.00*
The cousin to Thomas Bone . . . . *$ 70.00*
Hamilton, for shoes . . . . *$ 5.00*
John, that speaks English . . . . *$ 88.00*
The man that was lame . . . . *$ 16.00*
The Spaniard that took the jacket . . . . . . *$ 10.00*
Manual Salias, the Frenchman
*   who has the white wife* . . . . *$ 18.00*
and for two ounces of gold lent . . . . *$ 24.00*
*   in all.* . . . . *$ 42.00*
The man that set up the store in the new
diggins for what's due on hats, candies,
serapes, sardines, coffee, pants,pans, belts . *$300.00*

Here we see that this shop keeper not only sold on credit to persons whose name he did not even know, he also provided a portion of the opening stock for his competitor in a nearby camp.

As each camp grew, so did the camp store. The first addition might be an "official" brass-railed bar along one wall, followed by a felt-topped Monte' table. Three-card Monte' was a card game of Spanish origin, played with a deck of forty cards. Players bet against the banker on the color of the cards which would be turned from the deck. The Monte' dealer, usually a professional gambler who seldom lost, would pay a percentage of his winnings to the store owner for the use of his table and facilities.

The camp store was a gathering place for the miners after work and on Sundays. Note the stacked cots for weary travelers, the amateur barber and the Chinese cook preparing a meal. (Harpers Magazine)

Troupes of dancers, singers and actors traveled to camps which had facilities for such entertainment. Often, the dance hall was an addition to the camp store. (Harpers Magazine)

The liquor served at the bar was the cheapest available, often merely a concoction of grain alcohol and some sort of flavoring. Some store owners produced their own home brew from corn or potatoes and gave it a colorful name such as Devil's Dew or Tarantula Juice. The price of a shot and one refill was a pinch of gold dust – about one dollar. (Ingenious barkeeps placed blankets over the counter and floor to catch any fine dust that might fall during the day's many transactions, then washed the blankets and panned out the wash water.) Brandy was two dollars a glass and was very likely poured from the same barrel as the whiskey. The owner usually did keep a bottle or two of good champagne or rum hidden away in case some lucky miner wanted to celebrate with the "best."

Food of all types was expensive in mining camps, therefore the least expensive items were the most popular and easiest to obtain. Beans were the standard fare, with a small piece of pork fat if the previous week had been a productive one. Potatoes were prized in camp, as were milk products, butter and cheese. The storekeeper, if he had any cooking abilities at all, would usually bake bread or biscuits for sale. But if his price were too high the miner would buy flower and salt from which he could make "flap jacks." These were not pancakes as we know them, but a dry, nearly tasteless type of pan fried bread with practically no nutritional value. As one might expect, flavorings such as salt, pepper, and molasses were among the most important "staples." As with liquor, the store owner kept a few exotic foods for celebrations and special occasions. These included canned fish, oysters, beef tongue, chocolate, and sweet cakes.

As the camp grew and prospered, the availability of food improved and the store began to offer additional products and services. These might include an express service to transport gold dust and mail to San Francisco, medicines and basic medical services, and building supplies. During the mid-1850s, traveling troupes of entertainers began to make their way into the smaller mining towns of Calaveras County, necessitating the building of an addition to the little store with a small stage and perhaps a couple of upstairs rooms in which the performers could stay. At this point, the store had

evolved into a tavern, dance hall, and hotel, and the camp could now be called a "town."

Soon, other supporting businesses would begin to pop up along the town's main thoroughfare. A blacksmith shop might be the next building to rise, then as Adams & Co. and Wells Fargo began to monopolize the express business, each town got its own express office. The newly invented art of photography was a popular curiosity, and nearly every town of size had at least one "daguerreotypist." Doctors and lawyers, falling back on their old professions after dismal success in the mines, were the next to hang their "shingles." Then came a newspaper and a myriad of competing grocery stores, restaurants, hotels, and saloons. By 1852, many Calaveras towns had all these and more. In just three short years, the rush for gold had turned a dozen hastily constructed supply tents into a dozen booming gold towns – between the rivers.

17
A "Pleasant" Success

ATE in the spring of 1849, a group of emigrants left the state of Alabama for California. Among this band of gold-seekers were Dr. Adolph H. Hoerchner, a medical doctor, with his wife and child; Dr. D. L. Angier, a dentist, with his wife and three children; a Captain Tobin; and Charles Grunsky, a native of Germany. Throughout most of the gold rush years, travel to California was difficult and dangerous. This group chose the Panama route, which meant exposure to cholera, seasickness, and various tropical diseases. During the final leg of their journey, aboard a ship sailing from Panama to San Francisco, Dr. Hoerchner's child died, as did Dr. Angier's youngest son, Cutler.

The travelers became close friends as the long journey took its toll and upon reaching San Francisco they immediately set out together for the gold fields. They traveled by river schooner to Stockton, where tools of the mining trade were purchased and a five-way partnership was formed. The four men (Hoerchner, Tobin, Angier, and Grunsky) would each receive an equal portion of all mining proceeds. Mrs. Hoerchner would receive the fifth portion in exchange for services as cook.

The partners began working their claims on the Mokelumne River in October, 1849, but by early September, these claims were already exhausted and they moved on to Rich Gulch, twelve miles up the river. (It should be noted here that Calaveras County had many "Rich Gulches" -- one emptied into the Mokelumne near Middle Bar and was one of the richest mining camps during those early years; another, just to the east, emptied into the Calaveras River and was often called Upper Rich Gulch.) While the gold mining efforts of the group were moderately successful, they were greatly discouraged by the many hours of strenuous labor required to produce small quantities of gold. It was during that long winter of '49 that Grunsky decided to give up mining and open a store on Upper Rich Gulch.

This new business was so successful that in the spring of 1850 he once again formed a partnership with his old friends and began expanding. He turned over the Rich Gulch store to a new partner named Kohlberg and opened a second store just two miles away on Alabama Gulch, at a place he called Pleasant Springs.

In a letter to family in Germany (now at the Bancroft Library), Grunsky describes his new home:

Pleasant Springs is a beautiful spot. Do not imagine large and attractive buildings or handsome gardens. There are none. I still live in a tent whose walls, however, are made firm by means of a dozen or more hewn timbers. What I am praising is the beautiful scenery. Pleasant Springs is well up in the mountains, and we have a fine view from our store. . . . from points on the rim of the canyon, one can look down upon [the river] and hear its rushing waters. Upon both sides of the river are continuous mountain spurs into which the river's tributary streams have cut gorges almost as deep as that of the river itself. There are mountains in every direction.

Grunsky's store, a rough hewn building about thirty feet long and fifteen feet wide, sat on a hillside above Alabama Gulch flanked by small ravines on either side. In one of his letters he says that he could walk to the Mokelumne in about an hour --with the return trip requiring one half hour additional due to the strenuous climb. Grunsky's wood and canvas tent was just behind the store, under a large oak tree. The store provided a hot meal for $1.50 and apparently this sideline did well enough for Grunsky to hire a cook at $100 a month.

Two of the main reasons for the high cost of food and supplies in the gold fields was the expense of transporting these goods from San Francisco, and the percentage taken by the middleman, a wholesaler. Grunsky and his partners were able to eliminate both of those problems by opening a wholesale house in Stockton (run by Dr. Hoerchner) and by purchasing a pack of mules to haul the merchandise. D. L. Angier acted as mule handler. By mid-Summer of 1850, Grunsky and company were the primary suppliers for camp stores along the length of the Mokelumne River.

Among the primary patrons of Grunsky's Pleasant Springs store were Indians from a nearby Me-wuk village called Apautawilu. This village was typical of the Sierra Me-wuk, with several tepee shaped huts covered in skins and bark or planks; a Council House or "roundhouse", built over a large dugout and used for ceremonial gatherings; and one or more "grinding rocks." where the women would pound acorns into meal.

While the miners of Pleasant Springs did, on occasion, harass and take advantage of the Indians, both sides were surprisingly tolerant of each other. Many of the Indians worked for the miners, but some worked their own "claims," the location of which was always kept secret for fear that it would be stolen by whites. Their gold dust was traded for food and other goods at Grunsky's store, favorite purchases being, of course, those items which did their bodies the most harm -- sugar and whiskey. They were also fond of gambling, at which they were easily cheated. Sadly, within a few years of the village of Apautawilu had been reduced, through white man's diseases and mistreatment, to a handful of "Americanized" Me-wuk.

In the Fall of 1850, Grunsky turned over the operation of the store at Pleasant Springs to Angier, so that he could supervise the running of pack trains through the winter. Early in 1851, he traveled to his homeland of Germany, and in May of 1852, he came back to California with a new bride, Clotilde, along with one of D. L. Angier's cousins, who accompanied them on the return trip.

In 1852, the store at Pleasant Springs was enlarged to accommodate a boarding house and other services needed by the ever increasing population of the area. It was estimated that some 7000 miners resided in the numerous ravines that lined the Mokelumne River from Lower Rich Gulch to Mosquito Gulch, a distance of less than ten miles. In Grunsky's absence, the name Pleasant Springs fell into disuse for a period, giving way to Alabama Gulch, Alabama Hill, and Angier's Store.

(The name of Angier's Store became permanently entrenched in history in 1962 when Charles Camp and Fred Rosenstock published *John Doble's Journal and Letters from the Mines.* Doble left his Indiana home in 1851 for the California gold fields, keeping a journal and writing letters to a young lady in Pennsylvania whom he had never met. These writings are among the foremost "first hand" accounts of life in the gold fields ever been published. Doble wrote extensively about the Rich Gulch, Moke Hill, and Angier's Store areas, which he visited during the winter of 1852.)

In July, 1853, Dr. Hoerchner purchased the entire Pleasant Springs operation from Angier for $11,500, and later filed a land claim which encompassed the surrounding 160 acres, including Apautawilu. The profitable partnership was dissolved and holdings were split among the partners. Charles Grunsky and Angier retained Stockton properties and descendants of both families still reside in that city.

A post office was established at Pleasant Springs in 1855, with Dr. Hoerchner as postmaster. He also built a small community hospital there, which he operated until 1861 when he opened a practice in Mokelumne Hill. Later, Dr. Hoerchner's bid to

Carl Grunsky drew this representation of his father's store in Pleasant Springs as it looked in 1850. (Original in the Bancroft Library)

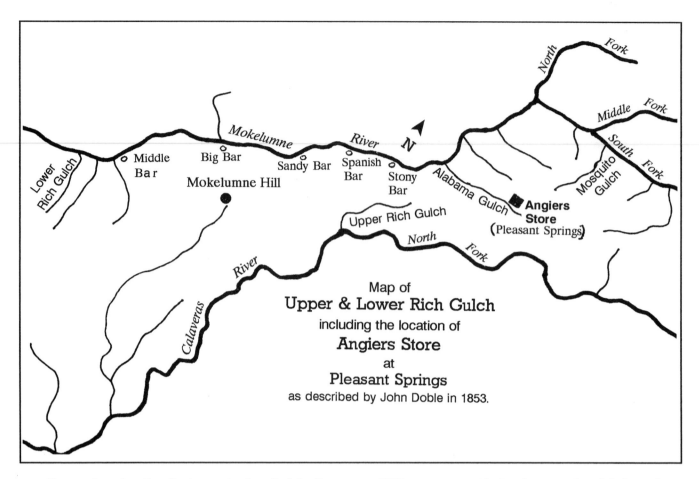

Map of
Upper & Lower Rich Gulch
including the location of
Angiers Store
at
Pleasant Springs
as described by John Doble in 1853.

provide services for the first county hospital in San Andreas was declined as too expensive.

Over the next few decades, the Pleasant Springs property would change hands several times and would boast several new buildings including Hoey's Hotel and Boarding House and the Pleasant Springs School. But eventually, commercial enterprises and educational facilities moved to the nearby business centers of Mokelumne Hill and San Andreas, the buildings were torn down or became victim to the elements, and the little community that was such an important part of early Calaveras County history disappeared from the map.

Still, some say that when you're driving along Highway 26 between Mok Hill and Glencoe, and you roll your windows down and listen very carefully, you may still hear the chants and ceremonial screams of Me-wuk Indians echoing through the hills, and you might even hear the snap of Grunsky's whip as he arrives with a mule train loaded with fresh supplies. And if you stare long enough through the trees, you may see the little shack on the hillside that was the beginning of young German emigrant's successful quest for fortune – between the rivers.

18
The Phoenix of Oregon Gulch

URING the first two years of the California Gold Rush, thousands of gold seekers settled along the banks of the Mokelumne River and its tributary streams and gulches. The camps they formed were the foundation for future towns and cities, some of which have survived, others of which have long since crumbled into dust. In most cases, the historical information relating to the first days and months of these camps is pure speculation.

It is interesting that among those first settlers of what would become Calaveras County were a group of former soldiers who had served in the war against Mexico under Colonel Stevenson; and at the same time, a number of their former enemies -- California Mexicans. It has been speculated that nearly every early camp along the Mokelumne was settled by one or the other of these groups.

By the fall of 1849, there were enough white Americans in the gold fields to make other ethnic groups feel extremely uncomfortable and unwelcome. This was especially true of those with Hispanic blood. Accordingly, it would not be hard to visualize a small band of Mexicans being chased from town to camp to town, never being allowed to stay in one place long enough to work a claim in peace. And it would perhaps be only logical to believe that this band would take refuge along a small gulch which, being totally dry, had been ignored by the other miners. And it would certainly be appropriate if they named the place "Campo Seco" -- dry camp.

However it came to be, by the winter of 1849 a large Spanish settlement of that name was in place on Oregon Gulch about a mile from the Mokelumne River. In the early part of 1850, there were Mexicans, Chileans, and Peruvians working claims there, and later in that year the camp boasted over 40 different nationalities (even though the camp lived up to its name during a year-long drought).

Despite dry spells and occasional visits by vigilante groups set on eliminating California's foreign population, Campo Seco flourished. And some who stuck it out did not go unrewarded for two of the largest nuggets ever found in Calaveras County were taken from the diggings there. One reported to be 118 ounces sold in 1853 for $940 and a second in 1854 weighed 93 ounces.

In December of 1853, the Campo Seco mining district was defined when the local miners established a code of laws. These boundaries were listed as follows: *On the north by Salt Gulch, on the west by the Mokelumne River, on the east by Cosgrave Creek, and on the south by the gulch known as Minter's Gulch.* Gulch claims were 100 feet long and 25 feet wide. Hillside claims were 75 feet square, while claims on the flats were 100 feet square.

As the town grew during the early 1850s, Adams and Company established an express office and a U.S. Post Office was opened in February 1854. But 1854 was not a good year for Campo Seco. During the long dry summer temperatures reached as high as 114 degrees and many of the miners set out for "wet" diggings along the major rivers. Then, on August 18, the town was wiped out by fire. While a few store owners rebuilt, this disaster was the final straw for many.

As was often the case in California mining towns, when other miners gave up, the Chinese took over, and Campo Seco soon developed a large "China-town" settlement. Two separate Chinese stores were built, one to service each of the two established "tongs" who worked the abandoned diggings. These buildings had sturdy rock walls with "chinking" in the cracks to help keep the building cool in summer and warm in winter. There was also a gambling hall, since games of chance were a popular Chinese pastime. (According to John McGill, who was an early resident of Campo Seco, the rock walls around the town were not, as is often assumed, built by the Chinese, but by Scottish farmers who came later.)

By 1857 the population of the town dwindled to a few hundred stubborn miners and business owners. In August of 1859, fire again visited Campo Seco, this time destroying all of Chinatown and a large portion of the rest of the community. Campo Seco again bounced back, as the San Andreas Independent reported a year later, on August 25, 1860:

The population of Campo Seco in the summer of 1860 is abut 300, including 50 Chinese and a sprinkling of Mexicans. The fire last year destroyed nearly the entire town, but most of it has been rebuilt. It contains a few fine gardens, two churches, (one used for a school house) two large hotels, one of them stone, owned by Mr. Nye, a number of saloons, and five stores. Mining is dull at present. A branch of the Mokelumne Hill Canal furnishes water for domestic use and irrigation purposes.

There were two important events which occurred late in 1859 that were, to a great degree, responsible for Campo Seco's recovery. One, referred to above, was the completion of the Mokelumne Hill Canal and Mining Company's water ditch extension from Moke Hill which supplied the community with its first permanent source of water. Campo Seco was no longer "seco."

The other event was the discovery of copper. According to published accounts, two Mexicans and a Chilean miner uncovered a rich deposit of copper ore and struck upon the idea of passing it off as gold. But after a Lancha Plana store owner discovered that they had sold him copper, they were arrested and tried for swindling. The trio managed to convince the judge that it was an honest mistake and the charges were dismissed on the condition that the money be returned to the store owner. They later sold their claim to J. K. Harmon, who operated a successful copper mine at the location for several years.

While copper never reached the value of gold, it was becoming more valuable with each passing year. Copper was one of the primary elements used in the production of brass, a metal that was seeing greater use for fittings in steam engines. Copper was also used for the thousands of miles of telegraph wires that were being strung between eastern cities and would soon traverse the entire continent. The community of Copperopolis, in the southwest corner of the county, owes its name to the large copper "lead" (pronounced "leed"; the term designates a "vein" of copper ore) discovered there in 1860.

In 1862, workers digging a drainage ditch struck a copper lead on the north side of Coon Gulch, near Campo Seco. Robert Eproson and a syndicate of 14 shareholders developed the lead by sinking a 30 foot shaft into the hillside from which tons of rich copper ore were extracted. But Campo Seco's roller coaster dipped to a new low in 1866

and 1867, when a glut on the copper market made it unprofitable to ship copper from California, and the mines closed down.

For 13 years the community of Campo Seco remained quiet. The townsite was surveyed in 1870 and was laid out into nine blocks with 67 lots. In 1880, the mining of California copper again became a viable business and many of the best mines around Campo Seco were bought up by the Penn Mining Company, whose holdings eventually totaled nearly 1200 acres. With two deep shafts on the site of Harmon's mine (J.K. Harmon would later become President and General Manager of the Penn Chemical Works), a large smelter and a tram to transport ore between the two, the Penn Mine was an extensive operation that helped to promote the recovery, and secure the economic future of Campo Seco into the 20th century.

Like doorways to the past, the ruins of Campo Seco stand as a reminder of the town's many lives.

This second copper boom lasted until 1919, when the mines once again closed down. But Campo Seco would see two more revivals; the first, not from mining this time, but from the construction of the nearby Pardee Dam in 1928. The community was host to hundreds of workers during the building of the dam and boasted four stores, a restaurant, two hotels, a dance hall, a speakeasy, and several moonshining operations. (Many of these were destroyed when another devastating fire occurred that same year.) After the dam was completed and the workers went on to their next project, the little town slept once more.

World War II brought a new demand for copper and the last awakening of Campo Seco. The Penn Mine reopened and continued its operation until 1959. Since that time, the commercial district has all but disappeared and today the community is inhabited by a few descendants of the early residents along with a small number of newcomers looking for peace and quiet and room to breath.

The history of Campo Seco is a story of boom and bust. Over the past century and a half, thousands of people of every race, creed, and color called the little town their home. Businesses were built and destroyed, fortunes were made and lost. And now, only a few crumbling walls of red stone mark the spot where a handful of persecuted Californios sought a place to settle and work in peace on a dry, dusty gulch -- between the rivers.

19
They Came Too

HEN one looks back at the changes that women as a group have gone through during the last quarter century, it perhaps seems easy to picture what women of the 19th century must have been like -- repressed, oppressed, dominated, having little or nothing to offer society other than their "feminine charms" and the performance of "womanly" duties. While this could certainly be said of a certain percentage of the female population of that period, so could it be said of some today. As it has been since the beginning of time, women of the 19th century, like the men of that time, came in a variety of shapes and sizes, with personalities, dispositions, character, demeanor, and tastes of an equally wide array. Nowhere was this more evident than with the women of California's Gold Rush era.

Many historians and writers have perhaps mislead their readers somewhat by "overplaying" the lack of women in the mining camps. There were certainly women residing in California throughout the Spanish period, and after the discovery of gold nearly every emigrant train or steamer arriving from the east included a number of women. In March of 1848, the population of San Francisco was 812 persons, of which an estimated 200 were females. This 3 to 1 ratio would remain more or less constant for larger California cities throughout the Gold Rush period. In the distant mines, however, there were 50 or even 100 men for each woman in 1848-49, with the percentage of women slightly increasing each year throughout the 1850s.

When did the first woman make her mark in the annals of Gold Rush history? Within hours of his discovery of a gold nugget in the millrace at Sutter's Mill, James Marshall showed the yellow metal to Elizabeth "Jennies" Wimmer, the camp cook and "washer-woman" who was at the time making some lye soap. In order to test the metal, she threw the nugget into the lye and allowed it to sit until the next morning when it was recovered unaffected. Encouraged by Jennie's test, Marshall set out for Sutter's Fort to report his findings, and the wheels of the Gold Rush were set in motion.

The early mining camps were rowdy, and many saw a direct relationship between the lack of women and the high spiritedness of the men. There were

two women of note that took it upon themselves to remedy that situation -- Mrs. Eliza Farnham and Miss Sarah Pellet. In 1849, Eliza published an open letter in several New York newspapers attempting to convince one hundred women to accompany her to the California gold fields, where they might become "one of the surest checks upon many of the evils that are apprehended there." While only three women made the trip, the strong willed Eliza continued to make her voice heard as writer, lecturer, and proponent of women's rights.

During the mid-1850s, Sarah Pellet's aspirations were a bit higher. It was her plan to import 5,000 women to the mining camps, but Sarah also found few volunteers. Her temperance lectures, however, drew large crowds, although the mostly male audiences were more interested in looking at the lady than in listening to what she had to say. At one such lecture, the introductory speaker wound up dead from a shotgun blast because he had taken too long to introduce the popular Ms. Pellet.

In his *Journal and Letters from the Mines*, prospector John Doble recognized the effect of women in camp:

The store [Angier's Store in Pleasant Springs] was crowded when we returned about dark, and a good many of [the miners] were tight--or in other words, half drunk--and after dark they got to singing sailor songs & playing games, etc, and got us all up and Tom Baldwin played the fiddle for them and they danced and sung till near morning, not letting us sleep any. Angiers has his wife here with him and she was greatly disturbed by the noise and language used. Such is California. Wherever women is not, there reigns vice and immorality.

Doble also records a tragic and all too common occurrence in the mines:

Mrs. [James] Holstead, that was married last fall here at the house by the spring, died today near eleven o'clock after an illness of some three months. She gave birth to a child about 2 weeks ago, which is supposed to have hastened her decease. The child died three days ago. I'm going to sit up tonight at the wake.

Five months later, Doble makes note of the marriage of James Holstead to a Miss Brown who "crossed the plains this season." In a place where

Nearly every wagon train bound for California carried a number of women. Unfortunately, women and children were the first to fall victim to cholera and other diseases of the trail. (Harpers Magazine)

single women were more precious than gold, Mr. James had found two wives in just over one year.

Most of the women who came to California during the early years of the Gold Rush were wives who had decided that, for better or worse, they would accompany their husbands on the "quest for El Dorado." In addition to performing the standard wifely duties, many contributed to the family income by doing laundry for the single miners of the camp or by selling bread and other baked goods. Miners who had not tasted a woman's cooking for several months paid as much as ten dollars for a pan of homemade biscuits or a loaf of bread. An apple pie might bring twice that.

A miner's wife might also help work the claim along side her husband, as a San Francisco newspaper observed in 1850:

We saw last April, a French woman, standing in Angel's Creek, dipping and pouring water into the washer, which her husband was rocking. She wore short boots, white duck pantaloons, a red flannel shirt, with a black leather belt and a Panama hat. Day after day she could be seen working quietly and steadily, performing her share of the gold digging labor. . . .

Single women came to the gold fields too, although they often ended up working at jobs that were not considered "proper" for a lady. Among the more lucrative positions were barmaid, card dealer, dancer, and prostitute. Less common, but still evident, were lady barbers, doctors, photographers, bullfighters, mule team drivers, and boat captains.

During the early years of the Gold Rush, hundreds of women arrived in California for the express purpose of engaging in the business of prostitution. Large numbers of these were Chinese women who had been sold into slavery, and would be sold again to California brothels. Others came, by force or by choice, from South America and France. The frequency of Chinese, Chilean, and French prostitutes added greatly to the already burgeoning prejudices against foreigners, so that almost any female who spoke with an accent was assumed to be a "fallen" woman.

Whether or not a prostitute would be allowed to stay in business depended not on the volume of clientele, but on the amount of influence wielded by the "moral minority" of the camp. Generally, this group would be led by a long time resident wife whose spouse had shown some degree of interest, however innocent, in the lady's wares. In smaller camps, the businesswoman might be given an enthusiastic escort out of town, preceded by a head shaving or tar and feathering, in the time-honored western tradition.

But in larger towns, the "immoral majority" ruled and the ladies freely displayed their charms in saloons and gambling halls, or in some cases, a full-fledged "women's boarding house" (the respectable synonym for brothel). Certain towns became widely known for the availability and abundance of their "soiled doves", among them, Sonora in Tuolumne County and Jackson in Amador County.

One of the most widely known women of the Gold Rush period was Eliza Gilbert. (Don't be surprised that you don't recognize the name.) She was born in Ireland and came to California in 1853, at the age of 35. She called herself the Countess of Landsfeldt, a title given to her by a lover, of which she had many. In San Francisco, she married a newspaperman named Patrick Hull – he was her fourth husband. Eliza was an entertainer, both on the stage and off, who under her stage name, Lola Montez, was widely known for her "scandalous" spider dance in which she pretended to be attacked by a hoard of tarantulas who made their way beneath her skirt to regions even spiders were not allowed during Victorian times.

After several months of touring the mining towns, with mixed reviews, Lola threw her new husband down the hotel stairs in Sacramento and bought a little house in Grass Valley. Her presence there influenced the youthful career of another of California's historic performers, Lotta Crabtree, who was only seven years old at the time. Within a year of the Countess' arrival, the little girl was performing her dances in the mining camps with each performance ending in a shower of gold from grateful miners. At the age of 17, she left for New York to become a stage actress, beginning an illustrious career that took her not only to the all the major cities of the U.S. but to London and Paris as well. Lotta retired in 1891, at the age of 44.

When the seventh Federal Census was taken in 1850, the population of the territory of California was officially counted for the first time. Calaveras County (which at that time included today's Amador County) held 18% of the total population of the state, including 16,884 men (excluding Chinese, Blacks, and Indians) and just 265 women. In the special census of 1852, the male population of the county had increased about 13%, but the female total had risen nearly 500%. Even so, the ratio of men to women was still 12 to 1.

For the most part, the Calaveras women were the wives and daughters of miners and storekeepers. They braved the treacherous journey across the plains or Panama isthmus only to find themselves stuck in a leaky leanto on the banks of a muddy foothill stream. They helped build the cabins, mended the clothes, cooked the meals, and raised the next generation of Californians. Many Calaveras women also started and ran successful businesses. Others simply provided feminine warmth and sympathy (if for a price) to lonely miners. Whatever their background or calling, the women of Calaveras County had one thing in common. . . .they came too, in search of a better life -- between the rivers.

Dancer/actress Lotta Crabtree began her long and successful career as a child star in the gold field camps of California.

20
Watery Ghosts of the Mok

N the early 1850s the Mokelumne River wound its way unobstructed through the canyons of central Calaveras County and was home to hundreds of miners who worked its bars and tributary gulches. Those gulches and the various camps which sprang up along the length of the river had mostly been named by the first miners who arrived there in late 1848 or early 1849. We can only guess at the source of those names. Some seem obvious, like those probably named for the miner's home country or state (ie. Alabama Gulch, Italian Bar, Spanish Bar). Others were apparently named for the miner himself (ie. Taylor's Bar, James' Bar). Other names appear to have been born of experience or pessimism (ie. Poverty Gulch, Humbug, Mosquito Gulch).

Many of the more successful early gold mining camps in Calaveras County were located along a ten mile stretch of the Mokelumne from the San Joaquin County border to Diamond Bar (where the Pardee Dam now sits). These included (among others less notable) Catts Camp, Camanche Diggings, Poverty Bar, Winter's Bar, Campo Seco, and Ragtown on the south side of the Mokelumne; and Putts Bar, Lancha Plana, Camp Union, and French Camp on the north. The westernmost of these was Catts Camp.

There were a number of resourceful individuals who, in the early years of the gold rush, recognized the commercial prospects of providing supplies to the distant camps. Among these was Samuel Catts, who was one of the first to transport goods by mule team from Stockton during the winter of 1848. He also established a general store on a hill about one mile east of the Calaveras County border and one mile south of the Mokelumne River that serviced the miners working along Camanche and Bear Creeks. The small community which grew up around the store became known as Catt's Camp.

Boasting a grocery store, saloon, and a number of log cabin homes, Catt's Camp remained a quiet stop on the road to Mokelumne Hill until the 1860s, when some 350 claims were filed on the surrounding land in anticipation of water being brought in by the Mokelumne Hill and Campo Seco Canal. An extension of the canal arrived in 1868, and did much to add to the development of the community throughout the 1870s. Catt's Camp ceased to exist shortly after 1883 when the nearby town of Wallace, created by the arrival of the narrow gauge railroad from Lodi to Valley Springs, became the center of commerce for the area.

Among the more notable historical events that took place in Wallace was a shootout that occurred between a Calaveras County Constable and two transient "toughs." On March 10, 1900, Constable S.D. Holman observed two men hanging around a way station that was under construction. After a minor confrontation with the pair, he went for help and returned that evening with three armed deputies. As the constable stepped onto the porch of the way-station, he was shot in the chest by one of the drifters. Under a cover of heavy fire from the three deputies, Holman was pulled away from the building and transported to his home where he died later that evening.

At daylight, County Sheriff Ben Thorn entered the way station and found one of the drifters dead of a gunshot wound to the head. The second man, Louis Dibble, had escaped, but was later arrested in Ione in Amador County. Since it was determined that his partner fired the shot that killed the constable, Dibble received only a 30 day sentence.

About a mile north and slightly east of Catt's Camp was Poverty Bar, one of two "bar" camps on the south bank of the Mokelumne river that saw significant growth during the early years of the gold rush. Its up-river twin, Winter's Bar was only slightly more productive, with significant amounts of gold being taken from both areas. These camps were all but abandoned when a major flood in 1862 sent residents heading for safer ground. Many staked new claims in and around what would become the town of Camanche.

There has been much speculation over the years as to how the town of Camanche got its name. The original settlement, located on Camanche Creek just south of the Mokelumne River, was called Limerick Camp, which would lead one to believe that the camp was founded by an Irishman although historical papers indicate that the early population of the town was primarily Chinese and Indian. Based on surviving journals and early maps, it appears that the name was changed to Camanche Camp (or Camanche Diggings) around 1856-57. At least one account says that a family named Bovard renamed the settlement for their home town in Iowa. (Since that Mississippi River town has also used the misspelling of the Indian tribal name "Comanche" for two centuries, this seems a logical possibility.)

The Sacramento Union for April 23, 1858, describes Camanche Camp:

A correspondent, writing to the Union April 21st from this camp in Calaveras County gives a very favorable account of the general business, as well as mining prospects of the place. . . . The camp boasts of four grocery stores, two clothing shops, two hotels, two blacksmith shops, one meat market, two drug stores, and billiard rooms and whiskey mills in abundance. . . . .The mines continue to pay well. The McGungle Brothers have struck dirt that pays from $1 to $8 to the pan.

The town continued to prosper throughout the 1860s, stimulated by the arrival of "washouts" from Poverty Bar in 1862, and the later arrival of the previously mentioned Mokelumne Hill and Campo Seco Canal. (Although Camanche Creek did contain water during the winter months, it tended to dry up early in the year.) A post office was opened in February of 1864. Like most gold rush towns with a large Chinese population, Camanche was the site of a "tong war" when, in 1865, rival clans met each other with clubs and knives on Main Street.

As surface placers began to wear out, Camanche Creek and the nearby Mokelumne River were

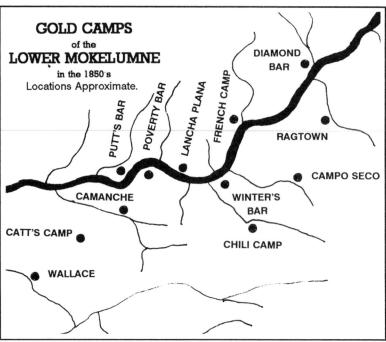

worked by dredging companies who continued to mine the area well into the 20th century. From the late 1870s the town's population became increasingly Italian, with many of the newcomers supplying fresh produce to surrounding communities from their "truck gardens." Another major crop grown near Comanche was a type of chrysanthemum (flower) used in production the insecticide "Buhach."

A number of important commercial enterprises began as a result of the Gold Rush. In addition to dry goods companies and freight carriers, there were also those who made a living by supplying water to dry camps like Catt's Camp and Campo Seco. As San

Before its evacuation and destruction in the 60's, Camanche was a typical quiet Mother Lode community.

A dark and rainy winter's day over the ruins of Camanche gives notice that the little town will soon sleep again beneath the lake's water.

Francisco, Oakland, and Stockton began to grow, they too were concerned with maintaining a good supply of water during dry months and the all too frequent droughts. Probably the most notable developers of water systems in the Bay Area was Anthony Chabot, who started the Contra Costa Water Company (CCWC) in 1866 and built both the Temescal and San Leandro Dams.

The CCWC went through a number of name changes over the years, becoming the East Bay Water Company in 1916, and eventually being absorbed by the East Bay Municipal Utilities District (E.B.M.U.D.), created in 1923. EBMUD's early priority was to locate distant river sources for fresh water and among the first to be considered was the Mokelumne. With George Pardee as President, EBMUD set in motion a project to build a major dam and reservoir at the site of the Gold Rush camp of Diamond Bar, northeast of Lancha Plana. After a number of lawsuits and other court actions, work on the Pardee Dam began in 1927.

According to officials at the time, the Pardee Reservoir would provide sufficient water supplies to the East Bay area for the next thirty years. But a study ordered in 1949 recommended the building of three additional dams on the Mokelumne: at Camanche, below Pardee Dam; at Middle Bar, above Pardee Reservoir; and near Railroad Flat, on the South Fork of the river. The resulting reservoirs, while providing sufficient water for the Bay Area's future, would virtually wipe the Mokelumne River from the Calaveras County map, and so the court battles began anew.

In 1959, EBMUD received final approval for the Camanche Dam project, and the dam was completed in 1964. The historic towns of Comanche, Lancha Plana, and Poverty Bar would soon be under 40 to 100 feet of water, along with a number of farms and ranches. Known Indian burial sites and pioneer graveyards were located and moved, although countless many were, no doubt, never found. 17 miles of county roads were relocated or eliminated, and landowners were given a "fair" price, as designated by the courts, with little or no significance given to the historical value of the land or the extensive gold deposits still buried there.

On June 22, 1962, members of the Calaveras Historical Society and the Chamber of Commerce met in Camanche to mark the closing of its post office. In the following months, Camanche's 500 residents would relocate to new homes, leaving the historic mining town to be razed by EBMUD demolition teams. Trees, shrubbery, and other "organic" materials were bulldozed away. Buildings were demolished and/or burned, leaving only the concrete sidewalks and foundations to mark the town's location. Within a few years, the rising waters of the lake crept up Camanche Creek and gradually, the remains of the little town disappeared.

Today, the Mokelumne River and its associated lakes and reservoirs provide 85% of the East Bay's water. Camanche Lake serves as flood control provides recreational facilities in the form of boating, fishing, and camping. Just as the river was the life blood of forty-niners, it is now the life blood of a million-plus East Bay water district consumers. Still, one can't help but question whether the result was worth the cost of the many historic gold rush camps that were forever lost to progress -- between the rivers.

21
High Expectations

URING the earliest years of the gold rush, the first permanent settlements in Calaveras County were naturally at the lower elevations of the foothills. As prospective miners worked their way up the rivers and tributaries, they stopped at the first spot that showed some promise of success -- and that was not already being worked by someone else. As the 1850s approached, with thousands of miners making their way to the gold fields, many new mining camps were being formed in the upper elevations of the Sierra Mountains near or above the winter snow line.

About two miles northeast of the gold rush camp called "Pleasant Springs" (also "Angier's Store"), the lower Mokelumne River was fed by its north, middle, and southern "forks". Starting in the latter part of 1849, a number of "diggings" were developed along these three branches and their associated gulches. As was typical in those days, the camps were given colorful names whose derivation can only be guessed at. Interestingly, most of those early names have fallen from use, replaced by the names of towns that came later.

In 1850, there were a number of miners working claims along a small gulch which emptied into the South Fork of the Mokelumne River. The area was especially wet and marshy during the summer, providing an extensive breeding ground for what contemporary accounts called "mighty big" mosquitos, prompting the name Mosquito Gulch (often spelled "Musquito" in those days). Like many early Mother Lode camps, it was apparently first settled by foreign miners who had been chased from American dominated diggings elsewhere. The area was occupied by a predominantly German population during the 1850s and a number of Mexicans and Chileans worked nearby claims with arrastras (ore crushers).

It is unknown exactly when the nearby town of Glencoe, at the upper end of the gulch, was founded. Local folklore says that it was named for a place described in a novel being read by an employee of the Mokelumne Ditch Company in the late 1850s. But the town does not appear on any early maps of the county and did not receive wide recognition until the Mosquito Gulch post office was transferred there in 1878 or 1879. There is little doubt, however, of the origin of the name itself which was given to

a place in Argylsire, Scotland where the Donald clan was massacred in 1692. Whether this name found its way to California via a 19th century novel or by some other means has been lost to history.

The origin of the name of Glencoe's neighbor, West Point, is equally as vague. As usual, local folk-lore has a colorful explanation -- that Kit Carson named the place when he visited that area during the winter of 1844. As of this writing, no solid evidence has been found to support this claim and in fact first-hand, contemporary accounts of the Fremont/Carson expeditions prove it unlikely.

When the first miners settled in that area during the spring or summer of 1849, they worked claims along Indian Gulch and Soap Gulch to the north of the Mokelumne's Middle Fork, and Sandy Gulch, which paralleled the river before entering it from the southeast. A number of nearby camps sprang up during the early 1850s, these included Camp Spirito, Camp Catarrah, Valentine Hill, and later, Bummerville, which would become home to a number of important quartz mines.

The earliest reference to West Point (located by local historian and educator, David Gano), appears to be from William Knight *Scrapbook: Calaveras County Vol.II.* It reads, in part:

In February, '54, Fernando and Ferrero came from Mosquito Gulch and established a provision store -- A blacksmith shop was started at the same time. The name of the place, which had before been known as Indian Gulch Precinct, was now changed to West Point. The store and shop being a central point, they naturally became a place of resort for the miners.

Due to the lack of established trails into the area, immigration to the town of West Point came primarily from, or through, the town of Volcano, across the Mokelumne River in newly-formed Amador County. On January 12, 1856, the following appeared in the Volcano Weekly Ledger:

WEST POINT - ITS RESOURCES AND WANTS
From a gentleman who has just returned from the above place we have received an account of the present condition and prospects of that new and interesting camp. Although it is situated in Calaveras County between the North and Middle Forks of the Mokelumne River. . . . its interests are

Mines of the West Point/Glencoe Area

According to the California Division of Mines and Geology, the West Point Mining District was one of the most productive districts in California, with an unusually large number of individual mines. The following list is presented not only for its historical value, but for the names themselves which are food for the imagination.

The Austrian	The Billy Williams	The Blackstone
The Carlton	The Blazing Star	The Buena Vista
The Centennial	The Corn Meal	The Chino
The Champion	The Continental	The Cross
The Etna	The Ever Ready	The Fidelity
The Garibaldi	The Gilded Age	The Glencoe
The Kelz	The Golden Rule	The Gold Star
The Lockwood	The Good Hope	The Lone Star
The Marquis	The Mina Rica	The Monte Cristo
The North Star	The Old Henry	The Rindge
The Riverside	The San Bruno	The San Pedro
The Scorpion	The Soap Root	The Star of the West
The Swallow	The Water Lily	The Wide West
The Woodhouse	The Yellow Aster	The John Henry
The Bald Eagle	The Matrimony	The Kaiser Wilhelm
The Mohawk	The Hazel Dell	The Petticoat
The Sanderson	The Lawson	The Poe
The Alpha	The Summit	The Old Gray

as completely identified with Volcano as that of any camp in our neighborhood. The great bridge which is now building across the river will affect an easy communication with us and will be their only road to the valleys.

The article goes on to describe the numerous water ditches in the area, the abundant quartz leads, and the need for a sawmill to provide lumber.

By July 1856, the population of the surrounding area had become sufficient to warrant the opening of a post office at West Point, with Augustus Walbaum as the first Postmaster. Roads into the area were constantly improving and soon the little town had stage coach service to Mokelumne Hill and points beyond. Its reduced dependence on Volcano is evident in a letter, written by a West Point resident to the editor of the Volcano Ledger. Published on February 21, 1857, it describes the improving conditions of the community, then concludes:

Thus you see West Point is a place of enterprise if not great wealth. Few men had much money in their purses when they begun these operations, but I think they are all in a fair way to become independent by exercising patience and industry.

Quartz leads are very numerous in this vicinity. . . . In placer mining a good business is being done in the numerous gulches around here. . . . all branches of business, appropriate to this section of the country are being advanced.

Although we are rough fragments of society, thrown off by Volcano during its different great mutations, yet we trust that there is still a sort of fraternal feeling entertained between us. . . .

West Point's population was typically multi-national, with a noticeable Chinatown section and large numbers of Mexicans and Chileans. The Chinese section was destroyed by fire in 1858 and all of the wooden building of the town were destroyed by another fire in the 1860s. The area was also widely populated by Me-wuk Indians who, if they survived the white man's diseases and mistreatment, quickly learned to make use of white man's food, clothing, guns, and liquor.

Mining in the West Point area continued to be successful into the 20th century, but residents also began to take advantage of the abundant timber in surrounding hills, with lumber and charcoal becoming major industries. Fruit and nut orchards are a fairly recent addition.

South of West Point and east of Glencoe were the neighboring camps of Independence and Railroad Flat, near the North Fork of the Calaveras River. Little information is available about the early years of these communities, but it is likely that the surrounding gulches were occupied by miners as early as 1849, and according to Doble (John Doble's *Journals and Letters from the Mines*), the camp of Independence (also called Independence Flat) was well established by 1852.

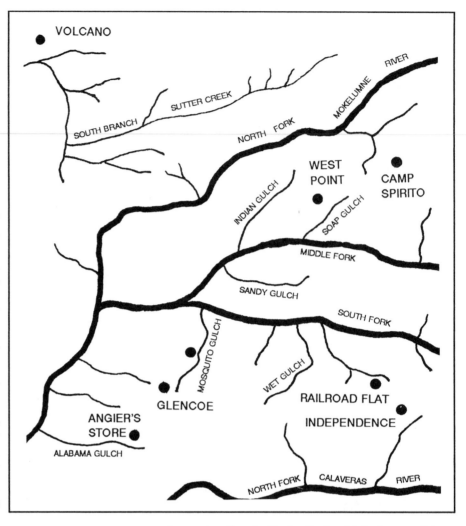

There is not now, nor has there ever been, a railroad in Railroad Flat. Again, there is no specific evidence of the origin of the name, but even the most staunch historian should have no problem accepting the simple, traditional explanation. Sometime very early in the gold rush, a miner constructed a set of wooden tracks upon which he could run an ore car (pulled by mules) across the flat from his diggings to the nearest water source. Thus, passersby came to call the place Railroad Flat.

Both towns continued to grow in size throughout the 1850s, boasting a number of stores and restaurants, a hotel, and numerous saloons. For reasons that remain a mystery, the Railroad Flat post office was in business for only one year, 1857. In October 1856, the Clark Ditch, which brought water to the area from the South Fork of the Mokelumne River was completed, contributing greatly to the economy of both Railroad Flat and Independence. Many of the workers who helped in the construction took their pay in the form of water "credits", to be used for washing gold when they returned to their diggings. Later, the ditch was extended to Glencoe and Rich Gulch.

While the Mokelumne River has always flowed down from the Sierra Mountains, the Gold Rush years saw a flow of humanity in the opposite direction, up into the hills. Thousands of men and women from all over the world left their comfortable homes and their successful farms and businesses to seek fortune in the gulches of the "Land of Skulls." Maps which once had only lines representing creeks and rivers were now dotted with new towns, and the lines were given names. While many of the dots have since disappeared, and the names are often forgotten, they are forever recorded in history -- between the rivers.

62

22
Down the River of Skulls

RIOR to the gold rush, only a handful of trappers and Spanish explorers made their way into the area which is now Calaveras County, mostly by following the three major rivers. The first group to attempt to map the area to any degree was the Spanish military, and many of the names used on those early maps have been long since replaced by later designations, primarily from the gold rush period.

According to the diary of the Spanish military explorer Gabriel Moraga, the Calaveras River, which they first named for St. Francis, was completely dry when first discovered in 1806. Interestingly, dairies of later Moraga expeditions make no mention of this river whatsoever and the name San Francisco was then given to what is now the Cosumnes River. None of the known maps, diaries, or documents from that period mention the name Calaveras.

Since the literal translation of the Spanish word "Calaveras" is "skulls," it has been assumed that the name was given to the river because a large number of skulls were found there. Again, there is no first hand evidence of when this might have occurred or who bestowed the name. However, sometime in 1833, a major epidemic swept through the Indian population of the Central Valley and foothills. With entire villages decimated, there was often no one left to bury the dead and subsequent explorers found large groupings of bones and skulls. Since John Fremont included the designation "Calaveras" on his map of 1844, one might conclude that someone gave the river that name between 1833 and 1844.

(Another logical theory, put forth by local historian/educator David Gano, is that when the river was dry, as it was during Moraga's first two visits, its bed of smooth round rocks were covered with a white deposit, giving the appearance of a "river of skulls" and thus inspiring the name.)

Nevertheless, while we may never know exactly how it came to be, by the start of the Gold Rush in 1848, the stream was called the Calaveras River and it quickly became dotted with mining camps along its length. Later, a few of these early camps grew into permanent settlements located along the river from the San Andreas area to the Stanislaus County line. The most important of these were North Branch, Latimer's, Greasertown, Petersburg,

Boston Bar, Taylor's Bar, and Jenny Lind. The early active camps of Rich Gulch, South Gulch, and Pleasant Valley faded as quickly as they boomed and little is know of their history other than short mentions in period diaries.

Almost everyone who has ever driven highway 12 from San Andreas to Stockton has seen the old Pioneer Cemetery which sets on a hill to the left of that road near its crossing of the Calaveras River. However, few know that it was built to service the town of North Branch, which sat in the little valley below. Evidence suggests that North Branch was one of the very first mining camps in what would become Calaveras County, with as many as 300 miners working there during 1848-49.

Like many gold rush camps, the settlement grew up around a store, established during those early years by E.T. Lake who was also later the postmaster. The town was also the site of an important toll bridge, which spanned the Calaveras at a point called "Second Crossing." With San Andreas quickly becoming an important commercial center and the road between that town and Stockton being heavily traveled, the toll bridge was a highly profitable venture for its builders and subsequent owners. To bring a wagon across the driver would have to pay $3.00 plus 25¢ for each 100 pounds of freight.

The North Branch post office, which had been installed in 1852, was removed to nearby Latimer's in 1859. The reason for this change may be found in an article from the San Andreas Independent of October 15, 1859 which indicates that the surface mining in North Branch was so vigorous that Lake's store was quickly becoming undermined. Also, the settlement around Daniel Latimer's ranch and store had grown to considerable size, with a large number of Irish families settling there.

While both of these communities were quite active in their day, the dwindling deposits of placer gold in the late '50s and early '60s led to an exodus of the population to other towns. Even though a number of successful nearby quartz mines were in operation well into the 20th century, the two towns quickly faded from the map. Today, there is little physical evidence that they ever existed.

Farther down the river, below the area called "Big Canyon," two camps grew to considerable size during the 1850s. The first was called Greasertown.

A sturdy, if somewhat perilous footbridge provided access to Petersburg, on one side of the Calaveras, and the numerous residences on the opposite bank.

(Shown on some maps of the period as "Greaserville," possibly due to confusion with a town by that name in Amador County, this highly derogatory appellation reflects the prevailing ethnic prejudices of those years and one wonders if the primarily Spanish and Chinese residents of that camp didn't have another name for it.)

The first residents of the camp, undoubtedly Mexican, arrived very early in the gold rush and the settlement quickly grew to considerable size. Citizens of the predominantly white camps of North Branch and Latimers were highly displeased with

having such a large congregation of foreigners nearby, and in 1853, a large mob from those communities marched to Greasertown and expelled a large portion of the population. Even so, the town remained an active mining camp into the 1860s, and boasted a number of stores, saloons, billiard parlors, and a hotel.

The town of Petersburg, about a mile up-river from Greasertown, sprang up in the late 1850's and probably did much to hasten Greasertown's demise. The town is believed to have been named for Peter Snyder, who had constructed a water ditch from near Latimer's to Greasertown. According to an article in a San Andreas newspaper of the period, by 1858 Petersburg had a store, a billiard room, and a number of families in residence.

As Greasertown dwindled to a few ranch owners, Petersburg grew and prospered. When placer gold began to play out, companies were formed to apply more aggressive mining methods. Others chose to take advantage of the high quality farmlands of the area and became ranchers. By 1864, the town had grown sufficiently to require the construction of a school house. Since there were numerous residences on both sides of the Calaveras, school children and others made frequent use of a well-constructed foot bridge which spanned the river.

Petersburg remained an active farming community into the 20th century, but in 1929 the land was condemned by the City of Stockton in preparation for the construction of the Hogan Reservoir. Despite the fact that the residents were not compensated for mineral rights when they were removed from their lands, the City of Stockton later leased dredging rights to a company that was able to pull over three quarters of a million dollars in gold from the river. Later, the area was inundated by the New Hogan Reservoir.

About a mile and a half below Greasertown was Boston Bar. Little is known about this camp except for an often mentioned but not very detailed account which says that Charles Johnson, owner of Johnson's Store was killed by Mexicans in 1866.

The area around Boston Bar, however, was the site of two large, early ranches; one claimed by Giacamo Leoni in 1849, and the other by Manuel Munoa in 1852. During the early years, the Leoni ranch was known as the "Swiss Ranch" or "Boston Ranch," but later came to be called the DeMartini Ranch for Leoni's partner, whose descendants resided on the ranch into the 20th century. A large portion of the DeMartini Ranch and all of the Munoa Ranch was inundated by the New Hogan Reservoir.

Erection of the New Hogan Dam was authorized by the Flood Control Act of 1944, but construction did not begin until 1960. Completed in 1964, the huge earth-fill dam sits just below its much smaller concrete predecessor, and stands 200 feet high and nearly 2000 feet long. (At the time of this writing, a severe drought has reduced the volume of New Hogan Reservoir to the point where even the original dam seems larger than needed.)

The New Hogan Dam lies just east of the former gold rush camp of Taylor's Bar. Little is known about the early years of this camp or of the person for whom it was named. Records show that there was a store located there in 1854, run by Vieussex Gaspard, and other names from those records indicate a largely French population. Like many "bar" camps, this community quickly disappeared with the placer deposits and the land was converted to ranch property.

While there were a few small camps located along the Calaveras River downstream from Taylor's Bar, the first early camp of note was Jenny's Bar. As is often the case, the origin of the name remains a mystery, but ironically, a Dr. John Y. Lind staked a claim nearby in 1849 and the town which sprang up at that location came to be called Jenny Lind.

The Pioneer Cemetery is all that is left to mark the little town of North Branch. But if desecration and removal of gravestones continues unchecked, it too may soon be only photographs and history.

23

She's No Lady....

ISS Jenny Lind was born in Stockholm, Sweden on October 6, 1821. From a very early age she showed a remarkable talent for singing and at age nine her parents enrolled her in the Stockholm Music Academy. By the end of her first year there she was already deemed fit for the stage and she soon began performing in local theater. At age 16, she was given an important role in a major opera and became recognized as Sweden's reigning "prima donna." After studying music in Paris for several years she appeared in Berlin, Vienna, London, and other European cities with ever-increasing renown.

In 1850, the American showman, P.T. Barnum engaged Miss Lind for an extended U.S. tour which was to include 150 concerts in Eastern cities. Due to the impressive combination of Miss Lind's talents and Mr. Barnum's showmanship, the tour was highly successful and financially rewarding (although the lion's share of Miss Lind's receipts were given, at her request, to charity.) In June 1851, Jenny Lind used a "loophole" in her agreement with Barnum to terminate her contract after the 95th performance. While she continued to give a limited number of performances on her own, she returned to Europe shortly after her Boston marriage to Otto Goldschmidt in 1852.

The reaction of 19th century audiences to Jenny Lind can only be compared to that of current day fans to stars such as Madonna or Michael Jackson. Concert tickets often sold for hundreds of dollars each and every city of any size wanted to be her next host. Articles about Miss Lind, written in newspapers of the day, were so complimentary of her abilities and her character that she quickly became a living legend -- and this was especially true in the gold fields of California where homesick miners, starved for feminine company, dreamed that this ultimate vision of femininity might someday perform here. But it was not to be.

Despite the efforts of a variety of San Francisco promoters (one of whom even built a magnificent theater which bore her name), Jenny Lind never came to California. In later years, it was discovered that Miss Lind had turned down offers far exceeding anything she had received in the east, citing her

fear of the arduous journey and the uncertainties of the "untamed west." Even so, her name appeared on theaters, river boats, and street signs throughout California, forever etched in the history of a state she never saw.

It is interesting that the Calaveras County town which bears the name Jenny Lind was most likely *not* named for that famous lady, although immediately after the name was chosen the connection was most certainly made. Early records indicate that before the town of Jenny Lind came to be, there were numerous mining camps along and near that area of the Calaveras River. One of these was called Jenny Bar, probably in reference to some incident involving a mule or donkey which occurred at that place (in those days, "Jenny" was a popular term for a female ass.)

According to the *Journals of Alfred Doten* (University of Nevada Press, 1973), the camps located in that area included North Gulch, Rich Gulch (one of three in the county), Chinn's Store, Perry's Store, Tremont House, North American House, Mexican Camp, Pleasant Valley, and Dry Diggin's (one of three in the county and probably more than a dozen in the state). Since Doten gives very descriptive accounts of his local travels during 1851-52, but does not mention Jenny Lind, one might assume that the town sprang to life sometime after he left the area in '53. It first appears on a map in 1854 and the first post office was opened there in 1857. Ironically, Doten does mention receiving a newspaper with an account of singer Jenny Lind's arrival in America.

Pleasant Valley, which was designated to be Calaveras' first county seat, was located about a mile or two northwest of the current site of Jenny Lind. While there is very little documentation of the town, it is mentioned in Doton's *Journal*, Book #7:

March 28. . . . AM early, Young and myself started off on foot. We walked down nearly to the Tremont House when the stages overtook us and I got on the first one, and Young on the second one. We had to ride outside, as they were full, and so we got quite wet. At Pleasant Valley, we met Currier bound home and he got on the coach with Young.

Since this incident occurred on the old Stockton Road, which ran east and west just north of Jenny Lind, this verifies Pleasant Valley's approximate location. It does, of course, leave many unanswered questions. . . . How large was the settlement there? Why was it chosen for the first county seat? Why was the seat never placed there? And, why did it so quickly fade from existence? Hopefully, future research will shed more light on the mystery of Pleasant Valley.

Exactly when the town of Jenny Lind came to be and how it came to be named will probably always be a matter of some debate. But knowing that a camp called Jenny Bar was already in existence, and that a gentleman named Doctor John Y. Lind resided there from about 1849 to 1854, it seems logical to assume that these two names were combined with or without a planned connection with the famous singer of the period. At any rate, newspaper accounts from 1856 show that Jenny Lind then boasted four general stores, two billiard halls, two hotels, a bowling alley, a blacksmith shop, a church, and several saloons. As the years progressed, the town grew to considerable size, with a significant Chinese and Mexican population.

In the 1870s and 80s, large mining companies began to move into the area, some of whom employed several hundred Chinese to strip the surface dirt and expose gold bearing bedrock. The land around Jenny Lind still bears the scars of the aggressive mining techniques used during those years. Several ditches and flumes were built to provided water for hydraulic mining, and during the early years of the twentieth century, dredging companies operated on the Calaveras River. As the gold played out, stores and businesses moved on leaving only a few scattered homes and old adobe walls to mark the location of that former bustling camp. Today, what remains of Jenny Lind sits on the edge of a massive modern housing development. Sadly, at the time of this writing little is being done to preserve the town's history, including the existing ruins of a single adobe building that is the only link with a glorious past.

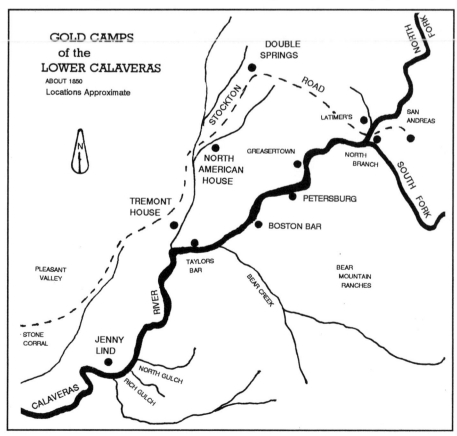

GOLD CAMPS
of the
LOWER CALAVERAS
ABOUT 1850
Locations Approximate

N

DOUBLE SPRINGS

NORTH FORK

STOCKTON ROAD

LATIMER'S

SAN ANDREAS

NORTH AMERICAN HOUSE

GREASERTOWN

NORTH BRANCH

SOUTH FORK

TREMONT HOUSE

PETERSBURG

BOSTON BAR

PLEASANT VALLEY

TAYLORS BAR

BEAR MOUNTAIN RANCHES

BEAR CREEK

RIVER

STONE CORRAL

JENNY LIND

NORTH GULCH

RICH GULCH

CALAVERAS

The town of Jenny Lind in the mid-1850s boasted a large number of miner's cabins and several businesses. (Calaveras Co. Historical Society)

One of the more successful sidelines of the gold rush was the operation of "road houses." These were a type of hotel situated along heavily traveled roads to provide meals and lodging to weary travelers. The *San Andreas Independent* of May 21, 1859, describes North American House, just north of Jenny Lind:

The house situated at the junction of the stage road via McDermott's Bridge and the new Stockton road is in successful operation and the proprietor is prepared to attend the wants of the traveling public. The bar is stocked with the choicest liquor and cigars and every accommodation appertaining to a road side hotel.

Another road house, called Tremont House, sat about a mile and a half south of North American House. Both establishments were frequented by miners from local "diggin's" who obviously appreciated the availability of good liquor and quality food. One of the earliest road houses in the area moved from Pleasant Valley to Stone Corral, about two miles west of Jenny Lind, in 1850 and by the 1870s a significant community had developed there.

In those days, the main road from Stockton followed much the same route as the current highway 26 except that where today's highway turns sharply north at Milton Road, the old one continued straight west, almost to the Calaveras River, before swinging north past Tremont and North American houses to Double Springs and eventually crossing the river at North Branch to terminate at San Andreas.

The close proximity of this road to the lower Calaveras camps contributed greatly to their constant state of activity. Stores and road houses seemed to change hands at least once every year and claims were bought and sold daily. A surprisingly large number of miners had claims on Rich Gulch or North Gulch yet also owned and worked claims along the Mokelumne River several miles to the north. Miners from the Jenny Lind area were frequently invited to activities at James and Winters Bars on the Mokelumne as well as Double Springs and Taylor's Bar. Americans from these camps were always ready to join together against Mexican aggressors (real or imagined), and large "vigilante" groups made frequent raids on predominatly Mexican Campo Seco and Greasertown.

Today, the lower Calaveras River is bounded on the south by large and well established ranches sitting in the shadow of Bear Mountain. There, the land remains rugged and relatively unchanged. In contrast, the area north of the river has fallen under the influence of commercial development, no doubt inspired by the creation of the New Hogan Reservoir. But on the banks of that historic stream sits a little town whose distinctive name serves to remind us of the area's colorful past and of a famous lady who turned down her chance to strike it rich -- between the rivers.

24
Mines, Miners, Mining and the Mother Lode
Part One

 F the thousands of individuals who came to California gold fields during the 1850s, very few had any experience in mining or for that matter even knew how gold was mined. When they arrived in San Francisco, Sacramento, or Stockton, they headed for the nearest "outfitter" who sold them what they needed and perhaps (but not always) gave them a quick lesson in how the equipment was used. During the first years of the gold rush, this equipment consisted of a pick, a shovel, a bucket, and a shallow pan. The instructions needed to operate these devices were equally as simple: stake a claim, loosen dirt with the pick, shovel it into the bucket, carry the dirt to the nearest water source, and use the pan to pan out the gold. A panning technique was perhaps the most complicated thing the miner had to learn, and this he usually picked up by watching the more experienced miners around him. During the early years, this equipment and methodology was not only sufficient for most miner's needs, it often paid off very quickly in great wealth for its owner. But those days were short lived.

In order to understand the various gold mining tools and methods, one must first know a little about where gold comes from. To begin with, gold was first discovered in California during the latter part of the 18th century by the Spanish, near Los Angeles. . . .long before Marshall's discovery at Sutter's Mill in 1848. (The Spanish had talked of the abundance of gold to be found here even before a thorough exploration of the area had begun, and one can only assume this information came from contact with California's native Indians.) Although gold was found in many areas throughout the state after 1848, the most productive regions were the northern and central portions of the Sierra Nevada mountain range, at lower elevations.

While the mountains themselves are composed of a wide variety of rocks and minerals, the crystalline rocks which make up their base are primarily what geologists call "metamorphics", which often contain quartz veins. Among the many minerals to be found within these veins is a soft and highly valuable metal called gold. Large belts of gold-bearing veins are called "lodes" and the belt which stretches along the foothills of the Sierra Mountain Range from near Georgetown in the north to Mariposa in the south is called the "Mother Lode." (It is interesting to note that, in Calaveras County, the gold rush towns of Murphys and Jenny Lind do not technically lie on the Mother Lode, but on the related East and West Gold Belts.)

The depth at which the Mother Lode lies beneath the surface varies widely throughout its length, but in many places rivers and their tributaries cut through the veins of gold and carry a quantity of the precious metal downstream. This gold, ranging in size from tiny flakes to nuggets weighing several pounds, is called "placer gold," and was the first gold mined by the Indians and later by the 49ers. Because it is extremely heavy, much of the placer gold settled into the bottom of the streams and eventually worked its way down to the bedrock. For this reason, only the very first miners were able to find gold lying on the surface, and this was quickly exhausted, necessitating the use of digging tools and giving birth to the term "diggings."

An area along a stream where large deposits of gravel and sand had built up, called a "bar", was one of the best places to stake a claim, and frequently a large mining camp developed on the bar. Deposits of placer gold could also be found well back from the water's edge. While many small gulches only had water running through them during stormy weather, the flow was sufficient to form significant placer deposits along their length, so that many of these gulches were heavily dotted with individual "digs" and small camps.

When placer gold was taken from its resting place, it was usually surrounded by large amounts of worthless dirt, sand, and gravel called "pay dirt" by miners. In order to extract the gold from these materials, miners used the same principal which created the placer deposits themselves -- the movement of water. Nearly everyone has seen a demonstration of panning, where excess sand and gravel is tossed out by a vigorous shaking of the pan, leaving heavy particles of gold lying on the bottom in a small swirl of black sand. While the process is much more difficult than it appears, it is easily learned by experience.

Devoting about ten minutes to each pan, the average 49er washed fifty pans during a good day and extracted a total of $7 to $15 worth of gold. But the panning method was hard easy work, requiring constant digging and squatting and long hours of dipping one's hands in cold water. Among the first devices which helped to diminish these problems and speed up the recovery of gold, was the "cradle" or "rocker." Without going into too much detail, this device looked much like its name implies and operated on the same principle as the pan. By rocking the cradle vigorously back and forth, the lighter sand and gravel were washed out, leaving the gold lodged behind "riffles" (small strips of wood) that were attached to the bottom. Although this method allowed more gold to be "accidentally" washed out with the gravel than did the pan method, larger quantities of pay dirt could be washed in a shorter amount of time, making a day's work much more profitable.

Still, the cradle had to be constantly rocked by hand and miners soon came upon an idea to let a steady stream of water do the work in a stable, lengthened version of the rocker called a "long tom." Placed in a small stream or at the end of a water ditch constructed specifically for the purpose, water rushed in one end of the tom carrying pay dirt over a series of riffles and out the other end. Later design changes allowed a number of similar devices, called "sluice boxes," to be attached together so that any gold which escaped one box might be caught in the next. Where sufficient water was readily available, sluice-box mining was the most efficient and profitable form of recovering placer gold.

The need for large quantities of water to operate these devices brought about the first organized commercial enterprize related to California gold mining -- the ditch companies. In Calaveras County during the dry season, the county's three major rivers became the primary source of water. During the early years of the gold rush, distant camps either had to haul water in themselves or buy water from one of the commercial haulers. But as the need for water increased, a few enterprising individuals banded together to affect the construction of canals or ditches to carry water from rivers to the camps. Individual miners or whole camps could then buy the right to use a certain amount of water from the ditch for mining and other purposes. These ditches were so numerous that today almost every major parcel of undeveloped land contains the remnants of one of these manmade waterways.

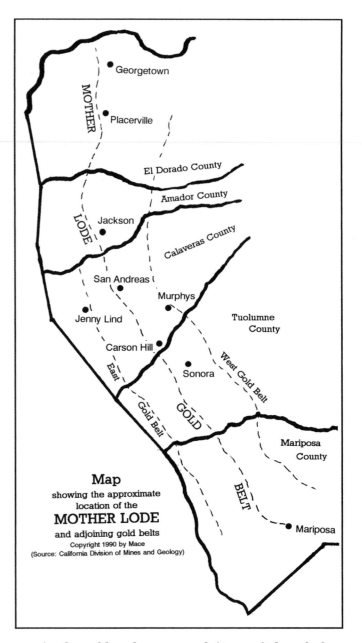

Map
showing the approximate location of the
MOTHER LODE
and adjoining gold belts
Copyright 1990 by Mace
(Source: California Division of Mines and Geology)

As the gold rush progressed, it wasn't long before some miners began to realize that if deposits of placer gold had arrived at their location by being washed downstream, then somewhere upstream there had to be a source -- the "mother" vein from which this gold came. And soon the search was on. What they found, at higher elevations on the hillsides above the stream beds, were areas of very old and highly compacted stream gravels from the Tertiary Age (12 to 65 million years old) that were extremely rich in gold. These large deposits could be several hundred feet long and deep, and were often buried under a large quantity of worthless dirt and gravel.

This exploration also eventually lead to the discovery of outcroppings of rock, primarily quartz,

An artist for Harper's New Monthly Magazine provided these engravings of early mining methods (panning, rocking the cradle, washing in the long tom) to accompany an April 1860 article entitled "How We Get Gold in California."

Long Tom

Rocking the cradle

that contained "veins" of gold. Although this was the "lode" gold they had been searching for, they also found that it was firmly embedded in hard rock. Mining and recovering this gold required laborious digging, chipping, pulverizing, and washing.

In April of 1860, one of the most widely read newspapers in the country, *Harper's New Monthly Magazine*, produced an article entitled "How We Get Gold in California," which described the various popular methods of gold mining in use at the time. In the opening paragraph, the author (described simply as "a miner of '49") gives his reason for writing the piece:

Of the thousands who note the semi-monthly arrivals of treasure, and who, from habit, have at last come to consider California a sort of gold pro-ducing Croton, whence the supply is expected as a matter of course, comparatively few are acquainted with the methods by which these riches are drawn from the bowels of the earth. I have even found men who supposed that the primitive rocker or cradle of 1849 is still in general use in 1860. I believe that it will be a service to our friends in the Atlantic States to set them right on various points connected with the miners of California.

In just slightly more than a decade, dozens of new mining methods had been introduced to increase the speed and efficiency of gold mining operations. While panning or sluicing methods were far from obsolete, the "big producers" in the California gold fields were now using modern equipment and techniques to sift through vast quantities of gold bearing material in just minutes. The individual miner, while not yet extinct, was fast becoming a thing of the past, and mechanized mining companies were the wave of the future.

25
Mines, Miners, Mining, and the Mother Lode
Conclusion

 N the Mother Lode area, gold was (and is) found in three basic locations; in and along the various streams and rivers which flow down from the mountains (placer gold); at various levels beneath surface material, in very old gravel deposits (Tertiary deposits or "cemented gravel"); and running in veins through "ledges" of quartz and other hard minerals (hard rock, lode, or quartz gold). Placer gold was recovered primarily by panning and by using simple sluicing methods such as the "rocker" and "long tom" (see Part I). While these methods were also used in the mining of Tertiary gravels and quartz gold the work was at the least, backbreaking and time consuming. Also, these mines were often located some distance from a water source, so that water had to be brought to the claim or pay dirt carried down to the water.

During the early years of the Gold Rush deep gravels were sometimes dug out by a method called "coyoteing." The miner would dig straight down into the earth until he reached bedrock. Then he would dig side tunnels into the pay dirt which was tossed or hoisted out. then panned or sluiced. Only occasionally was some sort of support used to hold up the clay overhead, therefore cave-ins were frequent and often deadly. Once the "pocket" had played out, the miner would then dig another hole nearby, in the direction that the gold deposit seemed to run.

Many stories were related in those days of visitors who, when approaching a large mining camp and seeing no miners or signs of activity, would call out to be greeted by a vast array of heads popping out of pockets like so many prairie dogs.

In places where Tertiary gold deposits were close enough to the surface and where water could be conveniently diverted to flow across the claim, the miner might use a method called "ground sluicing." In effect, he was creating his own stream which quickly ate away the surface covering and finally began to break up the tertiary gravels, carrying it to a sluice box waiting downstream. This method was a forerunner of the most powerful, productive, and destructive gold mining technique ever invented -- hydraulic mining.

Since high pressure water hoses had been in use for some time by fire departments in the East, it is perhaps surprising that their use in gold mining did not occur until the fourth year of the California Gold Rush. In fact, it was a combination of the quickly dwindling placer deposits, the increasing activity in mining Tertiary deposits, and the arrival of organized mining companies that prompted the invention and subsequent popularity of this technique. The name of the first person to use pressurized water in gold mining is lost to history, however, we do know that, sometime in 1852, a Frenchman named Chabot used a hose to direct water to his "digs" in Nevada County and in 1853, neighboring miner Edward Matteson used a nozzle to increase pressures and "propel" the water against ore-rich deposits on American Hill.

News of this innovative method spread quickly, and within months miners in the Mother Lode were using pressurized hoses and the improved variations which quickly followed. They learned that by diverting water into a large pipe at higher elevations, then channelling the flow into smaller and smaller pipes before it finally reached the nozzle, pressures of tremendous force could be created. To control this immense water pressure and direct its torrent to a specific area, large water "canons" were invented called "monitors." Controlled by a solitary operator, the flow from just one monitor could literally wash away an entire mountain in a single day. The stream of mud and debris was directed into huge sluices which trapped the gold in their riffles, then expelled the remaining silt (called "slickens") into the nearest stream.

While the owners of hydraulic mining operations quickly reaped the rewards of this most efficient of gold mining methods, its devastating effects on California's environment were far reaching. For the most part, hydraulic miners had little or no interest in what happened to the slickens after they left the sluice. Soon, sand and fine debris began to choke the rivers and streams, often causing floods and backing up into valley farmlands. The amount of silt created by hydraulic mining was so immense that its effects are still being felt today in areas of the Sacramento and San Joaquin Rivers, and even San Francisco Bay. Despite a quarter century of complaints from farmers and river navigators, it was 1884 before controlling government regulations were set in place.

Calaveras County had its share of hydraulic mines, (even though the method was never used here to the same degree as other gold producing counties) and the often eerie landscapes created by the monitor's blast can be seen in several locations. The most obvious and accessible site (called a "pit") is just off highway 49 in Chili Gulch, north of San Andreas. Hydraulic mining occurred along the length of this ravine from Mokelumne Hill to the Calaveras River's north branch and to a smaller degree, around Campo Seco, Camanche, Mountain Ranch, Railroad Flat, Murphys, Dogtown, and Calaveritas.

When people outside the Mother Lode area hear the word "mine," they probably think of long horizontal tunnels with ore cars running along railroad tracks. Even though, in 1852, placer mining produced the greatest annual yield of California gold, drift tunnels and deep rock (lode or quartz) mining have generated the largest portion of this state's total gold production to date. In Calaveras County, more than one-half of all gold recovered has come from drift and deep rock quartz mines.

(Note: The terms associated with mining are abundant and often confusing. While the term "tunnel mine" is generally used to designate any shaft dug *horizontally* into the *side* of a hill, it is used more frequently to describe "drift" mines than lode mines.)

Drift mining was just one more method of reaching the deep Tertiary gold deposits. Miners would dig a vertical or incline shaft, or tunnel into the side of a hill to reach the pocket itself. Once the gold bearing Tertiary deposit was located, the tunnel would be developed along the vein, "drifting" with the gold bearing channel. In Calaveras County, this technique was introduced in 1855 by the Murray Company at Douglas Hill near San Andreas. Within a few years, there were hundreds of drift mines across the county, with heavy concentrations near San Andreas, Mokelumne Hill, and Vallecito. This type of mining declined in the 1880s, then saw a short lived resurgence during the 1930s.

Quartz gold was discovered near Mariposa in 1849, and by 1850 there were attempts to mine this type of gold. The problems involved in hard rock mining during those early years were numerous -- including lack of proper tools and explosives to loosen the material, inefficient ore crushing methods,

A hydraulic monitor blasts away at a Chili Gulch "pit" in this late nineteenth century photo. (Calaveras County Historical Society)

and difficulty in extracting the gold from the crushed ore. Even so, there were notable early successes in Calaveras County, including mines of the Consolidated Mining Company in Carson Hill and the Winter Brothers in Angels Camp. Still, it would be the 1860s before quartz mining was executed on a large scale and most of the major lodes that were discovered in the early years remained underdeveloped until the advent of "deep rock" mining technology in late 1880s.

All of the gold that has ever been mined in California was part of, or originally came from, a "lode". While there are numerous lodes running throughout the state, our "Mother Lode" has been one of the most productive and is certainly the most famous. The geological explanation and description of this lode and how it came to be is complex and somewhat academic, as the following quote, taken from the *Gold Districts of California*, demonstrates: *The main mass of the Sierra Nevada is a huge batholith of granodiorite and related rock that is intrusive into metamorphosed rocks of Paleozoic and Mesozoic age. . . . Also,there are numerous dioritic and aplitic dikes that are closely related with gold-bearing veins.*

What does all this mean in simple terms? The Mother Lode is very old, very hard, and is made up of a variety of rocks and minerals through which an extensive gold bearing vein runs. The gold that exists in Tertiary deposits was washed out from the lode many thousands of years ago. Alluvial or placer gold was broken loose a bit more recently. Both of these types of gold are exhaustible and in fact the profitable mining of this gold has been all but abandoned. But deep within the bowels of the Sierra Nevada, vast amounts of gold remain buried in quartz and hard rock. The questions facing modern miners are the same ones that faced their 19th century predecessors -- how to find it, how to get to it, and how to profitably recover it. Thus, the age old quest continues -- between the rivers.

Glossary of Mining Terms*

Adit - Generally, a horizontal mine tunnel or drift. Often confused with "portal," the exterior opening of a mine tunnel.

Alluvial - Pertaining to rock, sand, gravel, and minerals that have been washed along and deposited by running water. Placer gold is found in alluvial deposits.

Bar - An extensive bank of deposited sand and gravel in or along a stream bed. Underwater bars are also called "shoals."

Batholith - A large, deep seated rock intrusion, often forming the base of a mountain range, and uncovered only by erosion.

Cement - Gold bearing Tertiary deposits which have been compressed over time into a concrete-like material.

Collar - The ground level opening to a vertical or incline mine shaft.

Decline - Any downward sloping portion of a horizontal mine tunnel.

Drift - A mine which follows the path or vein of gold bearing Tertiary gravel.

Dust - Fine particles of gold. A misleading term, since most "gold dust" is actually made up of flakes and grains of gold.

Hard Rock - A generic term for gold bearing rock, primarily quartz.

Lode - 1. A significant vein of gold running through fissures in the hard rock of the batholith. 2. A large belt of hard rock containing veins of gold.

Pay Dirt - Dirt, sand, gravel, and other materials dug from a claim to be panned for gold.

Pit - Site of hydraulic mining.

Placer - A concentrated gold bearing deposit of sand and gravel which eroded from the gold bearing lode and was carried and deposited by running water.

Riffles - Protruding wood or metal strips attached to gold recovery devices (sluices, rockers, etc.) designed to trap gold particles.

Slickens - The thick silt created by hydraulic mining.

Stope - An area within a mine from which ore has been or is being removed.

Sump - A pocket at the very bottom of a mine in which water collects and is pumped out.

Tertiary - In mining -- rock, sand, gravel, and minerals that were deposited by ancient drainage systems (12 to 60 million years old). Due to the major geological changes that have occurred since that time, Tertiary stream deposits are often found far from present drainage systems.

Winze - A passage from one level of a mine to another.

*Sources: *Webster's New Universal Unabridged Dictionary*; *Gold Districts of California*, and the *California Gold Rush* by John Walton Caughey.

26
Of Iron Rust and Iron Horses
Part One

 MINER Hiram Hughes returned to Calaveras County sometime in the spring of 1860. He had tried his hand at silver mining in Nevada's Comstock Lode, but after a year or so he decided he would give California gold another chance. In an area near the southwest corner of the county, Hiram found outcroppings of rock that closely resembled the formations he had seen near silver mines in Nevada and he quickly began prospecting along an area known as Gopher Ridge. In May 1860, he staked a claim on Quail Hill which yielded small amounts of both gold and silver, but even more of a reddish colored ore which he and other miners had seen before and had dubbed "iron rust" -- for that was exactly what it resembled.

At first, Hiram ignored the rusty material, just as those other miners had, for it was gold and silver that held his attention. But when his son, William Napoleon Bonaparte Hughes, discovered a lead containing enormous amounts of the red stuff later that year at a second claim on Hog Hill, Hiram decided to send it to San Francisco for analysis. When the assayer's report came back, Hiram opened his "Napoleon Mine" and began a new era in California mining -- the copper boom.

Hiram's discovery couldn't have come at a better time. In the East, preparations were being made for a great Civil War, and to the military machine, copper was a metal far more valuable than gold. During the 19th century, copper was already being used in great quantity in the production of steam boilers and tubing; sheathing, bolts, and nails for ships; protective boxes and storage cases for instruments; and for cooking and eating utensils as well. Copper was the principal ingredient in brass, bronze, and other metal alloys. Perhaps most importantly, copper was used for the wire which carried telegraph messages -- wire which already linked many of the major cities of the Eastern United States and would soon link both ends of the continent.

In August of 1860, two more claims were filed on rich copper leads about five miles northeast of the Napoleon by local miners Reed and McCarty. Soon, nearby landmarks began to take on the name of the red ore -- Copper Mountain, Copper Creek, and Copper Gulch. The community that quickly grew up around the Reed Claim took the name "Copper Cañon." By early 1861, Reed's mine, the Union, was producing vast amounts of "high yield" ore, bringing $125-150 a ton, and the little camp of Copper Cañon had become the bustling boom town of Copperopolis. The May 22, 1861 issue of the *San Francisco Bulletin* describes a flurry of activity in the place that nine months earlier was just an empty gulch:

A new hotel is in progress of erection by J. W. Bean, which will accommodate visitors to any extent in good style. The want of a good hotel has been much felt at the new town. Pike and Brothers have a good store, and a billiard saloon will soon be completed. There are several other buildings in the town which is now regularly laid out upon a beautiful flat, upon which there is a liberal number of oak trees. Great activity prevails at the town, and it is quite probable that 1000 tons of copper per month will be shipped from the vicinity to Stockton, during the coming summer. 250 men will be constantly engaged.

Later that year, the *Calaveras Chronicle* speaks of "the far-famed Copperopolis, a city in full bloom...," with several stores, a large assortment of billiard and drinking saloons, restaurants, meat markets, apothecaries, stables, barber shops, and a "first class hotel" with a restaurant that seats 100 to 200 people. The buildings in Copperopolis were cited as being among the "grandest" in the state. Four different stages included Copperopolis as one of their regular stops.

And so, within less than a year, the mining of "iron rust" had produced a notable new metropolis in Calaveras County and the copper boom was breathing new life into an area of the county that had been all but left out of the gold rush. By the mid-1860s, the Union Copper Mine had been joined by nearly two dozen competitors, including the highly productive Empire and Keystone mines.

In October of 1861, Hughes wrote to the Calaveras County Assessor: *"Our Napoleon lead on Hog Hill is proving No. 1. We are down thirty five feet on a level of copper ore varying from 2 to 3 feet in width. . . . Two men raise two tons per day, besides doing the timbering. . . . We have shipped 66 tons of copper ore from this claim and have forty more ready for sacking."*

This late nineteenth century view of Copperopolis shows that the town was still an active mining and commercial center. Note mine tailings to right. (Calaveras County Historical Society)

After the "Copper Bust" at the end of the Civil War, Telegraph City supported nearby ranches such as the E. Park residence shown here. (Calaveras Described, 1885)

While the area around the Napoleon never saw the same degree of growth as Copperopolis, a small community did develop on the slopes of Hog Hill called "Napoleon City." But a need to provision the substantial number of miners working in that locality resulted in the establishment of a larger commercial center on the road to Stockton at first called "Grasshopper City." When telegraph wires were stretched from Stockton to Sonora, the arrival of this communications marvel in Grasshopper City prompted a name change -- and Telegraph City was born. In its early days the town consisted of a single building -- a general store owned by Edward Laughlin. But by 1862, Laughlin had expanded his enterprise to include an express office and the town's first post office. A blacksmith shop, restaurant, and billiard saloon would soon follow.

As was generally the case in this part of the county during those years, a number of large and important ranches sprang up in the area as well. By the mid-1860s, Telegraph City's population had grown to several hundred persons, including enough families to justify the building of a schoolhouse. The construction and operation of the Reed Turnpike from Copperopolis to the main Stockton road in 1864-65, also provided a boon to Telegraph City's commerce. (This toll road was developed by the same Reed who was co-discoverer of the Union Copper Mine, and was built with profits from the sale of that mine. The turnpike operated until 1885.)

Because the military has always been one of the major users of copper and copper-related products, the boom years of copper mining in California have always coincided with wars. During the Civil War years (1861-65), a large number of copper mines were operating around Copperopolis and Telegraph City. After the war, the price of copper dropped from an all-time high of 55¢ to a mere 19¢ per pound. One by one, smaller mines began to shut down, and by the 1880s only six mines remained in operation.

Already feeling the post-war effects of the "copper bust," the business people of Copperopolis were struck a final blow on the night of August 28, 1867, when fire destroyed a large portion of the town. The conflagration began in the Copperopolis Hotel, cited by contemporary visitors as "the most elaborate building of its kind in the Southern Mines." Typical of town fires during this period, the flames jumped from one wood frame building to the next, stopping only where there was a large open space or "backburned" area. After the devastating effects of the fire and the closing of many of the mines, the town of Copperopolis never returned to its former grandeur, although later intermittent war-induced copper booms kept it alive into the twentieth century.

Telegraph City also felt the effects of mine closures. The nearby Napoleon Mine, where the Copper Boom began, went bankrupt in 1867, and although the little town continued as a commercial center for the surrounding ranch community, the 1880 census reported a population of only 49.

Today, Telegraph City's famous rock walls are the only obvious remains of this once bustling village. (These walls were built during the mid-to-late 19th century by a Scottish stone mason named James (Jimmy) Sykes (or Skeys), who employed a number of local men to help with the construction. Like many such stone structures which exist in

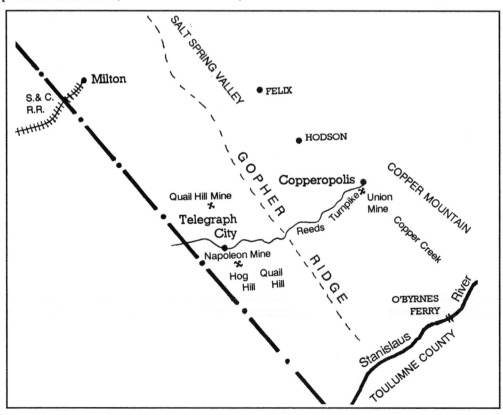

The remains of an old trestle reminds Copperopolis visitors that Main Street once paralleled a group of active copper mines.

the Mother Lode, these walls have often been misidentified as being Chinese in origin. While the Chinese did frequently use this type of rock construction, so did most Europeans. The Italians, Irish, Scots, and Germans (among others) were all known for their sturdy and visually distinctive stone walls.

Throughout the copper boom years, one of the major obstacles for mine owners was the transportation of ore to docks on the Stockton Channel from which it could be shipped to San Francisco and, eventually, the east. Reeds Turnpike did much to facilitate land travel from Copperopolis and Telegraph City, but what was really needed was a railroad line. And so, in 1862, the Stockton-Copperopolis Railroad Company was organized by Erastus S. Holden.

Had the proposed railroad been built during the copper boom of the Civil War period it would, no doubt, have added considerably to the profits of mine owners and the growth of southwestern Calaveras County. It might even have lessened the impact of the post-war bust. But initial opposition from teamsters, the primary haulers of copper ore, was followed by several years of political, financial, and corporate battles, and it was 1870 before Chinese workers began clearing land for the line. By February of 1871, the Stockton and Copperopolis Railroad was carrying passengers to the town of Peters, just 6 miles from Calaveras County, and by June it had crossed over to the Milton Ranch, just inside the county boundary. But this was, quite literally, the end of the line.

27

Of Iron Rust and Iron Horses
Conclusion

URING the gold rush years, the road to mining camps south of the Mokelumne River generally ran through Stockton, and for counties north of that river the road ran through Sacramento. This doesn't mean that people never came directly from Sacramento to Mokelumne Hill, San Andreas, or Angels Camp -- or from Stockton to Jackson or points north -- it simply means that most of the traffic into those areas came from those corresponding cities. Even today, the two counties still maintain an invisible tie to those cities. Ask any Jacksonian where he or she goes to shop and they'll most likely say Sacramento, despite the fact that Stockton is closer and less crowded. But in the 19th century, the transportation of people, equipment, and goods was highly affected by cost, distance, and the lay of the land.

During the earliest years of the Gold Rush, pack mules and mule teams carried supplies from the ports at Stockton to the Southern Mines and carried gold from those mines back to Stockton. Eventually, that gold would make its way up the delta to San Francisco for shipment to the east. As mining camps grew into large towns, roads were improved and transportation by wagon or stagecoach became common. It was gold that built the towns, gold that built the roads, and gold that kept the haulers in business. But the event that did the most to change transportation in Calaveras County was the copper boom of the 1860s.

In order to get their "iron rust" ore to Stockton during the early 1860s, the copper mines paid eight to ten dollars per ton by wagon. Assuming that the ore contained 12% to 15% copper (an average yield), it might bring $75 at market, meaning 10% or more of the mine's total sales could be spent on shipping.

And as the flow of copper grew, so did shipping costs. But in Stockton, one of the Mother Lode's first transportation pioneers was meeting with promoters who planned to cut those shipping costs in half.

The steam train as we know it was introduced into the United States in 1829. It connected the cities of Charleston and Hamburg in South Carolina. The first major railroad was the Baltimore and Ohio, which commenced operation in 1830 and transported over 80 thousand people during its first full year of business. By 1840, there were 1,843 miles of track in the U.S., and by the Civil War that figure had grown to more than 30,000.

The idea of connecting the full width of the United States by rail had been seriously considered as early as the 1830s, but the dream did not become reality until May 10, 1869, when east and west links of the transcontinental railroad were connected at Promontory, Utah, and tales of the monstrous, smoke belching, "Iron Horse" began to circulate among the Plains Indians. In California, Theodore Judah laid out the important (if somewhat small) Sacramento Valley Railroad in 1855. (Judah would later be instrumental in choosing the route of the transcontinental railroad over the Sierra Mountains into the state, and become the major figure in the development of California's railroads.) The West Coast Railroad Convention of 1859 marked the beginnings of a transportation revolution statewide, and the federal Pacific Railroad Bill of 1862 lead to the birth of the Union Pacific, Central Pacific, and Southern Pacific Railroads.

Meanwhile, in Stockton, Erastus Holden organized the Stockton-Copperopolis Railroad. In the early 1850s, Holden started the first stage service into Sonora and was now looking to improve transportation into the Southern Mines while at the same time providing a fast, high volume, and inexpensive way to haul copper ore to the shipping docks. Despite Holden's dedication to building a railroad into Calaveras, his plans suffered one defeat after another and appeared doomed to failure. In 1870, the project was taken over by a California Pacific official who finally got things moving.

By June of 1871, the Stockton-Copperopolis Railroad had finally crossed over into Calaveras County, but a major engineering obstacle still lay ahead -- the construction of a long and winding grade along Rock Creek, across Gopher Ridge into the Salt Spring Valley, and eventually to Copperopolis. That same year, federal funding which had been allocated to encourage the building of railroads during the 1860s expired, sounding the death toll for the Copperopolis line.

On the fourth of July, 1871, a great celebration was held in Calaveras County at a place called Rock Creek Grove, near the eastern terminus of the

Stockton-Copperopolis Railroad. Plans had already been laid out for a new town about a mile away, to be called "Milton" for the railroad's chief construction engineer, Milton Latham. The design for the new town was quite impressive, with three "tiers" of lots spreading outward from a large central plaza.

While the town never grew to match the designer's somewhat optimistic expectations, the Stockton-Copperopolis railroad began regular passenger and freight service to Milton, prompting the immediate construction of a railroad station, freight office (Wells Fargo, of course), and associated homes, stores, restaurants, and saloons. Connecting stage lines were quickly established with Copperopolis, Tuttletown, and Sonora.

Interestingly, many of the early travelers who passed through Milton were tourists, probably encouraged by an article which appeared in San Francisco's *Daily Alta California* newspaper on April 3, 1871, a full three months before the first train arrived there: *A new town called Milton has been laid off on the line of the Copperopolis Railroad, twenty-eight miles from Stockton. . . . These twenty-eight miles take the tourist across the hottest, dustiest, and most uninteresting portion of the distance from Stockton to the Big Trees and Yosemite, and will contribute to the pleasure of a trip to those natural wonders, as well as reduce the time and expense.*

Another article which ran in the *Daily Alta* two weeks later describes the Milton area: *About six hundred yards to the south of the town is Rock Creek Grove--a beautiful grove of oak trees, just the place for picnic parties. . . . To the northeast and south and almost into the town itself, mines are found and miners at work. . . . A great many lots are now sold, and house building is the order of the day. The railroad company has men at work building their depot. . . .*

By 1873, Milton was a well established railhead bustling with the comings and goings of travelers and freight. A new school house was under construction, as was a new hotel. The town boasted dozens of homes and businesses, including a number of hotels, restaurants, and saloons. But in late December, as the community was preparing for the Christmas holiday, it was struck by an extraordinary disaster. The *Calaveras Chronicle* of December 20th describes the event:

About 1 o'clock of the afternoon of Tuesday last, Milton in this county was visited by a tornado that resulted in the injury of several persons, and the destruction of a considerable amount of property. Several buildings were destroyed, others unroofed, and a number moved bodily from their foundations.

The [tornado], which apparently was about a quarter of a mile in width, was accompanied with wind and hail. It lasted but a few moments, long enough, however, to place at least half the town in ruins.

Once again, the people of Milton set about rebuilding their town. The new school house, which had been blown eight feet off its foundation, was set back in place and finally opened. The hotel that was under construction at the time of the storm was completely demolished, but was rebuilt with a new and appropriate name -- the Tornado Hotel.

Shown here in a photograph from the late 1800s, Milton was one of the busiest short-lived towns in Calaveras County. (Calaveras Historical Society)

With a constant flow of passengers and freight being transferred between trains, wagons, and stages, the little town of Milton remained in a constant state of activity. (Calaveras County Historical Society)

Even though Milton was active well into the twentieth century, little is left to indicate the former size and importance of Calaveras County's first railhead.

By 1875, Milton had been completely rebuilt and sported a number of additional new homes and businesses as well. But on the morning of May 20th, a disastrous fire laid the town in ashes. Only three buildings survived the fire--the railroad depot, the town hall, and the Tornado Hotel.

Still an important transportation center, Milton once again rebuilt, though apparently to a smaller degree, as evident in this 1882 report from the *Sacramento Record Union*.

Following is the number of business housed in Milton: Two hotels, 2 stores, 3 saloons, 2 blacksmith shops, 1 livery stable, 1 butcher shop, 1 barber shop, and 1 shoemaker.

Early in 1882, work began on a narrow gauge railroad which was expected to run through the northern portion of Calaveras County, eventually terminating at Big Trees. Like the proposed Copperopolis line, it too fell prey to lack of financing and stopped just inside the county line, giving birth to the town of Wallace. Three years later the narrow gauge reached Valley Springs, and shortly thereafter both it and the Copperopolis line were taken over by Southern Pacific.

When the Copperopolis mines reopened in the late 1880s, many of them had their own smelters, thereby eliminating the costly necessity of transporting the ore to Stockton. However, many of the smaller mines continued to use wagons, then later, steam driven tractors to pull ore cars along the dangerous Rock Creek Road to the railhead at Milton. This process would continue well into the 20th century.

In the late 19th and early 20th centuries, Calaveras County's first two railroads played an important role in maintaining the area's economic stability. Even though Southern Pacific promoters refused to extend the lines beyond Milton and Valley Springs, a steady flow of stage lines, ore shipments (gold and copper), and freight haulers kept those branches busy, if not profitable. A new railroad, the Sierra Railway, was completed into Angels Camp in 1902, but the line was so slow that passengers found they could take a stage from Milton in less time.

The mass-production of motorized vehicles in the twentieth century revolutionized transportation and brought about the demise of Calaveras County railroading. The Valley Springs line discontinued

The Milton schoolhouse is a distinctive and historically important landmark.

passenger service in 1932. Service to Milton was reduced to one train a week in 1933, and by 1940 even the rails were gone. The tracks of the Sierra Railway were pulled up in the late thirties as well. While Milton and Wallace have dwindled away to a few scattered homes and dilapidated buildings, Valley Springs has managed to forge its place in the 20th century. Telegraph City and the Napoleon are gone, while Copperopolis sits quietly in the shadow of mines that once provided the metal to win wars and brought railroads that were, for a time, the lifeline of the people -- between the rivers.

28
El Rio Guadalupe

The sun was low when he came to a mile-long slope, mostly covered with pines and studded with that white quartz, and knew that he was nearing his journey's end. Just as the sun touched the horizon, he emerged from the trees on the rim of an abyss, and his heart sank. What lay before him, a thousand feet deep, was the canyon of the Stanislaus River, which roared over its boulders and ledges at the bottom.

from *Bret Harte of the Old West*
by Alvin F. Harlow

N 1855, when the young Frank (Bret) Harte made his arduous walk from La Grange to Robinson's Ferry in patent leather shoes (see Chapter 8), the Stanislaus River (pronounced Stan-is-law) was already dotted with thousands of miners tents from the Big Trees to the San Joaquin River. Like most of the major rivers in the Sierra Foothills, the Stanislaus first saw mining activity early in the summer of 1848, and by the following year there were numerous well established camps along and within a few miles of its banks. But the history of this river starts well before the Gold Rush years.

When Jose' Joaquin' de Arrillaga became governor of Spanish California in 1806, he sent one of his most capable soldiers, Gabriel Moraga, to explore the valley of the San Joaquin River and its tributaries. Father Pedro Muñoz accompanied Moraga, hoping to convert the native Indians to Christianity. The diaries that Father Muñoz kept during the expedition are today treasured as the only surviving "first hand" history of the white man's earliest excursion into what would become the Mother Lode area.

After exploring small sections of the Merced River and the Tuolumne (which Muñoz called the "Delores"), the expedition continued northward and arrived at another large tributary of the San Joaquin, which according to father Muñoz diary, they named "Our Lady of Guadalupe." (Several historians, including Richard Coke Wood, have written that Moraga named the river "Lasquisimes.") Traveling upstream, Moraga discovered an Indian village which he called "Tuolumne" (apparently his adaptation of the Indian word "talmalamne", which

meant "rock village"), and found the natives cautious but friendly. For four days, Moraga and his men explored the areas on either side of the river and perhaps as far north as the Calaveras, before returning to the San Joaquin Valley.

Two years later, Moraga returned to the Guadalupe to search for Indians who had run away from the missions and to look for a possible mission site in that area. This time, Moraga himself kept a diary which describes the deep canyons of the river and the "pleasant meadows" nearby. In his report to Governor Arrillaga, however, Moraga indicated that the area would not be suitable for a mission. While a few Spanish and Mexican expeditions would pass through the area over the next twenty years, there are no records relating specifically to their excursions up the Guadalupe River until 1828.

In that year, a mission-born Indian named Estanislao, who had been living with others of his tribe at the Missions San Jose and Santa Clara, decided to return to his ancestral home on the Rio Guadalupe, much to the chagrin of the Padre Duran who sent a request to the Mexican governor for his capture. Estanislao, however, proved to be a skillful adversary and inflicted heavy casualties on the Mexican troops that were sent out over the next two years. Despite the fact that he was never captured, the Mexican government finally declared victory over Estanislao and his warriors and left him to live undisturbed in the land of his ancestors.

In March of 1844, the American explorer John C. Fremont traveled down the San Joaquin River from Sutter's Fort in search of a southern route across the Sierras. His southward path was blocked by the swollen Guadalupe and according to Fremont's diary, they proceeded to a point approximately 22 miles upstream to search for a fording place before returning to the San Joaquin. In his highly publicized reports, Fremont called the river "Stanislaus" for the Indian Estanislao, whose earlier clashes with the Mexican military had by then reached legendary status. (It should be noted here that the name "Estanislao" was given to this famed warrior by the Spanish as their translation of Poland's Saint Stanislaus Kostka (or Krakow), of which Fremont was apparently aware, as his spelling indicates.)

There is evidence to suggest that the Stanislaus was also visited by two other early western explorers in the pre-Gold Rush period. Trapper Jedediah

This photo from around the turn of the century shows Robinson's Ferry, one of the most important Stanislaus crossings. (Calaveras Historical Society)

Smith entered California during the latter part of 1826 and received a somewhat cold reception from the Mexican government which prompted his exit over the Sierra Mountains the following spring. It is believed that Smith hunted and trapped along the tributaries of the San Joaquin and camped on a river which he called the Appelamminy. It is quite possible that this river was the Stanislaus, and that Smith eventually used its course to guide him up the western slope of the Sierra Nevada when he made the crossing in May of 1827.

Over a decade later, in the Fall of 1841, the Bidwell-Bartleson emigrant party stumbled blindly into California over the crest of the Sierras, hopelessly lost. Because they had no idea where they actually were, historians have long argued over exactly where this crossing was made. However, based on their description of the various streams and landmarks, it seams likely that they eventually followed the Stanislaus down the western slope and into the San Joaquin Valley.

Nearly 10 years before the gold rush came along, a number of trappers had established semi-permanent residence in a place called French Camp, on the San Joaquin River approximately halfway between its intersection with the Stanislaus and Calaveras Rivers. Since the camp grew steadily over the years, it therefore seems only logical to assume that by 1848 white men were already using those rivers on a regular basis to guide them into the game-rich foothills of the Sierra Mountains.

During the years 1846-48, a number of individuals were encouraged to settle on land that was part of the French Camp Grant of 1844, belonging to Captain Charles M. Weber, who had arrived in California with the previously mentioned Bidwell-Bartleson party. Captain Weber established the town of Tuleberg (Stockton), and upon hearing in the Spring of 1848 of the discovery of gold at Sutter's Fort, he sent a number of men to prospect the foothill streams and rivers, including the Stanislaus.

Exactly where the first settlement on the Stanislaus was located and who settled it has been lost to history. It is believed that James Carson, George Angel, and others who had fought in Stevenson's Regiment during the Mexican war, entered the area in August of 1848 and found many Mexicans already working well-established claims. Byearly that fall, major camps had been established on both sides of the river, including Angels Camp, Murphys Diggings, Carson Creek, Tuttletown, Sonora, Woods Crossing, and Jamestown. A large number of claims were being worked along Mormon Creek, Angels Creek, Carson Creek, Coyote Creek, and the South Fork of the Stanislaus, many of which may have been initiated by Mexican miners as early as June of 1848.

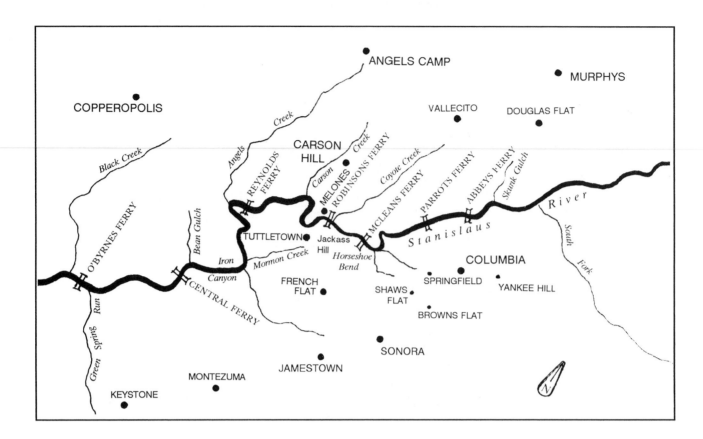

For prospective miners entering the foothills from the east, major rivers like the Stanislaus were an invaluable guide, leading them right to the heart of the Mother Lode. But for travelers from the north or south, they were often a major obstacle. Accordingly, one of the first businesses that a down and out miner might turn to was the operation of a river ferry, and the Stanislaus certainly had its fair share of ferries.

In his *Three Years in California* (pub.1857), J. D. Borthwick described his crossing of the Stanislaus by ferry in the early 1850s:

I crossed the Stanislaus -- a large river, which does not at any part of its course afford very rich diggings -- by a ferry which was the property of two or three Englishmen. . . .The force of the current was here very strong, and by an ingenious contrivance was made available for working the ferry. A stout cable was stretched across the river, and traversing on this were two blocks, to which were made fast the head and stern of a large scow. By lengthening the stern line, the scow assumed a diagonal position and, under the influence of the current and of the opposing force of the cable, she traveled rapidly across the river, very much on the same principle on which a ship holds her course with the wind abeam.

Some historians believe that Borthwick is describing the first ferry on the Stanislaus which was built by McLean, Jeffrey, and Company, probably in the spring of 1849, and which was located about 1/2 mile east of today's Stevenot Bridge (highway 49). McLean's Ferry primarily serviced Murphys to the north and Sonora to the South.

East of McLean's Ferry was Parrot's Ferry, which operated into the 20th century, and Abbey's Ferry, both of which serviced the towns of Murphys, Vallecito, and Columbia. Robinson's Ferry (located very near today's highway 49 crossing) was perhaps the most strategically located and heavily used of the Stanislaus Ferries. It serviced Angels Camp, Carson Hill, Jackass Hill, and Sonora. Downstream, Reynold's Ferry came much later, connecting the towns of Sonora and Tuttletown with Copperopolis and Milton, as did the Central Ferry and O'Byrnes Ferry, further to the west.

In the 20th century, the Stanislaus, like all of Calaveras County's rivers, has been the target of water and power developers. The reservoirs created as a result of this development always seem to target the most historical sections of our rivers. In fact, all of the historic Calaveras ferry sites along the Stanislaus have been lost through modern development, and a major piece of history has been taken from the people -- between the rivers.

29
The Crossing at Slumgullion

B Y the fall of 1848, just months after gold was discovered at Sutter's Mill, dozens of mining camps had already been established throughout the Mother Lode, and a flood of new miners was pouring in. Prospectors traveling to the north and south had to cross the many rivers that flowed down from the Sierra Mountains, and it wasn't long before some of those who had arrived earlier saw their chance to exploit these barriers to transportation through the operation of ferries.

One of the earliest ferries in Calaveras County was built on the Stanislaus River, probably during the winter of 1848, by George McLean and William Jeffrey. Because it connected the fast-growing town of Murphys with Sonora in Tuolumne County, it was often called the Murphys Ferry, although it is shown on maps of the period as McLean's Ferry. (While ferries were almost always named for their owners, the owner's name was not always properly spelled or pronounced. For example, McLean was often misspelled McLane.)

Shortly after McLean and his partner began operations, two gentlemen named John Robinson and Stephen Mead opened a tent store a few miles downstream, near a bustling mining camp that was establishing itself on the southerly side of Carson Hill. The Mexican miners called the widely scattered community "Melones". By the end of 1849, both the towns of Melones and neighboring Carson Hill had grown to significant size, prompting Robinson and Meade to establish a ferry across the Stanislaus to Jackass Hill and Tuttletown. And thus, Robinson's Ferry was born.

Like much of early Gold Rush history, there is considerable confusion over the original names and locations of these communities. Several historians state that Melones was called Slumgullion by the American miners. There is no evidence that this name was applied prior to its invention by the famed gold rush writer Bret Harte. Harte visited Robinson's Ferry during the early 1850s, and worked a nearby claim. In the latter part of the century, Harte based many of his stories on this experience, inventing fictitious names for what were, in many cases, real people and places. Slumgullion may have been Robinson's Ferry, Melones, or perhaps a composite of these and other gold rush towns.

Erwin Gudde (*California Gold Camps*) places the town of Melones "on the Stanislaus River, two miles north of Robinson's Ferry, and about two miles south of the town of Carson Hill." This, of course, is impossible since Robinson's Ferry is, itself, on the Stanislaus, and the town of Carson Hill is about two miles from that river. From "first person" accounts (miner's journals and letters) and 20th century archeological examinations of the area, it has been determined that three towns with significant commercial centers existed in close proximity to one another: Carson Hill, about two miles north of the Stanislaus on Carson Creek; Robinson' Ferry, running east and west along the banks of the Stanislaus; and Melones, on the southern skirt of Carson Hill somewhat northwest from Robinson's Ferry. (Adding to the confusion, the Melones Mining company moved to Robinson's Ferry just prior to the turn of the century and changed that town's name to Melones. It must be remembered that the Melones of the 20th century was not the same as the Melones of the Gold Rush era.)

Like Jenny Lind and West Point, the origin of Melones' name has also been a source of controversy and speculative oral tradition, with two theories receiving wide support. The more colorful explanation is that the Mexicans who first mined the area discovered "melon seed-shaped" gold nuggets. The "seeds," or nuggets, were taken from the hill, therefore the hill was the "melone", the melon. There is one early account which supports this theory, an article in San Francisco's *Daily Alta California*, dated June 16, 1851, which says that some of the former Spanish residents of "Camp Melone" had been attracted to a new strike south of the river, which they called "Sandias" (water-melon).

Another theory is based on recently uncovered genealogical information which indicates that a person or persons named "Meloney" lived in or near Robinson's Ferry during the early years of the Gold Rush, and perhaps a person by that name operated a saloon there. Also, the town was frequently called "Meloneys" during that period. It has even been speculated that John Robinson's wife had the maiden name Melone.

Even if all of this is true, it is less a reason for the naming of Melones than a reason for the abundant confusion over the name, as witness the following article which ran in the previously mentioned *Alta California* just two days after the article referring to "Camp Melone" and "Sandias":

Terrible Affray at Meloney's Diggings
A terrible affray took place at Meloney's Diggings, on Thursday evening last, in which one or two Americans and three or four Mexicans were killed and a number mortally wounded. The fight commenced about two women in a gambling saloon. The Mexicans drove the Americans from the house, and the latter in turn drove off the former and gained possession. The melee became general and an express was started for Angel's Camp for assistance.

Accounts of this incident were widely published, variously giving the site of the fight as Carsons, Carson Hill, Melone, Melones, Meloney's, and Santa Cruz (the name of a nearby mine). The following excerpt from the diary of L. Noyes describes the same episode in more detail, and gives us a better understanding of why Melones soon developed its reputation as a violent and lawless camp: *One night we were called out by someone and told that the Mexicans had rose in Malones and were murdering the Americans. We all got up, strapped on our pistols, took our rifles, and went down where we found there had been a bad row between Mexican and American Gamblers, which had originated by a Mexican woman striking another Mexican woman over the head with a handkerchief full of money. This was the occasion of several men being shot and cut. We concluded that it was best to let them fight it over, and no matter which got the worst of it.*

In 1851 Melones was described as "one of the largest mining camps in the state", with a population estimated to be as high as 5000. It is likely that this figure included the towns of Carson Hill and Robinson's Ferry and the hundreds of miners scattered along the creeks and gulches nearby. However, there is no doubt that Melones was a place of considerable activity during this period, due primarily to its close proximity to the rich quartz mines of Carson Hill, especially the "Morgan." And it is this connection that probably led to the town's early demise.

A dispute over claim rights led to the abrupt closing of the Morgan early in 1852, and by the end

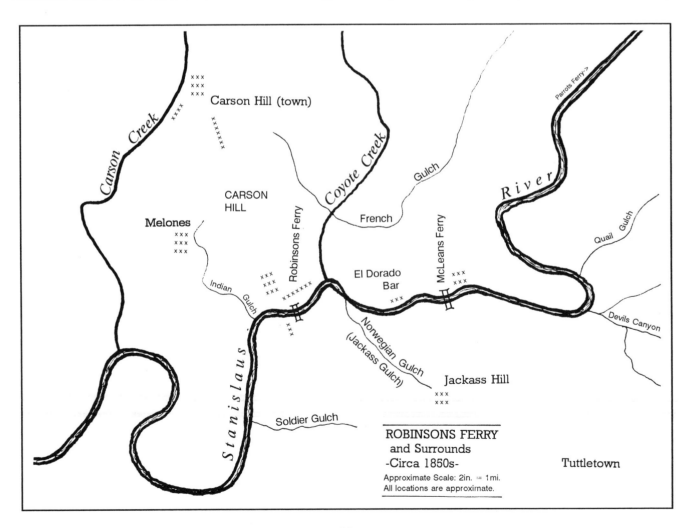

ROBINSONS FERRY
and Surrounds
-Circa 1850s-

Approximate Scale: 2in. = 1mi.
All locations are approximate.

By the turn of the century mining companies had turned Robinson's Ferry into the "new" Melones. (Calaveras County Historical Society)

of the year, the town of Melones was no more. A reporter for the *San Joaquin Republican* who passed through the area in June of 1853 wrote. . . . "now nothing remains except a few shanties inhabited by a few Mexicans." (In the years immediately following its abandonment, the Melones site was called "Maloney's Old Camp.") Just five years after the Gold Rush began, a gold rush ghost town sat decaying on the slope of Carson Hill.

While nearby Robinson's Ferry did not go unaffected by the mine closings, it remained the most active of the Stanislaus crossings throughout the 1850s. In fact, it appears to have put its upstream competitor (McLeans) out of business by 1854, although, by then Robinson and Mead had sold out their interests in the enterprise.

The various stores and saloons which sprang up along the river next to the ferry catered to the traveler and the new arrival, many of whom established semi-permanent residences near the ferry on either side of the river and tried their hand at mining the nearby gulches.

Although the ferry itself remained active throughout the 19th century, both it and the town of Robinson's Ferry went through a series of changes. Harvey Wood, who purchased a percentage of the business in 1856, became sole partner with J.M. French in 1860. The deed from that transaction lists the ferry and associated machinery, and a ferry house which included a "bar, bar fixtures, liquors,

provisions, and goods of every kind..." -- all the wants and needs of a miner on the move. But as the 1860s approached and placer mining dwindled, so did the population of Robinson's Ferry. Eventually it was reduced to a few transient miners and resident business owners.

The Civil War years seemed to have improved the economy of Robinson's Ferry, for an article in the Tuolumne Courier dated March 14, 1863 estimated 200 residents, of which 20 were women, and describes a town boasting four stores, two saloons, a restaurant, a butcher shop, and around forty private dwellings. No doubt the upswing was also partially due to the organization of the Melones and Stanislaus Gold, Silver, and Copper Mining Company that same year.

While the town of Robinson's Ferry still had lean years (in 1870 only the ferry house and ferry were in operation), Melones and Stanislaus Mining and their successors eventually helped to stabilize the growth of the community. Melones Mining built a large mill there, just after the turn of the century, and applied for a post office under the name "Melones", which opened in 1902. Harvey Wood, who had been sole owner of the ferry since 1881, passed away in 1895, and his wife and son continued to operate the ferry until 1904. Shortly thereafter, a bridge was constructed across the Stanislaus at Melones through a joint effort of Calaveras and Tuolumne counties.

Water from the first Melones Reservoir, constructed in 1926, covered the location of the old ferry, but were held back from the town of Melones by a retaining wall. The mill, then operated by Carson Hill Gold Mining, was destroyed by fire in 1942 and never reopened. There were only a few residents left to evacuate when the town was raised in the late 1970s in preparation for inundation by the New Melones Reservoir. The new dam was completed in 1979.

Even during extremely low water levels caused by past droughts, little could be seen of the historic sites of Robinson's Ferry and the second Melones. Old Maloney's Camp is long gone (its exact location is still a subject of some debate), and Carson Hill's littered rest stop does little to remind us of that town's historical significance. But if you study the photos on these pages, then grab a copy of Bret Harte's *Luck of Roaring Camp* or *Outcasts of Poker Flat*, you'll soon see it all in your mind's eye, just the way George McLean and John Robinson and Harvey Wood saw it when they first came to make their mark on the land -- between the rivers.

Addendum

After this article first ran in 1990 it was brought to the writer's attention that he had left out a very important name associated with the history of the Robinson's Ferry/Melones/Carson Hill area. Among the early settlers in this area was Gabriel Stevenot, who arrived at Melones in the spring of 1850, and shortly thereafter opened a store in or near that town. Stevenot was actively involved in numerous mining operations, and upon the arrival of his son, Emile, in 1863, organized the Melones and Stanislaus Gold, Silver, and Copper Mining Company, mentioned in the preceding text.

While the elder Stevenot died in 1885, his descendants continued to play an important role in the development of Calaveras County. His grandson, Archie, was actively involved in maintaining and promoting the history of the Gold Rush, and was officially recognized as "Mister Mother Lode" by the California legislature in 1961. His contributions were further recognized following his death through the dedication of the Archie D. Stevenot Memorial Bridge, which crosses the Stanislaus very near the original site of the town of Melones and the Stevenot Ranch.

Today's Stevenot Bridge over the Stanislaus River towers over the former sites of Robinson's Ferry and the "new" Melones.

30
Beside Valley Trails

HOUSANDS of years of geological evolution have created a great deal of interesting topography in Calaveras County, but perhaps none is more fascinating nor more beautiful than the high valley which lies between what we now call Gopher Ridge and the Bear Mountain Range in the southwestern part of the county. Long before even native Americans came to this land, the valley contained several large lakes. But through a process of natural erosion, the surrounding creeks and gulches gradually encroached upon them and drained their waters into the Calaveras and Stanislaus rivers. When white explorers first came to the valley (probably in the mid-1840s) only two small lakes remained. Later, the first settlers discovered a number of highly alkaline springs throughout the area which inspired them to call the place Salt Spring Valley.

The flood of miners who invaded the Sierra Foothills in 1848-49 might well have ignored the valley completely had it not been for a well established Indian trail that ran directly through its center. Called the Antelope Trail, this route had no doubt been used by both Spanish explorers and French trappers and now provided an easily followed pathway for 49ers traveling from Stockton to Angels and beyond. One of those early prospectors was Ben Marshall, who would later become Calaveras County's second sheriff.

Marshall came to California shortly after the end of the Mexican war and upon hearing of the discovery of gold in 1848, quickly set out for the foothills. In 1852, he bought a large parcel of land on the Antelope Trail near Rock Creek and opened a roadhouse there. The popular rest stop burned down in 1859 and Marshall began selling off parcels of the ranch in the 1860s. Because he actively promoted the Antelope route to the mines, it is sometimes called Marshall's Trail.

By 1850, numerous large mining camps had been established throughout the county and the easily traversed Salt Spring Valley provided a transportation "corridor" for new roads. The Calaveras Road crossed the northern section of the valley and connected Rich Gulch (near Jenny Lind) with the Antelope trail to Angels. Another road was also established to Boston Bar, further up the Calaveras

River. Those traveling this part of the valley could rest or take a meal at the Peach Orchard roadhouse, run by Harris Garcelon and Ossian Kallenbach. Their farm and hotel were probably the first "commercial" development of the Salt Spring Valley.

As more and more miners became disillusioned with their search for gold and turned to other ways of making a living, a number of small farms began to pop up across the valley. In 1852, on the Antelope Trail near Tule Lake, a Frenchman named Sylvester Felix established a ranch and sent for his wife, Josephine, to join him. She barely had a chance to settle in before Sylvester was killed in a teaming accident.

Ironically, the location that her husband had chosen for their home would be Josephine's saving grace, for shortly after his death she opened a roadhouse. The ranch was productive as well, with the help of the widow's neighbor Alban Hettick, whom she later married. In the years that followed, Madam Felix's roadhouse established itself as one of the most popular stops along the Antelope Trail and the lady herself became a legend. The respect of neighboring ranchers and miners is evident from the name chosen for their mining district during the copper boom of the '60s – the Madam Felix Copper Mining District.

Two other names that figure strongly in the history of Salt Spring Valley are Jacob Tower and Thomas McCarty. Both of these gentlemen had worked at Garcelon and Kallenbach's peach orchard during the early '50s and later settled on ranches of their own. McCarty's Log Cabin Ranch was located south of the valley and he would later become an important figure in the evolution of Copperopolis and its copper mines. His descendants would subsequently resettle in Salt Spring Valley and play an equally important role in the late development of valley ranches and mines.

Jacob Tower started his ranch in 1852 in the heart of the valley and entered into partnership with Wilson Bisbee around 1855. Consisting of over three thousand acres, this ranch was the largest in the area at the time and after Jacob married Mary Howard in 1864, the distinctive two-story Tower ranch house (built in 1860) would become a social center for the entire valley. Known as the "White House Ranch," the Tower residence, like others in

Salt Spring Valley's second schoolhouse, like the one built by Jacob Tower, sat on a knoll overlooking the Salt Spring Reservoir.

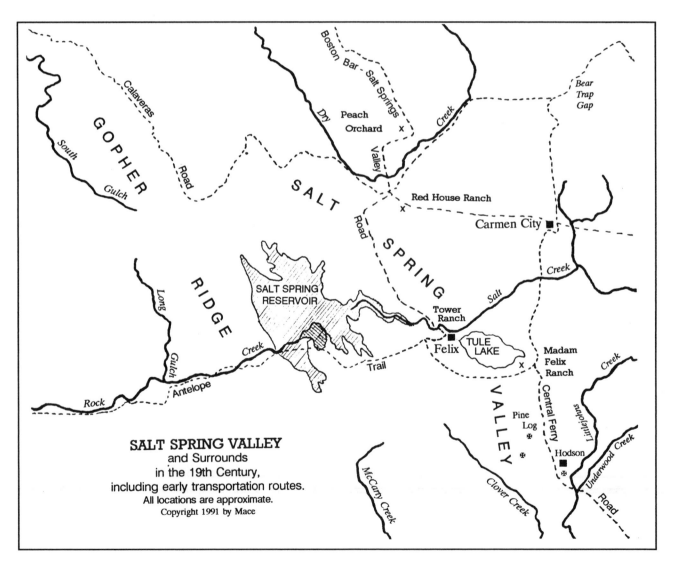

SALT SPRING VALLEY
and Surrounds
in the 19th Century,
including early transportation routes.
All locations are approximate.
Copyright 1991 by Mace

The scattered buildings of an impressive modern ranch mark the location of the Red House Ranch, which provided a rest stop for weary travelers passing through Salt Spring Valley during the late nineteenth century.

the valley, provided overnight accommodations for travelers at 50¢ a night, and a family style meal prepared by Chinese cooks was only 25¢.

In the 1860s, Jacob Tower built the valley's first schoolhouse on a knoll overlooking the Salt Spring Reservoir, but later had it removed to his ranch when it became apparent that other ranchers were not going to assist in its maintenance. A school district was eventually organized by group effort in 1869 and a new schoolhouse was built on the knoll. (Both buildings still survive on the Tower Ranch.)

As previously mentioned, there were two remaining lakes in the Salt Spring Valley -- Salt Spring Lake (possibly also called Tulare Lake), at the head of Rock Creek; and Tule Lake, south of Salt Creek. Both of these small basins would play an important role in the development of the valley. In 1858, an earth-fill dam was constructed on Rock Creek to enlarge Salt Spring Lake and create a reservoir containing 10,000 acre feet of water. This water was transported by ditch to various mining operations both in and outside of the valley well into the 20th century. Water from Tule Lake was also used to support mining operations.

Generally speaking, the earlier mining camps of Calaveras County developed along the rivers and their major tributaries and gulches. As placer deposits were used up, explorations were made into areas previously ignored by miners and new mining methods came into use which required large amounts of water. Around 1858, local papers began to carry stories about the discovery of moderate placer deposits and "free gold" (loose nuggets and

quartz rock containing gold) at a place called New Diggings between Littlejohns Creek and Clover Creek, in the lower Salt Spring Valley. Although the resulting rush was somewhat small and short-lived, it played a significant role in the valley's future.

The flow of water in the gulches of New Diggings was strictly seasonal, prompting the construction of ditches to carry water from Tule Lake, just to the north. The lake and ditch were described in a *San Andreas Independent*, November 1858:

Toward the eastern end of the [Salt Spring] *valley is situated Tule Lake -- a body of water fed in summer from a number of springs and in winter from five or six small creeks which empty into it. Tule Lake covers some 75 to 80 acres of space and when full, is from 6 to 8 feet in depth. In the early part of the past spring, Messrs. Dennis Corcoran and J. P. Haskill, of San Andreas, conceived the idea of cutting a ditch from the mining district below this lake, for the purpose of draining its waters for the use of the miners. The ditch will be finished next week; and will be three miles in length. . . .*

By 1860, New Diggings was the site of a store (owned by Jacob Pike), several miners cabins, and a small stamp mill. The Willow Grove quartz mill, near the later community of Hodson, was also able to operate with the arrival of water from Tule Lake. But in that year the face of mining in Calaveras County made an abrupt change when Hiram Hughes discovered copper across Gopher Ridge (see Chapter 26). Hoping to change their luck, the miners switched their efforts from digging gold to prospecting "iron rust."

New shafts were sunk, old claims were reactivated, and the Madam Felix Copper Mining District was created. But just as it had been with gold, the success of Salt Spring Valley copper mines was minimal.

When the copper "boom" ended, shortly after the conclusion of the Civil War, miners again turned their interests back to gold, but by 1871, mining of all types had pretty much come to a halt in the Salt Spring Valley. By then, the valley was dotted with ranches and crisscrossed with a "network" of roads. Despite the growing population and social atmosphere, the valley never developed a major commercial center. The "towns" of Felix and Carmen City never progressed beyond a store and a few outbuildings (although Felix did have a post office in the old Tower schoolhouse from 1896 to 1923). The town of Hodson, in the mining district, was a company town organized in association with the Royal Mine shortly after the turn of the century. There was never a church in the valley, although Mary Tower organized religious services in the schoolhouse.

When the Stockton and Copperopolis Railroad gave rise to the town of Milton in 1871, the importance of Salt Spring Valley as a transportation corridor greatly increased. It had been the intention of railroad promoters to continue their line along Rock Creek and through the valley to Copperopolis but lack of funds and the imposing prospect of constructing a grade up Gopher Ridge brought the project to an end.

In the years that followed, tourists in route to Calaveras Big Trees and Yosemite made extensive use of the Stockton-Copperopolis line and continued their journey by wagon or stagecoach through Salt Spring Valley. Teamsters also traveled the roads of the valley with shipments going to, and coming from the railhead. Tower's way station was quite active during this period, providing relief for the weary traveler and supplying fresh horses for teamsters and stage drivers. During certain times of the year it was advantageous to take a "northern" route through the valley to avoid flooded streams and muddy roads. One such road took wagons up

When early residents of Salt Spring Valley refused to support the school he had built, Jacob Tower moved it to his ranch, where it later served as post office for the town of Felix.

the eastern edge of the valley to Carmen City, then northwest across the valley to the old Calaveras Road near Dry Creek. The Red House Ranch provided a convenient rest stop for travelers using this route. (Many of the roads from this period are still used today and while paved, are probably about as rough as they were then.)

The Salt Spring Valley remains, to this day, virtually untouched by commercialization and modern development. The few large ranches which make up the valley's small population are in many cases owned by descendants of the pioneers mentioned here. Hidden between a large ridge and a mountain some miles distant from modern highways, the Salt Spring Valley is a magnificent reminder of the untamed and unspoiled land that preceded the rush for gold -- between the rivers.

31
The Business of Lodes

OTH historians and writers often seem to give the impression that "hard rock" or quartz gold mining did not begin until the mid-1850s, when stream-based placer gold deposits began to play out. Gold bearing outcroppings of quartz were most certainly noticed by the earliest prospectors and, according to Bancroft (whose early California histories are cherished by modern historians), the first quartz vein in the Mother Lode was discovered in 1849, near Mariposa.

In Calaveras County, during the fall of 1850, John Hance, James Finnegan, and others, were working the rich placers of Carson Creek when one or more of them came across quartz outcroppings on the slope of Carson Hill. On November 15, the following claim was drawn up:

We the undersigned, on behalf of the Carson Creek Consolidated Mining Company, do hereby claim by right of discovery and occupation all that certain ledge of quartz, rock. . . . .Gold having been discovered by members of the said company at different places of said ledge, all of which said ledge is within the said County of Calaveras, about two miles northwest from McLean's Ferry on the Stanislaus River and between Coyote Creek and Carson Creek tributaries of said river.

This notice was signed by the company officers: William Hance Jr., Jeremiah Austill, James Smith, William Rove, Duncan Murphys, James Nott, and A. Morgan. (James Finnegan's name does not appear on the notice, even though he was one of the original claimants. His exclusion from the company caused an ongoing argument over the legality of the claim.)

This "tunnel claim" on Carson Hill would come to be known as the Morgan Mine, one of the first lode mines in the county, and it would give birth to one of the largest early settlements in Calaveras County, the town of Melones. According to a 1905 article in the Calaveras Chronicle, Morgan, Hance, and the others took out $4 million before James Finnegan and his friends sent them packing. By 1851, news of the Morgan and other similar quartz mines had spread across the state, and the future of California gold mining had taken on a much wider scope.

In a lode mine, gold is trapped inside quartz and other "hard rock" materials. Accordingly, this gold bearing ore must be extracted from the earth, then crushed into smaller particles and the gold separated from accompanying worthless sand. In the earliest years of this type of mining, hand drills were used to bore holes into the rock, then large chunks were either busted loose with chisels and picks, or blown free with an explosive charge of black powder. While the owners of hard rock mines almost always worked their own claims, the work was often supervised by Mexicans who had more experience in this type of mining. It was a long, laborious process and was only worthwhile if the ore was "high grade" -- containing significant amounts of gold.

As anyone who has ever dug a deep hole or ditch is aware, the further down into the ground you go, the harder it is to dig -- and this is a hard fact (pun intended) in tunnel or shaft mining. Accordingly, those early mines seldom descended past 100 feet and many stopped far short of that. (Some of these mines were reopened in later years, with large amounts of gold being taken from well beyond the original terminus.) From deep shafts, ore was hauled to the surface by hand in leather bags, then transported to the crusher by pack mules.

For centuries, mining companies have searched for efficient methods to extract gold from gold ore, and even today's technology has not perfected a solution. Early miners were frustrated by the fact that only a small portion of the gold contained in the ore was being recovered in processing. They had pretty much solved the problem of crushing the ore through the use of the arrastra early on, and later with stamp mills. The arrastra, like much of early lode technology, came from the Mexicans who had worked quartz mines in their own country many years before California's Gold Rush. Relatively basic in design, the arrastra consisted of a large stone hanging from an "arm" that was attached to a central pivot. Walking in a continuous circle, a mule would pull the arm, dragging the stone over chunks of ore, eventually pulverizing them into fine sand.

Although the use of stamp mills was not as wide spread during the earliest years of quartz mining, they eventually would become the primary method of crushing gold ore. These machines consisted of a set of heavy iron "pistons" which were raised and lowered into a crushing bin (called a "battery") by mechanical means. The ore entered the bin from one

side and the crushed material came out the other side. By the mid-1850s, "stampers" of various size were operating throughout Calaveras County, and "milling" had become big business, often run totally independent from a specific mining operation.

The primary problem was not how to crush the ore, however, but how to extract the gold from the tons of other crushed minerals. Gold that had been freed from these other minerals in the crushing operation was recovered by a process called "amalgamation." It had been know for many years that gold and mercury were highly attracted to one another. (To illustrate, if one were to place a drop of mercury on a tin plate, the droplet would set upon the surface like a drop of water on wax paper. But when a drop of mercury is placed on gold, it spreads out over the surface, coating it like paint.)

When gold ore is placed in contact with mercury, the heavy gold particles sink into it and become one with it (an "amalgam" of gold and mercury), and the remaining minerals can then be washed away. The mercury can then be boiled off, leaving only the recovered gold. (It should be noted here that mercury is extremely poisonous, making this process not only tedious and time consuming, but also quite dangerous. Nearly every process ever used in the extraction of gold from crushed ore has required the handling of highly poisonous chemicals.)

This recovery process was used well into the 20th century, and is still used by amateur miners today. But even in the early days it was known that significant quantities of gold were being lost during this procedure. Some of the gold was still locked together with other minerals in the material that was being discarded -- the "tailings." While several attempts were made during the 1850's to recover gold from "complex ore," efficient extraction methods did not come along until late in the century.

History often mentions the huge "nuggets" that have been found at times throughout the Mother Lode. A great many of these were taken from lode mines and are not actually nuggets but big chunks of extremely high grade ore with predominant amounts of visible gold. One such "specimen" (as they are called today) was located on Carson Hill in 1854, and weighed in at a record 195 pounds troy.

By the late 1860s, the Calaveras countryside was dotted with lode mines from West Point to Melones and Sheep Ranch to Salt Spring Valley. From the earliest years of California gold mining, districts were drawn up immediately after each new strike was made to keep track of claims and establish mining laws. Unfortunately, the records of many early districts have been lost to time and we know very little about many of the thousands of mines that once existed in Calaveras County. Of those we do know about, many were short lived and unproductive. The top producing mines often changed owners many times over the years and almost always ended up in the hands of an organized mining company who had the money to introduce mechanics and technology that would assure maximum productivity.

Hardrock mining had its heyday at the peak of the Industrial Revolution, from the 1880s until just after the turn of the century. Improved drilling machines (pneumatic and hollow core drills) and explosives (dynamite) allowed miners to go deeper than they had ever gone before -- as far as 1000 feet and beyond. At these depths, air shafts were required for additional ventilation and accumulating ground water had to be pumped out. By way of steam or water powered hoists, men and machines were lowered into the mine in the same buckets that would later bring up the ore. Shortly after the turn of the century, electricity would power hoists, pumps, and ventilating fans and light the shaft.

Stamp mills remained the most popular method of crushing ore well into the 20th century. The crushed ore was washed directly out onto copper plates painted with mercury, where amalgamation took place. At predetermined periods, the stampers would be shut down so that the amalgam could be scraped up for processing. In larger operations where the stamps were set up in banks of five, only one bank was shut down at a time, allowing for non-stop operation of the mill. Some mines had as many as 100 stamps in continuous use.

Improvements were also made in the recovery of gold from complex ores, primarily through the use of "chlorination," a complex and expensive process; and through the cyanide bath, introduced in the late 1890s.

The top gold producing lode mines of Calaveras County were the Carson Hill group, including the Morgan and the Melones, which produced over

The mule powered arrastra was the primary method of crushing ore during the early years of quartz mining. (Harpers Magazine)

The Madison Mine at Angels Camp was representative of a "classic" lode mine. This photo shows from left, the mill building, headframe, and hoist shed. (Calaveras County Historical Society)

$26 million (5th largest in California); the Utica, in Angels Camp, which produced $17 million; and the Gwin (Paloma) and the Sheep Ranch, which brought out $7 million each. Other significant lode mines in the county included the Royal at Hodson, and the Angels, Lightner, Gold Cliff, and Madison at Angels Camp. A large number of hard rock mines operated near West Point, but few of those individual mine s produced more than $1/2 million in gold.

While many mines continued to operate well into the 20th century and a few mining companies are still squeezing out a few last ounces of Calaveras gold, most of the lode mines are long gone, their hoists torn down and their shafts covered over. But there are still those who vividly remember the familiar silhouette of their headframes and the thunderous beating of the stamp mills that transformed rock into riches -- between the rivers.

32
The Mother Lode's
Fourth Estate

During Medieval times, most of Europe was organized under a system of government called the "feudal system" which recognized three distinctive classes of people called "estates": First and foremost were the clergy, for religion was of primary importance during those times; second came the nobility, those persons of title who owned the land and controlled the political future of the country; and the third estate was made up of the common working class.

O one really knows when the first newspaper was produced but we do know that the ancient Romans distributed a hand written daily journal called *Acta Publica*, which reported births, deaths, festivals, and crimes, as well as local crop reports, financial news, and the progress of Rome's Imperial Arms. The first printed newspapers were probably issued in China during the 14th century, with each letter stamped by hand using carved wooden type.

After the invention of mechanical printing in the 15th century, town "gazettes" (so-called because the cost of the first Italian newspaper was a small coin called a "gazetta") became common, and even the discovery of America was chronicled in European newspapers. Newspapers were the earliest form of mass-communication and often had a major effect on the politics of nations. They not only informed the public of recent news events, they also provided a forum for the expression of thoughts and ideas.

In 19th century America, journalism had become a powerful institution and had earned the designation "fourth estate," in reference to the influence it wielded over all classes of people. The government of the United States, from its inception, sought to insure freedom of speech and freedom of the press. Being a government that was highly political in nature, its efforts were perhaps not solely unselfish, as the names of many early newspapers illustrate (i.e., the *Democrat*, the *Whig*, the *Independent*, the *Union*, etc.). Unfortunately, journalists and reporters of this period were not wholly concerned with how they got their stories or even whether or not they were accurate. Nevertheless, American newspapers of the 19th century were the only form of far-reaching

mass communication for a widely scattered and increasingly mobile population. Nowhere was this more important than in California and the West.

California's first English language newspaper was printed in Monterey on August 15, 1846, as American flags were being raised throughout the new California Republic . Using a badly worn press that had been left behind by the fleeing Mexicans, Rev. Walter Colton printed the first number of his *Californian* on sheets of paper intended for the wrapping of cigars. In his "prospectus," Colton dedicated the paper to maintaining "an entire and utter severance of all political connection with Mexico," and to the "establishment of a well organized government, and a universal obedience to its laws."

In May of 1847, the *Californian* was moved to Yerba Buena (soon to be San Francisco) where its only competitor to that point, the *California Star*, had been established in January by a Mormon elder named Samuel Brannan. Brannan and his editor, E. P. Jones, quickly developed a reputation for brashness and arrogance which this early editorial suggests they may have deserved: *We have received two late numbers of the Californian, a dim, dirty little paper printed at Monterey on the worn out material of one of the old California war presses. It is published and edited by Walter Colton and Robert Semple, the one a lying sycophant and the other an overgrown lickspittle. . . . we have concluded to give our paper to them this year so as to afford them some insight into the manner in which a Republican newspaper should be conducted.*

Both the *Star* and the *Californian* were well established in San Francisco when gold was found at Sutter's Mill in January, 1848. Upon hearing of the news, both papers attempted to play down the discovery, and the *Star* even went so far as to declare that it was a sham, magnified many times out of proportion. Within a few months, both papers would suspend operations because printers, typesetters, and nearly the entire staff had left for the gold fields.

In the latter part of 1848, California's first two newspapers returned, merged, and were soon read under a new banner -- the *Alta California*. As a variety of gold rush inspired newspapers appeared across the state, the *Alta* quickly established itself as the most influential and widely read West Coast publication. During the 1850s, the *Alta* had over 150 foreign and English language competitors who operated in the city of San Francisco alone. While most were in business for only a year or less, perhaps 40 of these newspapers were all operating at the same time. These included "dailies," "weeklies," "semi-monthlies," and "monthlies."

While it could not accurately be called a "Mother Lode" newspaper, the first paper which was widely read by those employed in the mining camps was an offshoot of the *Alta* called the *Placer Times*, published in Sacramento on the same worn press that first serviced the pioneering *Californian* in Monterey. (Interestingly, that tired old woodframe Ramage hand press would later produce the *Stockton Times*, the *Sonora Herald*, and the *Columbia Star*, before it was destroyed by vandals in Columbia.) Prior to the establishment of local publications in the gold fields (which were not long in coming), Sacramento and Stockton papers were delivered to the mines as soon as possible after printing.

The standard machinery of

The Calaveras Chronicle, the county's first newspaper, made its home in Mokelumne Hill for over half a century. (Calaveras Historical Society)

these early small newspapers was the Washington Hand Press, manufactured by R. Hoe and Co. of New York and shipped around the Horn of South America or across the Isthmus of Panama. There is an interesting story relating to one such press that was lost into the murky depths of Panama's Chagras River when the native canoe in which it was being carried capsized. After numerous unsuccessful attempts to pull the castiron contraption (which weighed nearly a ton) to the surface, it is said that the owner himself dove in and hauled it up. While the story is no doubt "embellished," as are many tales relating to the gold rush, it does illustrate the value placed on those few printing presses that survived the arduous journey.

The Washington Press was not so very different from the press invented by Gutenberg in the 15th century. Designed to print one page at a time, it consisted of a *bed*, which held the type-filled *form*. Paper was placed on the hinged *tympan*, that was then folded over the type, which had been inked with a roller. Then the entire bed slid along rails to a position under the lever-operated *platen*, which pressed the paper against the type. If the platen were large enough, two pages could be printed at a time, meaning that a four page newspaper could be produced on a single sheet of paper, requiring the setting of only two type-forms. Once the type was set, inked, and locked in place, a skilled printer could turn out four to six sheets per minute.

The type that came with the press was all that was available to the printer. If he was short on w's, he would use an upside-down m or set two v's together. If a c got broken, he would cut the side off an o. Often needed letters were simply carved out of wood with a penknife.

Few early California newspapers had illustrations, which required the skill of a master engraver. Images were carved into wooden printing blocks by cutting away tiny lines to form the highlights and shadows of the picture. Some newspapers bought "generic" woodcuts depicting characters or scenes which would appear in the paper several times over the year in connection with a variety of articles. Photography was still a fledgling art, and although daguerreotypes were used as the basis for many woodcuts, it would be several decades before a practical method of transferring photographs to the printed page would be developed.

The first Mother Lode newspaper was established in Sonora on July 4, 1850. Volume 1, number 1 of the *Sonora Herald* cost 50¢ and was printed in Stockton on a type of writing paper called "foolscap" for its watermark which depicted the head of a court jester. Although the *Herald* changed editors 12 times over the first 5 years, it quickly established itself as a voice of and for the common gold miner.

The honor of being the Mother Lode's second newspaper and Calaveras County's first, goes to the *Calaveras Chronicle*, which began operations in Mokelumne Hill on October 9, 1851. Editor H. A. DeCourcey, who had previously operated the *Nevada Journal*, quickly found that editorializing in gold country could be a dangerous business when a man named Carter challenged him to a duel. DeCourcey was only wounded in the incident, but shortly thereafter editorship of the *Chronicle* was turned over to H. Hamilton. The *Chronicle* building was destroyed in the fire of '54, but the paper came back and remained in production until just after the turn of the century. At the time of its demise (purchased by the *Calaveras Prospect*), it was hailed as California's oldest continuously printed newspaper.

Until the 1860s, the *Chronicle* was Calaveras' primary newspaper. Its nearest early competitors were the *Amador Sentinel* in Jackson (first printed January 1854), and the *San Andreas Independent*, which began operations in September 1856, as a weekly. The word "independent" in a newspaper's name meant that it intended to stay away from party politics and this San Andreas journal developed a reputation for its attention to social and intellectual topics. The *Independent* moved to Stockton in 1861.

One of the county's first foreign language newspaper was *Staats Zeitung* (State Newspaper), published for German-speaking residents of the Mokelumne Hill area from 1854 to 1858. Some early newspapers were based in humor, such as Mok Hill's *Quamkeag Coyote*, while others, like the *Calaveras*

Calaveras County Newspapers 1851 to 1990

ANGELS CAMP
Angels Camp Record 1899-1918
Calaveras Californian 1923-
Calaveras Democrat 1890-1891
Calaveras Mountaineer 1872-1873
Calaveras News 1906-1912
County Record 1887-1890
Mark Twain Times 1963
Monitor 1879-1889
Mountain Echo 1889-1907

COPPEROPOLIS
Copperopolis Courier 1865-1867

MOKELUMNE HILL
Calaveras Chronicle 1851-1908 (1951)
Calaveras Weekly 1940-1947
Quamkeag Coyote 1854
Staats-Zeitung 1854-1858

MURPHYS
Big Tree Bulletin 1858
Murphys Advertiser 1858
Semi-Weekly News 1858

SAN ANDREAS
Calaveras Advertiser 1879-1881
Calaveras Citizen 1871-1906
Calaveras Enterprise 1963-
Calaveras Prospect 1881-1926
Calaveras Prospect and Weekly Citizen 1926-
Calaveras Times 1863
Calaveras Union 1856
Foothill Democrat 1875-1876
Mountain News 1867-1868
San Andreas Independent 1856-1851
San Andreas Register 1863-1868
Weekly Citizen 1906-1926

All dates are approximate. Some current and small presses may have been missed.

Sources: Calaveras County Archives; *Las Calaveras*, Vol. XIII, No. 2; *History of Calaveras Newspapers*, Kemble, 1858.

Union, were election-year promotion sheets for the various political parties. (The Union Party's presidential candidate, an obscure backwoods Illinois lawyer named Abraham Lincoln, ran virtually unnoticed in the 1856 campaign.)

After the Civil War, dozens of newspapers sprang up across the county. Many only distributed a few issues before they were quickly lost to history, others managed to survive well into the 20th century. Today, the newspapers of Calaveras County continue a tradition which only its favorite son, Mark Twain, could describe with such painful honesty (and to which I humbly add my simple closure):

Our duty is to keep the universe thoroughly posted concerning murders and street fights, and balls, and theaters. . . . and a thousand other things which is in the province of local reporters to keep track of and magnify into undue importance for the instruction of the readers -- between the rivers.

33
From Saintly Beginnings

T is not surprising that no one knows how the town of San Andreas got its name. Many Mother Lode towns were named in the first days of the Gold Rush by a person or persons who may have only stayed in the area for a few weeks. In most cases, the first name given to a camp stuck with it over the years, but there are instances where those early names have been modified or even completely changed -- sometimes more than once. We know from period documents that the name San Andreas was being used as early as 1850, and we know of no other name that was used for that place. While anything more must be considered strictly conjecture, the story of the founding and naming of the town of San Andreas, as derived from local oral tradition, is as follows:

A group of Mexican gold miners located and worked the placers of what we now call San Andreas Creek, probably as early as the summer of 1848. As the year progressed, the size of the camp grew to a significant number and a French priest named Father Bouvard arrived and established a small tent church on the hill above the gulch (near today's Gatewood Ave.). The first mass was held there on November 30, 1848 -- Saint Andrew's Day, for which the church and the town were then christened by Father Bouvard. (As an interesting side-note of this story, Andrew is pronounced "Andres" in Spanish, and "Andre" in French -- "Andreas" is an Italian derivative.)

Although there were certainly richer diggings in the area, San Andreas accumulated a population of nearly 1000 by the winter of '49, and what had been a mostly Mexican camp was beginning to see a number of American, French, and Chinese arrivals. Both sides of the creek were dotted with miner's tents and leantos. Still, there were no permanent buildings or anything that would even suggest the beginnings of a town.

During the early part of 1850, the government of France dispatched one hundred officers from its Mobile Guard to work in the California gold fields. Along with several thousand French immigrants, they swarmed into the area around Mokelumne Hill and San Andreas, much to the displeasure of the established Mexican and American miners. In 1851, the Mokelumne Hill faction was driven out after a

fight with Irish miners over claim rights. They eventually banded with their countrymen in San Andreas, over which the French flag was defiantly hoisted until the matter was finally settled by the French consul from San Francisco.

By the Spring of 1851, San Andreas was ready for its first wood frame commercial building, the Bella Union. This simple structure, built as a saloon and gambling hall, also served as a sort of community center or town hall. The local miners met there on December 28, 1851, to establish a mining district and lay down district regulations. Some of the original claims, as large as one hundred feet square, were reduced considerably by these new regulations. The Americans (roughly defined in those days as not French, Indian, Mexican, or Chinese) wanted their fair share of the diggings. Interestingly, in a camp where prejudice and racism ruled, the first hotel, called the Main Street House, was built and run by a black man, Philip F. Piper.

Two water ditches were constructed into the San Andreas diggings during 1851 and 1852: one from Willow Creek, built by Captain Robert Pope and later called the "Silver Ditch"; and the other from Murray Creek, called the Union Ditch. (A third water source, the Table Mountain Ditch, reached San Andreas from San Antone Creek in 1856.)

By 1853, San Andreas was beginning to form some semblance of a town structure, with three main "streets" serving the ethnically segregated sections of the camp; Mexican Street (Main), French Street (Court), and China Street (St. Charles). Also during that year, two important "deep rock" gold discoveries were made: one on Douglas Hill (lower Showalter Hill); and the other on Gold Hill. Both of these finds would result in extensive new mining operations that would greatly boost San Andreas' prospects. A number of new commercial operations opened their doors, including Joseph Zwinge's American Hotel, a large canvas structure on Main Street.

San Andreas received official recognition in 1854, when the area post office was moved there from Third Crossing, where it had been established just two years previously. Prior to San Andreas' boom years, Kentucky House at Third Crossing served as the commercial center for this section of the county, and provided a popular "road house" rest stop for travelers heading south to Angels and Sonora.

There were at least two other important road houses near San Andreas during the early days; Gold Hill House, at the fork on the Pioneer Road (Stockton Road) just north of town; and Alabama House, on Calaveritas Creek just east of Kentucky House. Road houses not only provided rest and refreshment for the weary traveler, they also played an important role in the miner's social life, allowing him to get away from the diggings for a drink and some friendly conversation. (Much of the Mother Lode's colorful and somewhat "embellished" oral tradition originated in road house parlors.)

One of a series of devastating fires struck San Andreas in 1854, destroying a number of wood and canvas buildings including Zwinge's American Hotel. While those early conflagrations were certainly not deemed fortuitous by the town's early settlers, they did teach an important lesson. In 1855, from the ashes of Zwinge's tent hotel came the all-stone American Restaurant. Today housing the county library, it is San Andreas' oldest existing structure. (Unfortunately, two other stone buildings which were constructed that year have since succumbed to fire and "progress.") On February 2nd, 1856, fire again broke out on Main Street San Andreas and destroyed a large portion of the town after skipping over the "fire-resistant" American Restaurant.

Wise merchants who rebuilt in stone and brick during 1856 and 1857 were rewarded when still another devastating conflagration broke out in the early morning hours of June 8th, 1858. By this date, the town was of considerable size and included many private homes, commercial buildings, and an extensive Chinatown. When the flames were finally halted, only one major woodframe building was left standing -- the offices of the *San Andreas Independent*. To others of the town who had lost so much, that paper's decidedly optimistic statement from their same-day coverage might have seemed a bit indecorous:

San Andreas is in ruins. One of those terrible visitations that frequently visit California towns, and more particularly in the gold fields, has again chastened us with a fiery ordeal. Almost the whole camp is in ashes, yet from its ruins, like another Phoenix, a fairer and statelier "habitation and a name" will soon arise.

And arise it did. A great number of the town's existing buildings date from the period immediately following this fire, including the fabulous, thirty-room Metropolitan Hotel, which served as stage depot and community center for many years. Continued good luck in the mines did much to help San Andreas' recovery. In 1859, over a half million in gold dust was shipped by just one San Andreas freight hauler.

By the early 1860s, San Andreas was one of the largest and most active towns in Calaveras County, and its citizens felt that it should become the county's fifth relocation for the seat of government. A legislative act put the question before the people on May 25, 1863. Although the election was won by San Andreas, the county officials, then at Mokelumne Hill, refused to move, and the point was eventually taken up by the State Supreme Court. It was three years before a court order finally brought the county offices to San Andreas, and the first meeting of the Board of Supervisors convened there (in Sharpe's Theater) on November 5, 1866. A two-story courthouse building was completed the following year.

Very little has been written on the quartz mines of San Andreas,

Map of
SAN ANDREAS
AND SURROUNDS
in the early 19th Century
including primary transportation routes.
Locations are approximate.

San Andreas' namesake, St. Andrew's Church, sits watchfully on the distant hill in this nineteenth century panorama. Note the abundance of windmills scattered throughout the town. (Calaveras Historical Society)

probably because only one, the Union (not to be confused with the Union copper mine at Copperopolis), was notably successful. There were, however, quite a few other "deep rock" mines in the area, active primarily in the 1870s, '80s, and '90s. These included the Commodore, Etna, Everlasting, Fellowcraft, Ford, Gottschalk, Golden Hill, Helen, Holland, Kate Hageman, Lookout Mountain, Mester, Pioneer, Chief, Rathgeb, and Thorpe.

The names of two famous (if greatly dissimilar) outlaws have been connected with the town of San Andreas -- the very real and fascinating historical character, Black Bart, who was finally tried and convicted there in 1883; and the legendary Joaquin Murietta, who may or may not (this writer votes for the latter) have had a "hide out" near Yaqui Camp, south of town, in the early 1850s.

Like most Mother Lode towns of size, San Andreas has been subjected to a steady flow of "boom or bust." While the loss of mining has caused the town to dwindle somewhat from the "glory years," its dedication to preserving its colorful history and its capacity as the seat of county government help it to remain an active and distinguished link in the "golden chain" -- not to mention a great place to live, work, and play -- between the rivers.

104

Incident at Moonlight Flat

Sometime in the late summer of 1859, two men sat arguing politics. The likely location of this discussion was a San Andreas saloon, for both men were prominent in that community. Their names were William J. Gatewood, attorney at law, and Dr. Peterson Goodwyn, M.D. As the debate became increasingly heated, voices were raised and emotions exploded into a brief second of violence, as Gatewood reached out and struck Dr. Goodwyn with his hand. Whether or not he truly intended to do the good doctor any harm is doubtful, but being proud and honorable men, there would be no apology. In such a time, with such men, there could be only one solution -- Dr. Goodwyn demanded satisfaction!

Shortly after sunrise on September 16, 1859, several carriages quietly left San Andreas, rambling southward along the Pioneer Road in the direction of Third Crossing. A few miles past the Kentucky House, at a place called Moonlight Flat, the carriages stopped and their passengers stepped forth. Among them were Dr. Goodwyn, Mr. Gatewood, and their seconds, W. T. Lewis, Major Glenn, Captain Pope, and M. Rowan. Two surgeons and a few additional friends were also present. Within minutes, the ground had been marked off, and the two men stood, forty paces distant, with rifles in their hands.

"Are you ready?" the question was asked.

"I am," both parties replied.

"Fire, one, two, th....." At the beginning of the word three, both combatants pulled the triggers of their rifles. But only one shot was heard. Dr. Goodwyn's rifle had failed to discharge, and he now lay on the ground, shot through the abdomen. Within seconds, Gatewood stood over him.

"Doctor, I am indeed sorry that this affair terminated so -- very sorry indeed."

"I am glad to know that you acted like a gentleman," came the doctor's reply.

Doctor Goodwyn was transported back to San Andreas in Gatewood's buggy, which was more accommodating than his own. Despite the surgeons efforts, he died before noon. The following day, the *San Andreas Independent* provided details of the incident, concluding with this insightful statement on dueling and the "code of honor":

If the people desire to put an end to the 'Code', let them say so in some unmistakable manner; but so long as the record stands as it does, and the public are more eager to scorn him who refuses, than punish him who accepts a challenge, we challenge, we cannot hold dueling as a very obnoxious exception to our public morality, whatever may be said and written under the impulse which some great or good man's fall gives to our sympathies.

Wm. Gatewood became District Attorney, and later, editor of the San Andreas Register.

*   *   *

(Taken from details of the incident as related in the San Andreas Independent, with only slight "embellishment". Credit for the discovery of this story goes to the late and honorable Judge J. A. Smith.)

34
Tall Tales and
a Golden Ledge
Part One

AS the war between the United States and Mexico was winding down during the latter part of the 1840s, many military units were disbanded and a great number of former soldiers began to arrive in San Francisco. When news of the gold discovery at Sutter's Mill reached that city, hundreds of these men headed up the tributaries of the San Joaquin River into the Sierra Foothills. Many were formerly of Colonel Jonathan Stevenson's Seventh Regiment of the New York Volunteers, some were from a variety of other companies, and a few had arrived in California a bit ahead of the others -- as deserters.

Henry Angel may have been from any one of those three groups, but it is likely that he made his way into the foothills with a band of Stevenson's men that included James Carson, and John and Daniel Murphy. (Henry may have had a brother, George, who was also part of this troop. In the past, it was often assumed that George and Henry were the same man.) The group eventually began to break up as various members settled into diggings along streams and gulches throughout the area. Henry worked the creek that now bears his name, possibly as early as the summer of 1848. Carson went further south. The Murphy bothers went east.

Like many early prospectors who met with limited success, Henry Angel decided that there might be more money in selling provisions than in working the "digs" -- it was certainly less back-breaking. His "store" was a simple canvas building, sitting not far from the creek whose banks were by then crowded with perspective customers. However, Henry had apparently not shaken the gold bug, for in 1849 he sold his "Angel's Trading Post" to John C. Scribner. (The Scribners were very active in the early development of Angel's Camp -- John Scribner was the first Wells Fargo agent, both John and his brother Philip had a turn as Angels Camp Postmaster, and Philip was also the town's first druggist.) After lending his name to a booming gold town, Henry Angel tried his hand at several new enterprises around the area, none of which met with any great success. He passed away in the County Hospital on March 17, 1897, at the age of 72.

Many of the customers for Angels Trading Post came from the nearby early settlements of Slab Ranch and Albany Flat, both of which developed into sizable towns during the mid-1850s. The Slab Ranch diggings, less than a mile up the creek from Angels, were worked very early in the gold rush by four brothers, John, Joseph, James, and William Hill. Word of their success spread quickly and soon the area boasted numerous extensive placer mines. One of the more "notable" residents of Slab Ranch was the writer Myron Hill, whose work appeared in several East Coast publications as well as San Francisco and Calaveras newspapers. Slab Ranch remained an active "suburb" of Angels throughout the mid-nineteenth century, but slowly dwindled as placers wore out.

Albany Flat, south of Angels on the old Pioneer Road, is noted as the home of the Romaggi family (whose historic house stands today, badly needing preservation and protection). The community apparently also developed a significant commercial

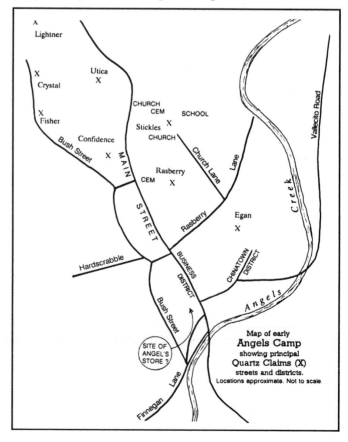

Map of early
Angels Camp
showing principal
Quartz Claims (X)
streets and districts.
Locations approximate. Not to scale.

Taken from a hill above old Main Street, this turn-of-the-century photo shows the famous "Chicken Ladder" walkway on Hardscrabble Lane. (Calaveras County Historical Society)

center in the 1850s, although nothing remains today to indicate where stores and saloons may have stood. According to local oral tradition, the camp was also a favorite rest stop for bands of Mexican bandits who frequently terrorized its residents.

When James Carson returned to Angels Creek in the spring of 1849, he wrote in his diary of the area's transformation:

When we reached the top of the mountains, we had to stand and gaze on the scene before us. The hillsides were dotted with tents, and the creeks filled with human beings to such a degree that it seemed as if a day's work of the mass would not leave a stone unturned in them.

It wasn't long before various other commercial structures joined the Angels Trading Post and the semblance of a town could be seen near the banks of Angels Creek. After major fires destroyed most of the early canvas and woodframe buildings in 1855 and again in 1856, a number of stone buildings went up, including Scribner's Wells Fargo building which occupied the former site of the trading post; and the Angels Hotel, to which a second story was added in 1857. The first Catholic church was built in 1854 and in that same year local children could receive schooling in a rented room on Rasberry Street. By 1857, Angels Camp had its first schoolhouse, on Main Street.

An unusual winter photo of old Angels Camp. (Calaveras County Historical Society)

In those early days there were two main trails that cut through Calaveras County; the Pioneer Road (also called the Stockton Road), which ran west to the San Andreas area then south to Angel's Camp and Sonora; and the Antelope Trail ("Marshall's Trail"), which ran thorough the Salt Spring Valley and over Bear Trap gap to intersect with the Pioneer road on Cherokee Flat at a place called "Forks in the Road" (today's Altaville). There is no doubt that the close proximity of this intersection had much to do with the rapid growth of Angels Camp, as did the early discovery of rich quartz leads running through the town.

There are numerous colorful tales relating to the accidental finding of gold. While most of these stories were no doubt born in gold rush saloons and roadhouses, it is certainly not infeasible that vast amounts of gold were discovered by accident in those days when it was so plentiful (if illusive). In Grass Valley, it is said that Mr. McNight went searching for his stray cow, and stumped his toe on a gold-rich quartz outcropping. At Yankee Jims, the burial of a departed miner was said to have led to the discovery of rich deposits at the bottom of the grave. And in Angel's Camp, it was Bennager Rasberry's ramrod.....

During the gold rush years, the standard weapon carried by miners was a single-shot muzzle-loading musket. It was loaded by pouring a measured amount of black powder into the barrel, followed by a lead ball which had to be shoved down the muzzle with a long metal "ramrod". While hunting rabbits one day, so the story goes, Bennager Rasberry got his ramrod stuck in the barrel of his rifle. Try as he might, he couldn't pull it out by hand so he decided to simply fire the gun, sending the ramrod spiraling into the roots of a manzanita bush. When he pulled the rod out, a chunk of quartz came along with it and...low and behold, the rock glittered with veins of gold.

Regardless of how the first quartz gold was discovered at Angels, by the mid-1850s two brothers named Winter were working a quartz lead lying just west of Main Street. Later known as the Davis-Winter ledge, this extensive lode eventually gave birth to a number of highly successful "deep rock" mines including the Angels, Lightner, and Utica. There were a total of eleven claims filed along this ledge during the years 1855-57. The Boulder Ledge, located further west, spawned the Gold Cliff, North Star, Angels Deep, and many others. In all, the Angels Camp Gold Mining District would generate more than 65 active lode mines.

35
Tall Tales and
a Golden Ledge
Conclusion

N an interesting article describing mining activities in and around Angel's Camp, the *San Andreas Independent* of October 17, 1857 makes a simple statement which now has important historical significance:

. . . . between Wintertown and Angels is the extensive lode which has given such impetus to trade and enterprise in the vicinity.

It was in 1857 that the growing community at "Forks in the Road" on Cherokee Flat chose the name Altaville over the above-inferred appellation which would have immortalized the area's first "hard rock" miners, the brothers Winter. Sitting on the hill above Angels Camp, the choice of Altaville, which means "upper town", was no less appropriate.

According to Calaveras pioneer Cornelius Demarest, prior to the name change, this camp was quite rowdy, frequented by gangs of Mexican outlaws and other "notorious" types. Demarest credits the local Vigilance Committee with having "cleared up the moral atmosphere" of the community, making it into "an ideal place for a home, away from the roar and racket of the ordinary mining town. . . . "

The Altaville area did, however, have its share of mines, including the Cherokee, on Cherokee Creek; the Hog Pen Mine and the Keystone in the town itself; and a number of mines which were worked on nearby Bald Hill, including the Etna and Victor, which were operated well into the 20th century.

Annexed into Angels Camp in 1972, Altaville in the 19th century was very much an independent town, its growth stimulated by a prime location at the intersection of two important trails and the placer mines of nearby Cherokee Creek, as well as the quartz mines mentioned above. At one time the town included a public school, a blacksmith and livery stable, a wagon maker, a dance hall, and several stores and saloons. (The Altaville schoolhouse, built in 1858, is today preserved as a historical site.) In later years, Altaville would boast an important foundry, and an enterprise that was no doubt quite rare in the Mother Lode, a silk farm. The area acquired great notoriety in 1866, with the discovery of the "Calaveras Skull" on nearby Bald Hill.

Outside of working, drinking, and gambling, there was very little to occupy a miner's mind, and one of his most enjoyable pastimes was the practical joke. There were always a few gullible souls upon which some hoax could be effected with relative ease and many of these pranks were quite elaborate. It is unlikely, however, that the perpetrators of the Calaveras Skull hoax could have foreseen the wide-reaching and totally disproportionate commotion their scheme would generate.

It is unknown exactly who, or even how many individuals may have been involved in the hoax. The provenance of the skull, by the time it arrived at the California Academy of Natural Sciences in San Francisco, was that it had been found at the bottom of a mine shaft on Bald Hill by Jim Matson, a miner, who presented it to his friends, who then took it to Dr. William Jones of Murphys. Dr. Jones, supposedly believing the skull to be of ancient origin, sent it to the academy for study. Within weeks, San Francisco newspapers were touting the discovery of "the skull of the world's oldest human being." Eventually the skull made its way to the National Museum in Washington, D.C, where it continued to receive serious consideration for many years thereafter. Finally, it was proven that the skull was that of an Indian and was of relatively recent origin.

The writer Bret Harte, having lived and worked among the miners of Calaveras County, was not at all taken in by the hoax and wrote his now famous poem, "To the Pliocene Skull", which lampoons the discovery. In the final stanza, the skull speaks:

"Which my name is Bowers and my crust was busted
Falling down a shaft in Calaveras County;
But I'd take it kindly if you'd send the pieces
Home to old Missouri!"

During the 1860s and 70s, the hills of Angels Camp fell conspicuously quiet, as the stamp mills began shutting down. The gold rush of the '50s became the Copper Boom of the '60s, and Angels Camp had no copper. Much of the gold then being mined was tied up in complex ores which were not easily recovered. Over the next two decades, mining properties changed hands several times, but most mines remained relatively unproductive until the 1880s.

With the advent of new mining technology and equipment, the Angels mines saw their most productive period from the mid-1880s until the start of World War I. Many of the mines produced millions of dollars in gold during this period, operating seven days a week, with two - ten hour shifts each day. These were truly the "glory years" of Angels Camp.

It should be mentioned here that Angels Camp has had a number of fires in the "modern era" which have destroyed important historical buildings. The fire of 1885 destroyed 15 commercial buildings and all of Chinatown. Other significant fires occurred in 1931, 1938, and 1941. Fortunately, many of the brick and stone buildings erected after the fires of 1855 and 1856 have survived succeeding blazes to provide us with a historic glimpse of Angels Camp in the gold rush years.

The penchant of early Angels Camp miners for pranks and "tall tales" is today the foundation of that town's primary claim to fame -- the jumping frog story, made famous by Mark Twain. By his own admission, Twain (a.k.a. Samuel Clemens) seldom told the truth in its truest form. In other words, he often "embellished" the truth to make it more interesting and readable. Even the story of where and how the jumping frog tale came to be, as told by Twain, is likely "embellished" to some degree.

According to Twain, he and his friend Jim Gillis walked from Jackass Hill to Angels Camp on a wet January day in 1865. In the rainy weeks that followed, they stayed in two or more different hotels, waiting for the weather to break. Finally, in February, they began prospecting the nearby hills for possible "pocket mines". On February 20th, Sam Clemens returned to Jackass Hill, and within a few days, had set out for San Francisco. All that we really know for sure is that sometime during his short stay in Angels, Twain heard the story of the "Jumping Frog" and made a note of it in his diary. Throughout his life, Twain wrote several different accounts of the origin of the Jumping Frog story -- always set in the Angels Hotel.

"Jim Smiley and His Jumping Frog" was published in New York's *Saturday Press* on November 18, 1865, and eventually precipitated world wide fame for Mark Twain and (if to a lesser degree) Angels Camp. The story was a very simple one. In

Little is left of Main Street Altaville, shown here in a nineteenth century photograph. (Calaveras County Historical Society)

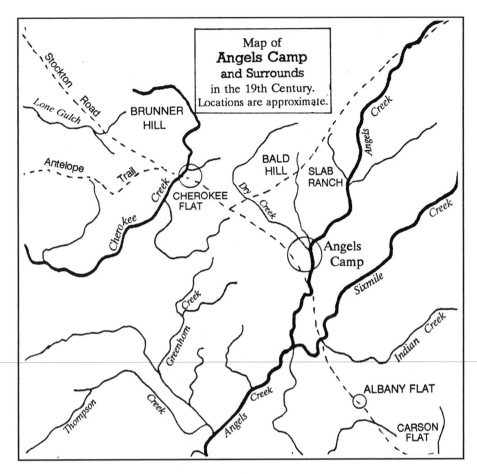

Map of
Angels Camp
and Surrounds
in the 19th Century.
Locations are approximate.

fact, Clemens himself admitted that he did not understand why it was so well received. When he made note of the story in his diary that winter's evening, probably in his room at the Angels Hotel, he used only 35 words (See Chapter 9).

Was it bartender Ben Coon, hotel owner Ross Coon, or local barfly Simon Wheeler who related the Jumping Frog story to Sam Clemens? Or perhaps some other local character whom Twain never credited. As with most of his work, the truth lies hidden somewhere among his bountiful fiction. Regardless, the question probably never came up at the meeting of the Angels Camp Booster Club in 1928, when they organized the first Jumping Frog Jubilee, a two day "fun-fest" of eating, drinking, games, and entertainment. Today, the Jubilee has become the Mother Lode's "premier" event, attracting an international crowd numbering in the tens of thousands, and has established the "City of Angels" as the most famous of the many historical towns -- between the rivers.

36
Fevers, Quacks, and Healers

URING California's gold rush years, almost no one died of old age. If an emigrant survived the "arduous journey" across the plains or through the jungles of Panama or Nicaragua, he or she could consider themselves lucky indeed -- and while their greatest challenge may have been behind them, the perils of life in this wilderness territory might still bring an early and "permanent" end to their adventure. Death and sickness were as much a part of the gold rush experience as dance-hall girls, bandits, and striking it rich -- perhaps more.

Gold fever, the lure of envisioned riches which captured the nation and brought thousands to California during the early 1850s, was not really a disease. Yet if any real affliction ever deserved that appellation, it was cholera. In many cases, ships were barely out of eastern ports and wagons only days from Missouri when this disease struck. In a time when medicine was only beginning to advance from the dark ages, a severe outbreak of cholera would kill one-half of those afflicted. In some cases, a person who began to show symptoms before noon would die by midnight.

Cholera was born of filth. During the early 19th century, large sections of the world's major cities were made up of shabby huts and tenements, their streets and alleys paved with swill and garbage. In the United States, a devastating cholera epidemic in 1832-34 killed thousands, and in 1848 the disease was brought in by emigrants from Germany and France -- just in time for the gold rush. As they headed for California by land and by sea, the 49ers would carry it with them, suffer from it, pass it on to others, and often die of it. Like many afflictions of the period, there was little that could be done about cholera. No one knew for sure what caused it, and therefore no one knew how to cure it. The extent of damage it caused depended almost solely on the health of the body it invaded. The strongest and healthiest survived, the weak did not.

Cholera devastated the cities of Sacramento and San Francisco in the fall of 1850, killing perhaps as much as ten percent of the total population. Among the dead were sixteen doctors -- men who had come to California in search of riches, but who instead gave their last full measure in dedication to the obligations of their profession.

It has been estimated that some 1500 early California emigrants called themselves "doctors." At this stage of medical history, the only "degree" a doctor needed was a certain degree of ability in tending wounds and dispensing medicine. For many centuries, the primary treatments for disease were bleeding, blistering, and purging, all of which required little knowledge of medicine and most of which were ultimately more harmful than the illness itself.

It has often been said that a little knowledge is a dangerous thing, and no where is this more obvious than in 19th century medicine. Doctors of that time knew that some infections were carried by the blood. It therefore seemed logical to them that the best way to cure a patient was to remove that infected blood. This was done very simply by piercing a vein and allowing the "bad blood" to drain out, or by attaching one or more parasitic leaches. As much as ten to twelve ounces of blood might be drained in a single session, and these bleeding sessions would continue until the patient either died or was cured. Many 49ers whose cause of death was listed as cholera, malaria, or other fevers were, in fact, bled to death.

Patients with symptoms relating to the stomach and bowels were usually treated by "purging" with laxative drugs or chemicals. The most popular of these was called "calomel" which contained large quantities of poisonous mercury, the effects of which went far beyond the intended result, including internal bleeding and tooth loss.

Wounds and infections were often treated by "cauterizing" with a hot iron, or "blistering" with smoldering cotton. While painful and archaic, these treatments were probably among the most effective procedures performed by the gold rush doctor. The primary anaesthetic, antiseptic, and disinfectant used for this and other operative procedures was commercial alcoholic distillates -- good drinking whiskey.

Most of the medicines dispensed by gold rush doctors were old time herbal remedies and "quack" tonics containing a high percentage of alcohol. The one true "miracle drug" of the period was quinine, which was of great value in the treating of cholera, malaria, and other fevers. During the early years of the gold rush, quinine was in such demand that it was selling in San Francisco for four-times its weight in gold. Perhaps fortunately for the 49ers, pain relievers, primarily addictive opiate derivatives such as laudanum, were equally hard to come by.

The availability of medical help in the gold fields was, at most, dubious. There might be one town where two or three doctors were in residence, while in another area the nearest physician was at least a day's ride away. It would not be unheard of for a "quack" with absolutely no medical background to be dispensing "patent" medicines in a town where five qualified physicians were quietly working their diggings. While a doctor's dedication to the healing art might be strong, the lure of gold was stronger.

It wasn't long before doctors, like many others, realized that it was far easier to make a living at their chosen profession than by toiling in the mines. Almost every town that had grown to any size had a doctor's office, although there was always some risk in visiting such an establishment, for as many as one out of five were probably fakes.

One such quack, who set up his practice in a growing camp, was doing quite well dispensing tonics, patent medicines, and "miracle cures" when one day a patient came along with an obviously serious disease. Afraid of doing the fellow in, or even worse being exposed as the charlatan he was, the "doc" set out

Gold Rush physicians, both real and self-proclaimed, relied heavily on a good set of medical books for diagnosis and treatment. (Harpers Weekly Magazine)

for the nearest town with a physicians office, ten miles distant. He quickly realized his efforts were in vain when to his surprise and dismay, the consultant agreed completely with his diagnosis and treatment. He, too, was an imposter.

Some such "physicians" dispensed medicine "by the number", having purchased a kit containing various medicines in numbered containers. The patient's symptoms were located in the accompanying manual which, for example, might suggest that medicine number 32 be taken once a day for seven days as treatment for that particular ailment. The system might actually have worked had it not been for "enterprising" quacks who, when faced with a shortage of number 26 simply dispensed a dose of number 10 and a dose of number 16.

Without statutes regulating the medical profession, gold rush towns were ripe for such quackery. The average doctor in a camp of any size could take in $75 to $100 a day and all that was really needed to appear convincing was a frock coat and the impression of being knowledgeable. A legitimate San Francisco physician estimated that of that town's two hundred practicing doctors in 1851, no more than thirty were genuine.

The office of a legitimate gold rush doctor might consist of a simple canvas tent with a cot and table and all the doctor's tools and medicines contained in a single bag. In the best of circumstances the doctor might have a small office upstairs over the barber shop with a table, a desk, and a cabinet filled with the tools of the trade: a stethoscope, a microscope, a mortar and pestle, splints, a saw, forceps, tweezers, knives, and scalpels. In another locked cabinet were the doctor's treasured bottles of laudanum, quinine, alcohol, calomel, chloroform, Dover's powder, sulphur pills, and camphor balls; along with jars of mustard plasts, red pepper poultices, and leaches.

The complaints received by gold camp physicians tell us much about the lifestyle of the miners. Here is a list of ailments treated by a gold rush doctor in 1852, as taken from his records for that year, starting with the problems seen most frequently:

Diarrhea, contusions, fractures, dysentery, intermittent fever, typhus, acute rheumatism, chronic rheumatism, gonorrhea, bronchitis, pneumonia, scurvy, colic, hepatitis, asthma, hemorrhoids, cholera, jaundice, syphilis, cystitis, burns, knife wounds, childbirth, gunshot, post-mortem, & delirium tremens.

For a single visit or a case in which follow-up was not required, doctors generally charged $32. For ongoing cases, he charged $16 per visit -- $32 if it lasted more than one hour. Charges for a night call were $50 to $100; delivery of a baby, $200; for basic surgery, $500; and for major surgery, $1000 and up. (These fees varied widely throughout California, to both lesser and greater degrees.)

No one really knows who the first doctor to arrive in Calaveras County was. There is no doubt that there were several physicians here in the first days of the gold rush (1848), although at this time they were more likely concerned with mining than with doctoring. One of the earliest must have been Dr. Richard Somerset Den, who mined near Angels Camp in 1848-49 and later opened a practice there. In his book, *El Dorado*, Bayard Taylor mentions Dr. Gillette and Dr. Gwin, who were working claims on the Mokelumne River in 1849-50, and Dr. Hugh Toland was in that same area in 1852.

Probably the best known of early Calaveras physicians was Doctor Adolph H. Hoerchner who braved the Isthmus of Panama route to California with a group of immigrants from Alabama in the spring of 1849 (See Chapter 17). Doctor Hoerchner must have felt great frustration and grief in his inability to save his own child and that of his friend and traveling companion D. L. Angier, when both children died of cholera during the final leg of the journey. Once in California, Dr. Hoerchner and his wife entered into a five-way mining partnership with Angier, Charles Grunsky, and a Captain Tobin. After meeting with moderate success, the partners went into the supply business, with Grunsky operating a store at Pleasant Springs, and Dr. Hoerchner running their wholesale house in Stockton.

Eventually Hoerchner bought out the entire Pleasant Springs operation. He became postmaster there in 1855, and also began operating a small community hospital. In 1858, he contracted with the county to care for the indigent sick and elderly at his Pleasant Springs facility. Three years later, he opened a drug store and clinic in Mokelumne Hill. Sadly, the widely respected Dr. Hoerchner died in 1870 at the relatively young age of 49.

Dr. Hoerchner was the only physician to bid for the county contract in 1868, but his bid was refused because the county could not afford his fee. County patients were then moved from Pleasant Springs to the Gold Hill House near San Andreas, which had been donated to the county to serve as a hospital. Dr. E. B. Robertson was appointed county physician. Two years later, the Gold Hill house burned to the ground, killing two patients.

Medical science made great strides during the second half of the 19th century, and new government regulations did much to eliminate medical fraud. The last big outbreak of Cholera struck the U.S. in 1866, and by the 1880s its cause had been identified and prevention methods were defined. California's first medical school was founded at the University of the Pacific in 1859, and quality hospitals were established throughout the state during the 1860s.

Today, many of California's doctors are recognized as being among the best in the world. Even in the small towns of Calaveras County some of the best men in the medical profession perform healing miracles that only a few years ago were deemed impossible. As for gold fever -- people are still rushing to California to search for wealth and success. And if growth and development is any gauge, many of them still hope to find it -- between the rivers.

37
Out of the Silent Wood

Like Arabs first, we pitched our tent
Where smiling nature stood,
And soon a city's walls upwent
From out the silent wood.

James H. Carson, Murphys Camp
November 13, 1852

 N November of 1852, Stockton's *San Joaquin Republican* published "Scenes in the Mines", a description and short history of Murphys, written by one of the best known 49ers, James Carson. From this and other writings it is apparent that Carson was a romantic. With poetic articulation, he describes the "beautiful little valley at the head of Angels Creek," as it appeared in the spring of 1849:

The wild deer was playing with its fawn amongst the tall green grass that thickly clothed it; the turtle doves cooed together as they built their nests in the tall old oaks, and the stillness of the pretty scene was only broken by the sighing of the summer breeze amongst the tops of the tall green pines.

Prior to the gold rush, this area of the lower Sierra Mountains was occupied by several villages of Me-Wuk Indians, who hunted, fished, and lived a serene existence among those tall green pines. The Me-Wuks knew about gold long before the white man ever sat foot in California. For them its value was purely ornamental so they did not spend too much time or effort in trying to find it. But in those days flakes of gold were easily found in local stream beds and these were often placed inside the transparent tip of a feather (quill) which could be worn on a cord about the neck. Had the Me-Wuks known the misfortune this shiny metal would soon bring upon them, they would no doubt have chosen to hide it, rather than display it.

Like most early mining camps, the first miners to work the Murphys area were probably Mexicans who were quickly pushed out by the rush of American prospectors arriving in the spring and summer of 1848. Among those early arrivals were John and Daniel Murphy, who had split from a prospecting party that included Henry Angel and the aforementioned James Carson. The Murphys were members of Charles Weber's Stockton Mining Company, which had already established several trading posts near other gold field camps. Various gold rush journals place the Murphys first at Dry Creek near Vallecito (Murphys Old Diggins) -- later they moved north to Angels Creek at what is now the town of Murphys (Murphys New Diggins).

There is considerable confusion about the names and locations of these early mining camps. James Carson says that the town of Murphys was first called "Stoutenburg" and was changed to Murphys Camp when Murphy opened his trading post there. However, records indicate that both Murphy boys were gone from the area by the end of 1849 (Daniel moved to San Jose late in '48, followed by Henry in December 1849), and in November of that year election returns were filed from "Stoutonburgh's Diggins" precinct. According to the *San Andreas Independent* (May 1, 1858), William Stoutenberg, of the West Coast Mining Company, discovered gold in Vallecito during the spring of 1849.

Much of the confusion over Stoutenburg comes from the journals of Friedreich Gerstaecker (*Narrative of a Journey Round the World*, Harper, 1853), who visited the Murphys area in the summer of 1850 and used the name interchangeably with Murphys New Diggins. However, Gerstaecker places Stoutenburg on Coyote Creek, not Angels Creek, which would lead one to believe that when he is using that name he is talking about Murphys Old Diggins. . . . Dry Creek or Vallecito. (The Vallecito appellation does not appear in print until 1852, and even then was frequently "corrupted" as Biacete, Bayecito, or Vallesietta.)

At both his "Old Diggins" on Dry Creek and his "New Diggins" on Angels Creek, John Murphy quickly established a rapport with the local Indians, to whom he traded blankets and trinkets for gold nuggets and dust. It was the abundant success of this enterprise that led to his quick exit from the area. After less than two years, Murphy had accumulated a fortune estimated in excess of $2 million and his name had become forever etched in Gold Rush history.

The changes that Murphys Camp went through over the next two years can best be illustrated by the "first hand" descriptions of two early visitors. First, Gerstaecker in 1850:

Although consisting only of tents, (Murphys New Diggins) had, during the summer of 1849, been raised to the rank of a real town, where an alcalde,

a sheriff, and a constable were duly elected. The whole town comprised about fifty tents, two or three blockhouses, and a house built of planks; yet, it already boasted nearly as many "bars" as tents, besides three American and four French dining rooms, two doctor's shops, at least twenty gambling tables, and a skittle ground where you might have three throws for the reasonable price of 25 cents.

In his *Scenes in the Mines*, James Carson describes Murphys as it appeared in 1852:

. . . . containing upwards of five hundred frame houses, large and substantially built, and a permanent and floating population of near three thousand. The town contains eight taverns besides private boarding houses, two restaurants; one express and banking house; one livery stable; seven blacksmith shops; nine carpenter shops; four bakeries; five butcher shops and markets; two steam saw-mills; one cider and syrup factory; one bowling alley, besides dance and drinking houses innumerable.

Already considered among the richest camps in the Mother Lode, Murphys prosperity was boosted further by the construction of a water ditch by the Union Water Company, which was completed in January of 1853. Eventually, this ditch from the upper Stanislaus River would also provide water to Douglas, Vallecito, Altaville, Angels Camp, and Carson Hill.

During the 1850s, two small "suburbs" grew up on either side of Murphys' central business district in connection with successful mining operations: Owlsberg, which extended up the ridge north of town to the Oro y Plata Mine; and Algiers, south of town near the Central Hill Mining District. In 1857, a group of miners organized a small camp southeast of town at the intersection of Pennsylvania and Missouri Gulch, called Brownsville. While this "town" never really expanded beyond a few tent-stores and shanties, it was the site of successful placer mining operations and was later expanded into an important ranching enterprise. George and Alfred Brown, for whom the town was named, played an important role in the early development of the Murphys area. Browns Express provide early local competition for Adams & Co., Todds, and Wells Fargo.

Mining was also continuously successful at neighboring Douglas Flat and Valecito. In the mid-1850s, a number of tunnel companies were organized

to tap the riches of nearby Table Mountain. In 1856, it was reported that one such company was bringing out fifty ounces of gold each day.

On August 12, 1859, the town of Vallecito burned to the ground. On the 20th, it was Murphys' turn. The conflagration began in the Magnolia Saloon, near the west end of town. Within minutes, fire had spread to the surrounding woodframe buildings and soon a brisk wind had carried it into the main business district. In less than forty minutes only three buildings remained standing to represent what was once downtown Murphys. The *San Andreas Independent* wrote:

The affliction is severe and general, but it is borne with a fortitude and nonchalance nowhere so admirably exhibited as among California pioneers overtaken by adversity.

Many of the replacement buildings which arose from the ashes were built of stone and are today the charm of Murphys.

Two other fires would wipe out most of Murphys' early woodframe buildings built prior to the twentieth century -- one in 1874 and the other in 1893. Many of these structures were never replaced.

No history of Murphys would be complete without a mention of the legendary bandit Joaquin Murietta who, it is said, began his career in this town when his brother was unjustly hanged and his sister attacked. While there is no proof that the incident ever occurred (or, for that matter, that one specific Joaquin Murietta ever existed) the tale is an important part of Murphys' "color," and is certainly representative of the actual prejudices that existed in the gold camps. (For the complete Murietta story, see Chapter 6)

The construction of a railroad to Milton in the early 1870s, along with the turnpike that connected Murphys with Altaville, encouraged a regular flow of tourists up the mountain to the Big Trees resort area. Murphys became a popular "rest stop" for those traveling in both directions and the register at Sperry and Perry's Hotel was soon filled with the names of many famous 19th century celebrities out for a bit of excitement in California's "wilderness."

Several large caverns in the Murphys area have also been promoted to tourists over two centuries. Even Carson recognized their lure in his 1852 description:

Besides the beauties of nature so profusely lavished around this pretty mountain city, she has placed also beneath the earth strange things to invite the geologist and naturalist to this her richest field of study....two beautiful caves that are of great magnitude, and as yet but partially exposed.

The Moaning Cave, near Vallecito, was once called Solomons Hole and was believed to hold vast riches that had been tapped by the Indians and early Spanish explorers -- a legend that was later disproved.

Like most of Calaveras County, Murphys today owes much of its commercial success to both the fact and fiction of history. When Bret Harte published "A Night at Wingdam" in 1860, Murphys' residents apparently saw some similarity between his "Arcadian hamlet" and their own bustling camp, for shortly thereafter the stage from Milton to Murphys became the "Wingdam Stage," and Murphys added one more nugget to its wealth of legends.

During the early years of the Gold Rush, Murphys Diggins was among the richest camps in Calaveras County. Today, it is equally as rich in history and gold rush lore. It has truly lived up to James Carson's prediction of 1852: *"The sun of Murphys greatness has just risen; a short time and she will take the sceptre of the Mountain Queen."*

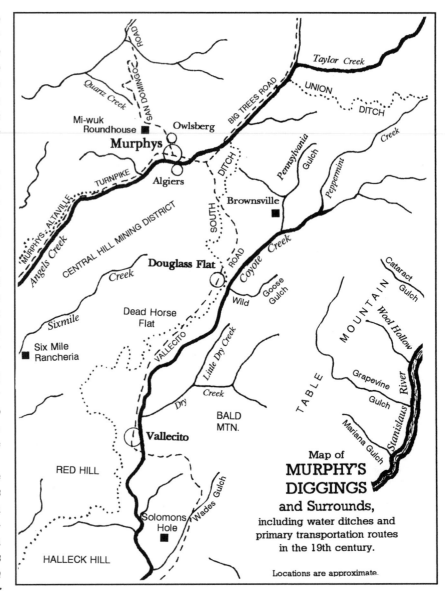

Map of
MURPHY'S DIGGINGS
and Surrounds,
including water ditches and primary transportation routes in the 19th century.

Locations are approximate.

38
The Hill

HE *Calaveras Weekly* for Friday, January 23, 1948, displayed the following bold headline: **Pioneer Mokelumne Hill Family Records Dispute Coloma Claim.** An accompanying story tells of a group of pioneer French trappers who settled in the area of Mokelumne Hill during the early 1840s, and who allegedly were mining gold there as early as 1845 -- three years before the discovery at Coloma that initiated the Gold Rush. While that claim of precedence has never been proven or disproved, it does raise an interesting question: Does anyone really know when the first white men settled in the area that is now Calaveras County?

The simple answer to that question is -- no. What we do know, is that during the early 1840s there were several camps of French and American trappers along the San Joaquin River near the forks of the Stanislaus, Calaveras, and Mokelumne; also the ranch of Captain Charles Weber at what is now Stockton. Other ranches were established in the area throughout the 1840s.

While there were problems with the local Indians, Captain Weber had developed a rapport with several of the chiefs and the trappers quickly learned that these natives were generally peaceful, tending to run rather than fight. Accordingly, it seems illogical to assume that none of those people living along the San Joaquin ventured into the foothills. The trappers, no doubt, trapped along the Mokelumne; and the more adventurous, perhaps, settled there.

Most of what we know of California before the Gold Rush comes from the diaries and papers of the mission padres, and it is in these papers that many of California's place-names have their origin. The name "Mokelumne" was first written in 1817 by Father Narciso Duran, president of the missions. He spelled it "Muquelemnes," and it is believed that the name originated from one of the Me-wuk villages located on the valley portion of the river, possibly at Lodi or Lockeford.

The suggestion that Mokelumne is a corruption of the Me-wuk word for "big river" (Utawahkaloo or Wakalumitah) is perhaps a bit far-fetched, since the Mokelumne is hardly "big" compared to the San Joaquin. California Indian dialects were so varied and abundant, it is easy to find such "similarities."

It seem more logical to assume that there existed a village of "Mokels" -- the Me-wuk suffix for "people" is "umne".

In the journal of Captain John C. Fremont, we find this entry for March 25, 1844:

We traveled for twenty-eight miles over the same delightful country as yesterday, and halted in a beautiful bottom at the ford of the Rio de los Mukelemnes, receiving its name from another Indian tribe living on the river. The bottoms on the stream are extremely broad, rich, and fertile; and the uplands are shaded with oak groves. A showy lupinus of extraordinary beauty, growing four or five feet in height, and covered with spikes in bloom, adorned the banks of the river, and filled the air with a light and graceful perfume.

When news of the discovery of gold at Sutter's Mill (Coloma) reached Captain Weber at Tuleburgh (Stockton), he immediately sent out a scouting party to see if that precious metal existed in the nearby streams. They soon returned with news that nearly every river, creek, and gulch contained gold to some degree. (There is no mention of whether or not they found white settlers already on the rivers.) Weber quickly organized a mining expedition for the Mokelumne and others of his party headed south to the Calaveras and Stanislaus.

It is difficult to understand how, in a period when communication was practically non-existent and travel was at best slow and tedious, so many people made their way into the gold fields in such a short amount of time. By the spring and summer of 1848, the Mokelumne River was dotted with miners tents and organized camps were already being established. The first to arrive were, of course, those who were already nearby -- French trappers from the Hudson Bay Company; and Mexican and American settlers from the Central Valley. Next to arrive were Colonel Jonathan Stevenson and his men, recently mustered out of military service following the war with Mexico.

During the first months of the rush, mining was generally confined to the rich placers of river shoals, giving birth to camps such as Poverty Bar, Middle Bar, and Big Bar. As river claims became harder to come by, the gulches were explored and found equally as rich -- in Calaveras County alone, there were five separate mining camps called "Rich Gulch."

Old Brewery ruins at Mokelumne Hill. (Calaveras Historical Society)

Late in 1848, rich deposits of gold were discovered beneath the lava flows in the hills south of Big Bar and by November about two dozen men were working claims on Stockton Hill. Within only a few months the "tent city" of Mokelumne Hill had established itself nearby, providing food, lodging (Dickinson's Boarding Tent), and supplies (Syree's Store) to the ever-increasing flow of miners. Immediately to the east, Les Fourcades would later provide the same services for a large assembly of French miners working the rich diggings of French Hill and Happy Valley. (If the antecedence of the French in Calaveras County can ever be proven, it may be found that Les Fourcades was, in fact, the first established non-Indian community in the Mother Lode region.)

During the Gold Rush years, the entire state of California became a melting pot. While this diversity of races could be found in nearly all of Calaveras county's gold towns, it was nowhere more evident than in Mokelumne Hill, where each group seemed to find their own separate "niche." In addition to French Hill and Les Fourcades, there came to be an extensive Chinatown in "China Gulch" and a large Chilean population just south of town on "Chili Gulch." The Irish and Jewish communities, being better tolerated by the Americans, were contained within the streets of Mok Hill itself. The

Mexican population, for which the American miners generally had great contempt, remained mobile or settled at distant Campo Seco.

One of the richest mining areas of Mokelumne Hill obtained an unfortunate appellation based in racial bigotry. The oft-repeated story of "Nigger Hill" is related here in the words of a miner who visited Mok Hill in 1852 (Keep in mind that prejudices against free Blacks were probably greater during this period - pre-Civil War - than at any time in the history of the United States.):

. . . . having learned its name, I must know how or why it was bestowed. I inquired of a miner, and this was the history. . . . When these diggins [Mokelumne Hill] was first discovered and the miners were making an owner to the man doing well, two niggers came up the ravine and staked off their claims. Their neighbor mines being prejudiced against the ebony colored gents ordered them off. . . . the darkies had to obey. One of them ventured to ask where they should go. One of the whites pointing up the hill, told them they could go there, as they never thought of there being gold up there. The niggers went up on the side of the hill and went to work, the whites expecting to see them gather their traps and leave. The darkies remained, and on the third day, they thought they would go up and see what they were doing. The first one

addressed the niggers with: "How are you, you old fellow. . . what luck?" "Pretty good, sir. This much in this pan," which was about one third full, "that one full", pointing to another that was heaped full. Then there was a rush! They surrounded the niggers and soon dug them out, but they had made their piles.

(From the diary of Richard Augustus Keen, 1852, courtesy of the Calaveras Historical Society.)

There were two notable conflicts that occurred during the early years between American miners at Mok Hill and their foreign counterparts. In 1849, Chilean miners who had settled into diggings along the gulch named for their home country attempted to gain additional land by staking claims in the names of their Indian slaves -- a defiance of established miner's law. The conflict turned into a small "war" with a number of deaths on both sides and eventually the Chileans were overcome by organized American "justice." Justice in this case meant stealing everything the Chileans owned and the application of tortuous physical punishment.

In 1851, the "French War" was far less devastating. It appears that the primary cause of the disagreement was simple jealousy of the rich claims on French Hill. Whatever the cause, two large groups of armed French and American miners were prepared to do battle when cooler heads prevailed (including the French Consul and other government officials) and the incident came to an uneventful, and timely conclusion.

By 1850, Mokelumne Hill was the largest organized community in the region with a population numbering in the thousands. (Estimates of 10 to 15 thousand are highly exaggerated -- in 1850, the entire population of the county including present day Amador was only 16,884). One can imagine their surprise and disappointment when the state legislature chose first the practically unknown camp of Pleasant Valley; then the tiny neighboring camp of Double Springs as county seat for newly created Calaveras County. On "the Hill" plans were immediately set in motion to have the seat changed. Unfortunately, the town of Jackson had the same idea, and it was 1852 before "the Hill" finally became the home of county government.

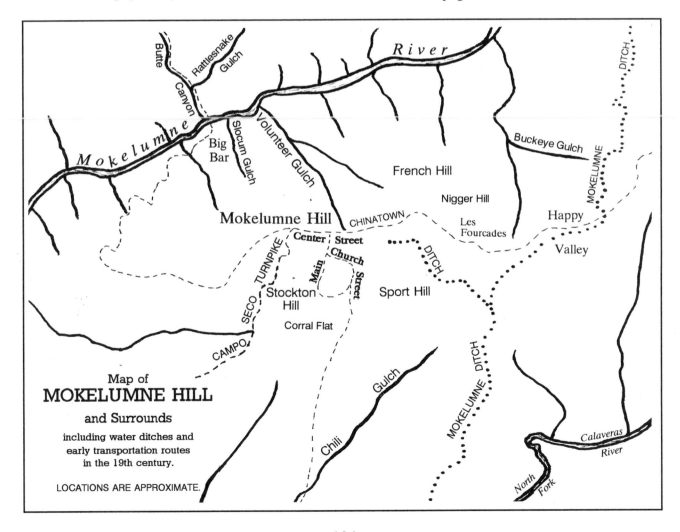

Map of
MOKELUMNE HILL
and Surrounds
including water ditches and
early transportation routes
in the 19th century.

LOCATIONS ARE APPROXIMATE.

As one of the richest camps in the Mother Lode and county seat for Calaveras County, Mokelumne Hill thrived. Despite its deserved reputation as a wild and often dangerous place to reside, it soon developed a more "civilized" segment of society (perhaps steadily improving in direct proportion to the increase in the female population). Soon the town boasted numerous hotels and saloons, various stores, express offices, social clubs, schools, and churches. Like most gold rush towns, Mok Hill's early buildings were constructed of wood and most of the town burned to the ground more than once -- notably 1854, 1865, and 1874.

While several early stone and brick buildings still stand as reminders of the Hill's historic past, the scattered, sleepy village of today bears little resemblance to the boisterous boom town of the 1850s and '60s. Nature has reclaimed and covered the scarred hills that gave up their treasure to two decades of dedicated, if rowdy, inhabitants. When the county seat was moved to San Andreas in 1866, perhaps a bit of Mok Hill's spirit went along. It was no longer the largest; it was no longer the richest; it was no longer the wildest. But one thing that Mokelumne Hill had then, it still has today -- its colorful history. Any book about the gold rush that doesn't mention Mok Hill is a poor history indeed. It was the largest; it was the richest; it was the wildest; and it was the first -- between the rivers.

39
Stars of the Stage

HEN the Gold Rush began in 1848, there were only three notable towns in Northern California; San Francisco, San Jose, and Monterey. Even these were little more than semi-organized villages. By late in 1849, however, the rush to California's gold fields had increased the population of those communities tenfold and a number of other burgeoning settlements were well on their way to becoming important cities. Among these were Sacramento and Stockton, who owed their popularity to locations on navigable river channels near the northern and southern mines. Argonauts in route to the northern mines from San Francisco took a steamer to Sacramento, then followed established trails to Marysville, Bidwells Bar, Grass Valley, Placerville, and other camps. Those who chose the southern route took a boat to Stockton, then continued by foot, mule, or wagon to Jackson, Mok Hill, Angels Camp, Sonoran Camp, etc.

The trails from Stockton and Sacramento to the mines were just that. . . . worn and winding pathways over jagged rocks, through heavy brush, and across swift river fords. During those early years, mules were the most convenient and reliable form of transportation. A stout mule could carry the miner and his small pack of supplies from Stockton to Mokelumne Hill in one long day or two short ones. Later, parallel pathways were created as teams of mules and oxen began to haul supplies by wagon to the mines, and the foothills resounded with the crack of the muleteer's whip and shouts of "Hippah ..mulah!" Dusty in summer, boggy in winter, these double-rut trails were the first Mother Lode roads.

During the fall of 1849, the first California stagecoach went into service between San Francisco and San Jose. The fifty mile trip was made in nine hours and there was no specific schedule kept. During the rainy season, the stage might bog down well short of its intended destination, leaving the passengers to fend for themselves. And the cost of the trip was not cheap. . . . thirty-two dollars or two ounces of gold dust. In the Spring of 1850, however, competition from other new stage lines improved service among all the competitors, and brought the price down to $16 or "an ounce," and service was extended southward to Monterey.

By the end of 1851, numerous stage lines were in operation from San Francisco, Sacramento, and Stockton to camps throughout the mining region. The *Alta California* newspaper reported on November 12, 1851 that there were six daily stages from Sacramento to Marysville; one to Nevada City; two to Coloma; one to Placerville; one to Auburn; one to Stockton; and one to Drytown and Jackson. Early in 1851, Kelly, Reynolds, and Company established a stage service from Stockton to Sonora, which soon branched out to Mokelumne Hill, Angels Camp, and Carsons Creek.

In 1853, Charles Green and John Vogan began a stage line which connected Sonora and the Southern Mines with Sacramento, by way of Jackson and Drytown. Nineteenth century historian J. D. Mason described a journey on Green and Vogan's Lines:

There were no roads, the coaches following the trails, zigzagging around the dust-holes in Summer and mud-holes in winter. There were no bridges, and sometimes driver and horses were lost. During the summer season the trip was rather pleasant, but when the coach stuck in a raging stream of water four or five feet deep, the situation made a timid man pray and a wicked one swear. The highwaymen occasionally levied tribute on the passengers, who, though armed, would find themselves unexpectedly confronted with a pistol in such close proximity that it was useless to resist.

A top coach driver averaged ten miles per hour, which generally meant showing little or no regard for the comfort of his passengers. Early coaches were little more than covered wagons with a hard roof and canvas sides. Heavy springs beneath the coach, meant to absorb some of the bumps and dips of the road, bounced the passengers about and often shot them straight up into the roof. The gradual introduction of now-famous Concord coaches did much to improve passenger comfort, primarily due to their leather strap suspension system which once prompted Mark Twain to call the Concord a "cradle on wheels." The Concord is the style of stagecoach most often associated with the Old West, although it is seldom shown in movies loaded to full capacity with nine passengers inside and a dozen or more others on the roof hanging on for dear life, as was often the case.

Preparations for a stagecoach ride to the mines generally began long before dawn. If you had spent the night at a hotel, you would be awakened for breakfast at about four or five a.m., then make your way in the morning twilight to the nearby stage office where the coach and its six horse team was waiting. If other coaches were in line, yours would be easily located by the destination painted boldly on each one. In a few minutes, you would hear the driver call out something like: "Board up for Angels, Carsons, and Sonoran Camp. . . . .All aboard!" You and your fellow passengers would barely be settled in your seats when the driver (called a "whip" or "jehu" – pronounced "yea-who")would call out to his groom, who held the horses steady, "Let 'em go, Johnny!. . . . Feet off the seats inside. . . . and grab t'hold!" Almost as the last word is shouted, the driver snaps his whip, the coach lurches forward, and your journey begins.

Soon the coach interior is filled with dust and you quickly learn that the only way to stay off other passengers laps is to clutch the edge of the window. There are two people next to you, three more on the opposite side, and three more sitting in the center of the coach on seats that fold out of the doors. The person in the middle of the coach can do little more than wedge himself between those on either side and apologize continuously as he is tossed about. As the sun peeks over the distant Sierras, the temperature in the coach begins to rise steadily.

Always room for one more.
(Harpers Magazine)

After two or three hours, the coach arrives at its first stop, a road house or way-station where the passengers can stretch their legs and take some refreshment while fresh horses are hitched up. You're in the mines now, and a "lunch" of tough beefsteak, boiled potatoes, undercooked beans, and strong coffee costs $2.50. . . . five times what you would pay in the East. You were lucky indeed if you had time to finish this fare before the familiar call is shouted... "All aboard!"

A miner described the final leg to Sonora: *At about twelve o'clock, the stage reached the Stanislaus River, where lunch was served and another fresh team secured. With the approach to Sonora, the terrain changed from level plains to rugged slopes and woodlands, and the road, which had been disagreeably dusty but smooth and straight, now became winding as it advanced over rocky glades, hills, and gullies, with the result that the passengers were jarred and shaken without mercy.*

This portion of the trek is slow and tedious and it is near sundown before the stagecoach arrives at its final destination. Some of the passengers head for the nearest hotel. For others, who have come to stake their claims in distant gulches, the journey has just begun.

Stagecoach drivers were a special breed. Early historian George Bancroft says that the average driver was "lord of his way, the captain of his craft, the fear of timid passengers, the admiration of

stable boys, and the trusty agent of his employer." Basically, the requirements to be a stage driver were minimal but stringent; dependability, honesty, sobriety, and a certain degree of driving ability, although this latter quality was often developed first-hand after the driver was hired. Called by familiar "nicknames" for most of their lives, many drivers went to their deaths after their given names were long forgotten, their tombstones engraved with "Curly Dan," "Sage Brush Bill," "Buffalo Bob," "The Dutchman," "Dusty," and other such "handles."

Probably the most famous of California stage drivers was Charlie Parkhurst, a loner who drove nearly every major run in the northern part of the state, including Santa Cruz, San Jose, Sacramento, Stockton, Mariposa, Placerville, and many others. It was once said that Charlie could drive a route with closed eyes, simply by listening to the sound of the wheels on the trail. After more than thirty years, Charlie was forced to retire due to ill health, and died in 1879 from tongue cancer brought on by decades of tobacco chewing. When Charlie was being prepared for burial, it was discovered that "One-Eyed Charlie," California's most revered stage driver was, in fact, a woman.

One of the most hilarious accounts of a ride on a California stage comes from Mark Twain's associate, Artemus Ward, who wrote of Horace Greely's visit to this state in 1872. According to the highly "embellished" tale, on a trip from Sacramento to Placerville, Greely was assigned to the care of Henry Monk, a highly dedicated stage driver who had been given orders to have "this great man" there by seven p.m. Monk drove with such ferocity that, at one point it is said that Mr. Greely's head was actually thrust through the top of the coach. Despite continuous pleas from Greely to "Stop, you maniac!", Monk simply yelled back, "I've got my orders! Keep your seat, Horace!" Upon reaching Placerville (on time of course) Monk was asked if Mr. Greely was aboard, to which he replied, "He was a few miles back."

By the 1860s, nearly every California town of size had stage service, often from several competing companies. In the Mother Lode region, stagecoaches were often filled with tourists in route to Yosemite or Calaveras Big Trees. T. J. Matteson of Murphys established his coach line

Accident on a mountain trail. (Harpers Magazine, 1862)

A GENERAL SMASH

in the early 1850s, and was one of the most active carriers of tourists from the rail terminus at Milton to the Mammoth Grove Hotel at Big Trees.

Also active in Calaveras County during the latter part of the century were the Raggio Brothers, who began a stage line between San Andreas and Sheep Ranch in 1882, and eventually bought out Matteson at the turn of the century.

The proliferation of railroads and the introduction of the automobile in the 20th century signaled the end of the stagecoach era. Only a few of those early coaches have been preserved to this day, mostly by Wells Fargo for museum displays. The passing of this picturesque symbol of the Old West is perhaps best epitomized in this bit of a poem by Sidney Dyer:

The old stagecoach, as it came, of old,
*   Each idler roused with its noisy din;*
With cracking whip,
*   how it briskly rolled,*
With conscious pride,
*   to the village inn!*
But now it stands in the stable yard,
*   With dusty seats and a rusty tire;*
And we this friend of youth discard,
*   For railway cars and a stead of fire.*

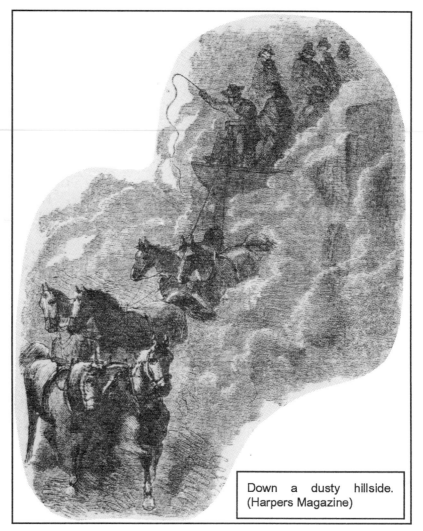

Down a dusty hillside.
(Harpers Magazine)

126

40
The Mountain Mines

ROBABLY the most amazing aspect of Gold Rush history is the speed at which the land we now call the Mother Lode was settled. In the winter of 1847, there were a few scattered Indian villages in the foothills and perhaps one or two small settlements of French trappers. By the fall of 1848, the hills were crowded with miner's tents and shacks, and by early 1849 there were organized communities with stores, houses, and streets. When California was divided into counties in 1849-50, Calaveras County already boasted hundreds of established towns. This, just two short years after the discovery of gold at Sutter's Mill.

Because miners settled at the first available spot that seemed likely to produce rich diggings, the county's oldest and largest towns are located at the lower elevations, near major foothill streams. Starting in the early 1850s, as these areas became crowded and as gold mining began to make the transition from placer (surface streams) to quartz (tunnels and shafts), new settlements began to appear higher in the mountains. Also, many Gold Rush immigrants to California quickly learned that the life of a gold miner was not easy, nor necessarily profitable, and therefore turned to farming and ranching, for which the low Sierra Mountains seemed ideally suited. One such enterprise, located about eight miles west/northwest of San Andreas, was appropriately called "Mountain Ranch."

No one really knows when Mountain Ranch was first established. It is likely that miners had prospected nearby creeks and gulches by 1850 and farming may have begun shortly thereafter by a man named John Sullivan. A supply store was built there, probably around 1852, and was sold by W. D. Atterbury to Sullivan and partner John McKeon early in 1853. This establishment served the growing community of miners and farmers for several decades and McKeon became the town's first postmaster when the Mountain Ranch Post Office was established in 1856-57. About a mile to the east another community had begun to take shape during the early '50s, called El Dorado. (As an interesting side-note, there were seven California towns named El Dorado during the gold rush period, in addition to innumerable canyons, bars, flats, creeks, "diggins", and gulches. Also, the Calaveras town of El Dorado

should not be confused with El Dorado Bar and Flat on the Stanislaus River.) This town thrived during the mid-nineteenth century, primarily due to the operation of a steam-powered quartz mill and successful nearby lumbering operations. Having significantly outgrown nearby Mountain Ranch over the years, that town's post office was moved to El Dorado in 1868.

Typical of early mining camps, El Dorado's ethnic diversity occasionally led to fights, murders, and lynchings. The *San Andreas Independent* for December 4, 1858, published a lengthy account of an elaborate incident which began:

A DESPERATE FIGHT AT EL DORADO

On Sunday night last, a most desperate fight came off at the little mining camp of El Dorado in this county, between three Americans, on the one side, and a Spaniard, a Portuguese, and a Mexican on the other. Two of the Americans were killed, one instantly, and the other died twenty-four hours later. From the best information we could obtain, all parties were in liquor at the time.

El Dorado had intermittent periods of boom and bust throughout the latter half of the nineteenth century and like most small towns with direct ties to quartz mining, gradually dwindled away during the modern era. The Mountain Ranch store changed hands a number of times and, subjected to numerous "additions" and "remodelings," survived into the twentieth century as a private residence.

The necessity of separating unsubstantiated local tradition from proven history has been mentioned by this author more than once -- and so has the importance of preserving these "tall tales" for their contribution to the color and romance of the Mother Lode. The following story is related here with the latter purpose in mind:

The true gold rush had already run its course when, in 1866, a young prospector name Tom Smith and an "old timer" named Furguson formed an unlikely partnership. Having worked the placers of "Jackey Camp," near Calaveritas, with little success, the two decided to begin prospecting in higher elevations to the east where the old man had heard there were great hidden ledges of gold. Being the more knowledgeable of the two, the old man followed the established rules of gold prospecting --

A turn of the century view shows the Sheepranch Mine with the Pioneer Hotel visible to the left. (Calaveras County Historical Society)

watching for likely geological formations and the types of minerals that were known to bear the elusive metal. Meanwhile, young Tom rambled over the hills and gulches, spending as much time admiring the scenery as looking for gold.

After the pair had been in the mountains for a few weeks, Tom came upon a small ranch with a corral containing a number of sheep and decided to drop in at the nearby sheepherder's cabin for a friendly visit. Finding the inhabitant far from hospitable, Tom made a quick exit across the corral and in his haste, stubbed his toe and fell to the ground. As he lifted himself up, he noticed a stone had been knocked loose and he picked it up to give it an angry toss. But when he glanced down, he saw that it was covered with tiny golden flecks.

Even as a tenderfoot prospector, Tom knew better than to assume that what he had found was gold, so he pocketed the stone taking care to remember exactly where he had found it. That evening at camp, he placed the specimen where the old timer would be sure to spot it, to test his reaction. He wasn't disappointed. The old man danced and shouted, "Gold, boy. . . real gold. . . a gold mine. . . millions . . . right here close by!"

Tom explained to Furguson that he had found the rock earlier and promised to take him to the exact spot the next day. The old man kept Tom awake all night, spinning yarns of the riches that would soon be theirs. At the crack of dawn they went to the corral and Furguson located the ledge, staking their claim just beyond the sheepherder's property. Eventually, the ledge generated nearly a dozen successful mines, including one of the richest on the Mother Lode's East Belt – and the town that sprang up nearby was called Sheep Ranch.

We do know, for a fact, that there is some truth in the above story. The town of Sheep Ranch was named for a summer grazing range which was used as early as the 1850s. Gold was first discovered there April 19, 1867 by A. P. Furguson, long after numerous other less productive mountain mines had run their course. As news of the discovery spread, the area was soon covered with claim stakes. One Sheep Ranch history says that the first gold was discovered by the ranchers themselves and that Furguson and Smith's claim came later. In any case, it was their claim which would later become the rich "Sheepranch Mine". Smith sold out his interest in the mine to Calaveras County Clerk, W. A. Wallace, in 1872. Other nearby mines included the Lodi, Loon, Hurricane, Bean, Mason, Elk, Alabama, Tom Smith, Pioche, Golden Eagle, Aspinwall, Roscoe, Franklin, Salamander, Q.M., Tong, and Chavanne, among others. (Some of these names may refer to the same mine under different owners.)

In 1877, the mining company of Hearst, Haggin, and Tevis bought the Sheepranch Mine, and in the years that followed most of the above-mentioned mines came into their control. These three men would not only play an important role in the development of Sheep Ranch, but were also notable players in the history of the State of California and the West. Lloyd Tevis helped to develop the first telegraph over the Sierra Mountains, was instrumental in the founding of the Pony Express, and was once President of Wells Fargo. His long time partner, Ben Ali Haggin, was active in horse racing, and was a successful California entrepreneur for whom Stockton's Haggin Museum and Library are named. Probably the most familiar of the three was George Hearst, father of then future newspaper mogul William Randolph Hearst.

128

George Hearst came to California in 1850, during the height of the early Gold Rush. He mined in the Placerville area for a time and by careful management of his profits was able to begin a successful mining career that would take him to Nevada, Utah, Montana, and South Dakota. Hearst was actively involved in the Sheepranch Mine project when he was appointed California State Senator in 1886. It was also during this period that he purchased the *San Francisco Examiner*, which would eventually become the first building block in his son's multimillion dollar newspaper empire.

George Hearst passed away in 1891 and the mines were shut down until 1896 when they were purchased by the Sheepranch Mining Co. who worked the operation with modernized equipment until 1907. The Sheepranch mine went through a series of owners until 1942 when it was closed by Executive Order because, according to President Roosevelt, gold was not a strategic war metal.

During its heyday, the town of Sheep Ranch boasted two hotels, both of which were converted from other uses -- the Anderson or Pioneer Hotel, and the Eagle. Originally built as the Oddfellows Hall lodge, the Eagle Hotel continued to operate into the 20th century under various owners until it burned in 1952. Anderson's Saloon and Hall was originally constructed on Chee Chee Flat, near Mountain Ranch, but was moved next to the Furguson and Wallace Mine in Sheep Ranch sometime in 1868 or 1869, and became the Pioneer Hotel. In 1899, the original structure was jacked up and a lower story and surrounding porches constructed. During the late 1930s, the building was leased by the St. Joseph Lead Company for use as a boarding house for the Sheep Ranch Mines. The old Pioneer Hotel still stands next to the remains of the Sheepranch Mine.

Throughout the Mother Lode, many of the mines which were closed at the outbreak of World War II were never reopened, especially those which were badly flooded. Mountain mines were especially susceptible to this problem and practically none have operated with any amount of success since 1950. Towns that once boasted populations in the thousands have been reduced to a few dozen and some have completely disappeared. Today's mountain residents are much like those early pioneers. They brave the long and winding roads, the cold winters, and the lack of shopping and other conveniences in order to live in the peace and quite of California's dwindling wilderness -- between the rivers.

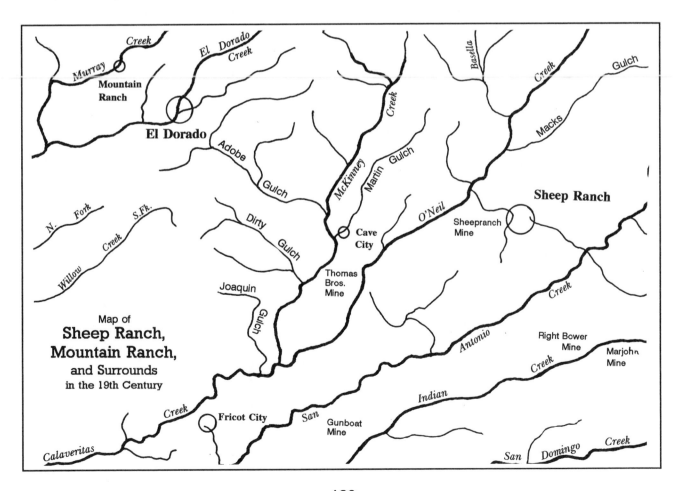

Map of
**Sheep Ranch,
Mountain Ranch,**
and Surrounds
in the 19th Century

41
Creekside Camps
Part One
Calaveritas, Fourth Crossing, Dogtown

EFORE Calaveras County had roads or towns, mining camps or "digs" were associated with nearby geographical landmarks such as mountains, hills, flats, bars, creeks, and gulches. Often, but not always, the settlement and the creek, gulch, etc., bore the same name and for the most part, no one today really knows which came first. This is the case with the little mining town of Calaveritas.

It seems logical that early explorers/prospectors traveled up the Calaveras River and taking its southern fork, named the first notable tributary Calaveritas or "little" Calaveras. On some early maps, the small stream is designated as the "Calaveritas River." Surprisingly, the same stream has been called O'Neil Creek as well, although today that name is given to a branch of Calaveritas Creek which lies further up in the mountains. The name Calaveritas was apparently quite popular, since both of the earliest camps on the creek were given the same appellation: first Lower Calaveritas, established by a group of Mexicans around 1849; then Upper Calaveritas, which was settled about a mile further upstream, reportedly by an American miner named William Workman in 1850.

By 1851, Upper Calaveritas was growing into a bustling mining camp while Lower Calaveritas had developed a reputation rivaling nearby Yaqui Camp as a hangout for "cutthroats and thieves," and was quickly losing its "respectable" residents to its upstream counterpart. Several permanent adobe buildings were constructed by Mexicans very early in the town's history and within a couple of years Upper Calaveritas boasted a livery stable, restaurants, saloons, fandango houses, and a number of stores. By the mid-1850s, Lower Calaveritas had all but faded from memory and Upper Calaveritas became simply Calaveritas.

During the mid-1850s, Calaveritas thrived as a commercial center, due primarily to mining successes along the nearby creek and gulches and the popularity of the town's gambling and fandango houses. Early Calaveras pioneer Wade Johnston described his visit to one such establishment:

One time when the boys were in Upper Calaveritas, we saw a terrific fight between two Mexican women at a fandango house. First one, then the other would have the best of it. The boys refused to interfere, finally one got the other by the hair and was twisting her head down on the banister and she was taking aim behind her ear with a revolver when one of the men present rushed in, threw up her arm and separated them just in time to save the woman's life.

(from "Wade Johnston Talks to His Daughter", Courtesy Calaveras Historical Society)

The glory of Calaveritas would be short-lived, however, for in 1858 more than 50 of the town's buildings were destroyed by fire. Local oral tradition says that the fire was started by a "poor loser" from the gambling tables. Whatever the cause, it marked the demise of Calaveritas as a notable mining camp. Almost none of the burned buildings were replaced and with nearby placers playing out, most of the miners moved on to richer diggings.

A few stores (notably that of John Sharp/Luigi Costa) continued to operate in Calaveritas through the period of hydraulic mining, which was conducted with meager success into the 20th century. The town was also kept alive by activities at the nearby

The Costa Store at Calaveritas.

Calaveras Cement Company quarry. Today, only a few of Calaveritas' original buildings remain standing in the shadow of the Calaveras Cement Company's distinctive and picturesque old wooden trestle.

Northeast of Calaveritas was a small camp called Old Gulch, which also developed a number of commercial establishments early in the Gold Rush, including a saloon, butcher shop, blacksmith, and two general stores owned by Agostini and Thompson. The gulch itself was extensively mined throughout the 19th century, as was nearby Washington Flat. Like many little camps of this type, when the mines played out the land was used for ranching and farming into the 20th century and little evidence of the town itself remains. Old Gulch was located near the edge of the Calaveras Cement Co. quarry.

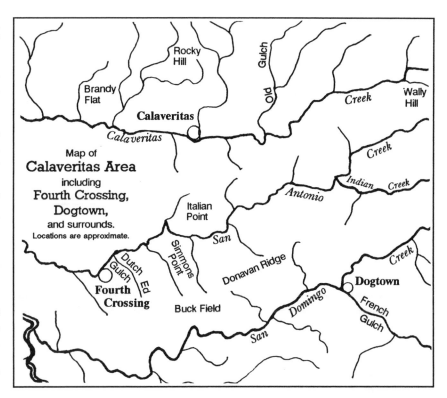

Map of
Calaveritas Area
including
Fourth Crossing, Dogtown,
and surrounds.
Locations are approximate.

One of the earliest roads in Calaveras County came from Stockton, following the Calaveras River to near San Andreas, then along that river's South Fork and eventually turning eastward to Murphys. Apparently, there were four notable stream crossings along that route, three of which were designated on maps of the period: Second Crossing, at North Branch just west of San Andreas; Third Crossing, at Kentucky House and Calaveritas Creek; and Fourth Crossing, at Foreman's Upper Ranch on San Antonio Creek two miles south of Lower Calaveritas.

It is not known exactly when Fourth Crossing was first settled, however, rich placers were likely located in San Antonio Creek as early as 1848 and David Foreman and Alexander Beritzhoff operated a ferry and hotel at the crossing very early in the Gold Rush. Later, Foreman established a toll bridge, store, saloon, and stage depot as well. (Foreman's Lower Ranch was located near what is now the town of Linden, in San Joaquin County.) Fourth Crossing established one of the first organized schools in Calaveras County and received a post office in 1855 which operated (except for a four-year closure) until 1925.

With improvements in transportation achieved by the 1860s, Fourth Crossing, then owned by William Reddick, quickly became an important rest stop on the route to the southern mines, providing refreshment and accommodations for weary travelers, as well as fresh horses and blacksmith services for the stage lines. The stores, restaurants, saloons, and dance halls also provided sustenance and entertainment for the large number of miners working San Antonio Creek and camps along the nearby Calaveras River. During the 1860s and '70s, Foreman's Mining District around Fourth Crossing contained nearly 200 separate mining claims.

According to the San Andreas Independent of June 20, 1861, the town was still growing:

New Hotel at Fourth Crossing

We learn that Mr. William Reddick, proprietor of the place known as Foreman's, or Fourth Crossing, contemplates erecting a new and commodious hotel this summer.

William Reddick settled in Fourth Crossing after a short stint working the placers of Angels Camp. He first came to California in 1849 with a band of immigrants he had personally organized. He would repeat the arduous journey three more times, in 1851 and 1853 with two more companies of immigrants and finally in 1854 with his own family. (Also of note, William Reddick served as Lieutenant Governor of California, the highest political position ever held by a Calaveras County resident.) Reddick passed the Fourth Crossing property on to his sons in 1884 and it remained in the Reddick family until the 1930s. The toll bridge at Fourth Crossing continued in operation until 1888 when it was taken over by the county and opened to free traffic. Reddick

Fourth Crossing Hotel. (Calaveras Historical Society)

passed away in the 1890s, after which the old Foreman Ranch was used as a base of operations for a major mining company and eventually returned to ranch and farming use, as it is today. In recognition of its significance in the early development of Calaveras County, a historical plaque was dedicated near Fourth Crossing on October 23, 1965.

South of San Antonio Creek is San Domingo Creek, which was also the site of many placer mining operations, none of which evolved into towns at lower elevations (the towns of San Antonio and San Domingo will be discussed in the next chapter). Later in the 19th century, a small community named Dogtown developed on the creek directly north of Altaville and at one time boasted a blacksmith shop, a store, a school house, a number of woodframe homes and a large Chinatown. A man named La Riviere operated a successful roadhouse at Dogtown for several years and the area was the site of successful hydraulic mining operations.

There are several interesting newsworthy incidents associated with Dogtown, one of which was related in the *Calaveras Prospect* of March 27, 1897:

William A. Keefer, the Secretary of the Jupiter Gravel Mining and Water Company, who's works are located in Dogtown in this county, is missing. Nobody seems to know what has become of him and his sudden disappearance gives rise to much speculation and conjecture. . . . By some it is believed he had been ambushed and killed by an enemy, and by others that he had fallen into some prospect hole, while others think he is all right and has absented himself only for the purpose of carrying out the details of some scheme he had on foot. . . .

San Francisco detectives were hired to locate Keefer, but no trace of him was found. It wasn't until eight years later that he was discovered in Paris, alive and well and living on his ill-gotten gains. At the time of Keefer's disappearance, the Jupiter and the Monarch hydraulic operations were among the largest and most modern in the county.

In the 1880s, La Riviere, the primary land owner in Dogtown sold out and eventually the property ended up in the hands of Pacific Gas and Electric. The little community all but disappeared during the early part of the 20th century. (Note: There were seven different Dogtowns located throughout California during the Gold Rush years.)

It is hard for us, today, to imagine the immensity of the Gold Rush. A miner of 1852, traveling the length of San Antonio Creek from its convergence with the Calaveras River to what is now Sheep Ranch, could not have passed more than a few hundred yards at a time without running into another miner or crossing a claim. And the same was true of Calaveritas and San Domingo creeks. With such a wide-spread abundance of population, it is nearly impossible to determine why camps with stores and saloons popped up at specific locations along these streams. Perhaps it was the richness of nearby diggings, or perhaps it was just the place where a discouraged miner decided to change occupations. And why did some towns develop and prosper while other seemingly identical camps failed and faded from existence? The answer applies to nearly every story of boom and bust in the gold rush. . . . it was pure luck.

42
Creekside Camps
Conclusion
Fricot City, Cave City, San Antone

N the upper elevations of the Central Calaveras foothills, three creek tributaries of the Calaveras River's South Fork are fed by several notable branch streams. McKinney and O'Neil Creeks merge to form the Calaveritas; Indian Creek feeds the San Antonio; and the San Domingo is supported by French Gulch, near Dogtown. Each of these streams (called "rivers" in the early days) was home to at least one important mining camp during the Gold Rush years.

The two earliest camps of this area were probably two who bore the name of the streams on which they sat; San Antonio (sometimes called San Antone) and San Domingo. It is hard to say which were named first, the camps or the streams. It is likely that Mexican miners were already in residence when the first Americans came to this area and while the hispanics were not especially well-liked or well-treated, the 49ers did tend to accept and use the names they had already assigned to camps and geographical features.

While details of its beginnings are unknown, San Antonio Camp quickly established itself as a booming mining town in the early 1850s. The camp's "commercial" section was at one time quite large, with saloons, gambling houses, dance halls, and numerous stores typical of camps situated near extensive mining operations. Nearby gulches were heavily worked during the placer mining period (one of Calaveras County's five "Rich Gulches" was located here) and later, numerous quartz mines were established along the San Antone Ridge between San Antonio and Calaveritas Creeks. These quartz mines, while abundant, were not especially successful and San Antonio Camp quickly dwindled, as the *San Andreas Independent* of January 29, 1859 reported:

On Monday we visited San Antonio. The old camp looks deserted. The bed of the river opposite, above, and below the town has been worked annually for eight years. Still it pays wages and will for the most part be worked again this spring. A new wagon road is in the course of construction down to town from the ridge on the north. The place contains two stores and some twenty to thirty dwelling

houses. . . . The mines in this district are mostly of the character which require patience and energy in their development, and many years of constant labor to develop them.

Among the more successful of these early mines were the Railroad Hill, Hope Hill, Tunnel Hill, and Chase's Diggings, which the article also described:

The celebrated Chase Claim is up the river a mile from San Antonio. It is located on a bar and runs into the point of a hill, crossing the mouth of a small ravine, obliquely following a lode of hard crystallized limestone. The outside of the bar was shallow and has long since been worked out but as the operations were extended toward the point of the hill, the limestone pitched off at an abrupt angle, rendering the diggings very deep and more expensive to work. However, the dirt becomes richer with depth. Some of the gold is course and one nugget weighed 19 ounces.

While little remains of San Antonio Camp (like other camps of its type, it burned down and was not rebuilt), its memory has been kept alive through a tale of unfound buried treasure, centering around a black miner who came to San Antonio Camp from Mok Hill in the early 1850s. When white miners of the Hill realized that several blacks were working a rich claim on a nearby knoll, to which they had been directed as a joke . . . they quickly swarmed the area and pushed the blacks out, but not before the men had accumulated a large amount of gold. When Dan Buster took up his new claim near San Antonio Camp, he was said to have over $50,000 in his possession. According to legend, the gold was seen and weighed by San Antone store owner Frank Cuneo and when word got out, Buster had to bury his treasure so that no one could steal it. The old man refused to reveal its location, even under torture, and when he died in 1863 he took the secret with him to his grave.

Slightly to the southeast of San Antonio Camp, a small community called Indian Creek also developed on a stream of the same name. Consisting of only a few tents and miner's shacks during the early years, a small commercial center eventually developed and the town came to be called Esmeralda. Canavero and Segale operated a saloon and general store from approximately 1864 to 1874, and a post office was established at Esmeralda in 1887 and continued in operation until 1943. The town supported nearby placer mines during the 1850s and 60s and quartz mines from the 1880s.

An interesting legend connected with Esmeralda concerns an Italian miner who traveled from there to Duck Bar on the Stanislaus, using a walking stick cut from Mrs. Canavero's fig tree. Upon reaching the river he stuck the stick in the sand, where it took root and eventually grew into a massive tree and familiar landmark. The fig tree was so large and the limb and root system so complex, children used to play on it like a jungle-gym and travelers used it as shelter from the elements. (Along with other important bits of Calaveras history, the Duck Bar fig tree was destroyed by the New Melones Reservoir.)

South of Esmeralda were the creek and town of San Domingo. Little has been recorded of this town's beginnings, which likely parallel that of San Antonio and Esmeralda to some degree. The camp was still quite small in the late 1850s, and while there were a number of relatively successful mines in the area, most of the miners probably got their supplies from nearby San Antonio, Dogtown, or Altaville. The San Domingo Mine was active into the 20th century.

North of San Antone Ridge, between McKinney and O'Neil Creeks was the little town of Cave City. Its name came from an impressive nearby cavern, said to have been discovered in October, 1850, by a miner named Captain Taylor. Recognized as a tourist attraction even in the 1850s, a hotel was erected nearby and the cave opened to tours in 1853. Cave City prospered as both as a tourist attraction and a mining community, with numerous saloons and gambling houses, until the 1860s when the mines began to play out and the old cave became its only draw. Although the original Cave City Hotel burned down, a new structure built in 1881 continued to cater to the tourist's needs. An article in the *Calaveras Weekly Citizen* of December 29, 1883 describes the town and cave:

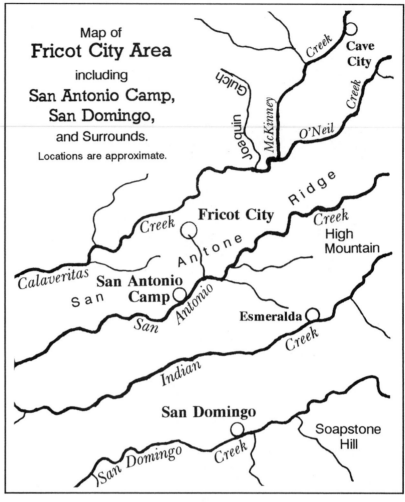

Map of
Fricot City Area
including
**San Antonio Camp,
San Domingo,**
and Surrounds.
Locations are approximate.

Cave City is in the eastern part of Calaveras County. It once contained 1000 inhabitants but in the failure of the gravel mines the population diminished as in other mining towns, till at present the "city" consists of a hotel, a saloon, and a haystack. A few of the curiosities of early times still remain at the place. . . . The cave has the appearance of having been at some time the subterranean outlet for some large river or lake. . . . There are 12 large chambers with narrow passages leading from one to another. The roofs and sides are covered with beautiful formations. Many of them three feet in length are pendant from the ceiling and glitter in the lamplight like thousands of diamonds.

A second cave, also discovered in the area was said to contain the remains of over 100 human bodies (some estimates ran as high as 1000 skeletons). "Skull Cave" was greatly puzzling to archaeologists of the 19th century who believed that a large number of Indians might have been sealed in the cave and perished from starvation or disease. Thinking the skeletons were of relatively recent origin,

Old store at Esmeralda on Indian Creek.
(Calaveras County Historical Society)

investigators were puzzled by the lack of clothingremains and other artifacts. Today we know that this cave and others like it throughout Calaveras County were "mortuary caves," dating back many centuries. Because so little is known about Indian lifestyles prior to the arrival of the white man, we can only assume that the bodies were deposited there after death and the skeletons accumulated over the centuries (probably between 1000 B.C and 500 A.D.).

In closing this review of the creekside camps of Calaveras, mention must be made of Fricot City. While it was never really a "city" or even a town, and although it actually came into existence long after the Gold Rush years, Fricot City and its founder are an important part of this county's history. In the 1890s, Desire' Fricot established eight mining claims along San Antone Ridge, and in 1897 he constructed an impressive home into which he would move with his new bride in 1898. Both Fricot and his father had been partners of Andre Chavanne (once owner of the Chavanne Mine at Sheepranch) in his Grass Valley mining operations. As a successful mine owner and businessman, Desire' controlled an extensive financial empire before the

age of 30. The Fricot mansion accidentally burned while Desire' was away actively supporting the French and their allies during WWI, but was rebuilt to even greater splendor after the war.

In the 1930s, the Fricot home became an important center for social and cultural activities and soon the Fricot complex came to be called Fricot City. Desire' constructed a number of buildings for use by the Boy Scouts and established himself as a selfless contributor to the advancement of scouting in California. Fricot was also an active and influential participant in efforts to establish a state park at Calaveras Big Trees, as well as other conservation and humanitarian causes. Desire' Fricot passed away in 1940, followed by his wife in 1942. The Fricot Ranch was used as a residence for homeless boys from 1944 until 1972.

During the 1850s, hundreds of California towns grew to notable size, then just as quickly became ghost towns as the gold disappeared and the miners moved on. Today, only a few of their names remain on maps to mark a fork in the road or a few crumbling historic walls that were once bustling creekside camps -- between the rivers.

43
The Producers
Part One

HE exact definition of the "Gold Rush," in years, has always been a subject of debate among historians and scholars. Almost everyone knows the story of how James Marshall plucked a nugget from the millrace at Sutters Mill in 1848 and how this singular event triggered an unprecedented westward migration of gold seekers. Therefore, the Gold Rush most certainly began in 1848 -- but when did it end? The mining of gold reached an all-time annual high of $81 million in 1852 and then began to decline as the rich surface placers wore out. New methods of mining then took the place of the shovel and pan. Hydraulic mines produced huge amounts of gold until they were shut down by the government in the 1880s. From that point on, quartz mines and dredging operations were the big "producers" of California gold. As long as gold was being produced, people were still rushing to California and both miners and investors were still rushing to find the gold.

From the early years, the state of California has done its best to keep track of gold production. The early miners unknowingly made this task easier through the creation of mining "districts." Originally, the purpose of a mining district was to organize the miners by setting down maximum claim sizes and establishing a strict set of rules and regulations. (These laws not only pertained to mining, but to all community-related matters.) In later years, mining districts provided a method of demarcating specific active mining areas. These were the recognized gold producing zones.

During the 1850s, nearly every mining camp of size had its own district and Calaveras County had hundreds of districts. Some of their names have been maintained into the 20th century, others have long since faded into history. Each, in its time, was a "producer".

The Alto District - During the first years of the Gold Rush, this area in the southwest corner of the county was placer-mined with minimal success, then worked using "drift" mining during the 1850s. The Alto Lode was discovered in 1886, but it wasn't until the 1890s that a shaft was sunk and the "Alta" Mine became a producer. The mine started out with a 10-stamp mill and by the turn of the

century had 40 stamps being operated by electrical engines. The Alta milled nearly 80 thousand tons of ore in 1906, its last full year of operation. Located just south of Copperopolis, it reached a depth of 400 feet, and produced nearly $1 million in gold.

The Angels Camp District — Containing 40 major mines, this district encompassed the towns of Angels Camp and Altaville as well as nearby hills and gulches. Some of the earliest quartz mines in the county were initiated in this district on what would later come to be called the Davis-Winter ledge (see Chapter 34). Three of the largest and most productive mines of the county were located here, the Utica, the Lightner, and the Angels. The Utica Mining Company was originally organized in the 1850s and the mine was worked with intermittent success (and occasionally under other names) into the latter part of the century. Aggressive deep rock mining began in the 1880s and during the period 1893-95 the Utica produced more than $4 million in gold. At its closing in 1915, the Utica reached a depth of 3050 feet and had yielded over $13 million.

The Angels Mine was worked extensively from 1866, but was not known as the Angels until 1884. When it closed, during World War I, it held the distinction of having been in continuous operation longer than any mine in the county. The final depth of the Angels Mine was 1050 feet and it had produced nearly $3.5 million. Its next-door neighbor, the Lightner, operated for only 20 years, during which the shaft had to be re-sunk due to cave-ins. Despite this setback, the Lighter's new shaft reached 900 feet and the mine produced a total of $3 million in gold by 1915.

Because of the size of this district and the large number of mines which were in operation since the very early days of gold mining, its total production was probably much higher than the "official" estimate of $30 million.

Blue Mountain District — The Blue Mountain Range is southeast of West Point between the Middle and South Forks of the Mokelumne River. This area was extensively prospected during the 1860s, giving rise to a bustling camp called Blue Mountain City. Typical of many gold rush towns, it grew to considerable size then just as quickly disappeared. Its post office was in operation for just

The Alta Mine, Scorpion Gulch, 1907
(Calaveras County Historical Society)

Angels Mine and mill buildings.
(Calaveras Historical Society)

one year -- from 1863 to 1864. The major mine of the district was the Heckendorn Mine, whose namesake owner later published the *Big Tree Bulletin*. Interestingly, the Heckendorn and other nearby mines produced significant amounts of silver, as well as gold. After the early 1870s, it was worked intermittently until World War I.

Calaveritas District – The streams around Calaveritas were worked extensively by placer miners during the 1850s and nearby areas were the site of ground sluicing and hydraulic mining during the second half of the 19th century. Early 20th century dredging operations met with modest success. Principal mines were the Barnhardt, Calaveritas Hill, Consolidated, Oro Fino, Railroad Hill, and Richie Hill.

Camanche District – Heavily prospected and worked during the placer mining period, this district extended over three counties (Calaveras, Amador, and San Joaquin) and was later home to dredging operations by American Dredging and others. Working the Mokelumne River from 1904 to 1951, these dredges produced an estimated $10 million in gold,

San Domingo hydraulic mine, 1908
(Calaveras County Historical Society)

benefiting the nearby towns of Camanche and Lancha Plana. The two towns and most of the district now lie beneath Camanche Reservoir.

Campo Seco District — The principal mine of this district was the Penn, and while it was primarily a copper mine, it did produce significant amounts of gold (60,000 ounces). Nearly every type of gold mining used during the 19th century was tried at Campo Seco, all with minimal success.

Carson Hill/Melones District —This district was the richest in the county and was home to the earliest quartz mines. Carson Hill, the geographical feature, slopes southward to the Stanislaus River, eastward to Coyote Creek and westward to Carson Creek. Most of the principal mines were located on the western and southern slopes. The first rich quartz strike, later to become the Morgan Mine, was discovered late in 1850 and was the object of almost continuous claim disputes.

Several quartz veins of the Carson District were quite rich and early pocket mining was highly successful. A record 195 troy pound mass of gold-bearing quartz was removed from one such pocket in 1854. Over 50 arastras were operating on Carson Hill in the early '50s and a water powered stamp mill (one of the first in Calaveras County) was erected on nearby Carson Creek in 1856 by Gabriel Stevenot to facilitate the crushing of ore.

During the late 1850s and early 1860s, extensive mining and milling operations were brought into use, several under the direction of the Stevenot family. Most of the mines in the district changed hands several times during the 19th century and were frequently combined to form various mining companies such as Melones and Stanislaus Mining and Melones Consolidated.

The Carson Hill mines were particularly active during the late 1870s and early 1880s, with William Irvine operating the Morgan and Gabriel Stevenot and partners running the Reserve. The Melones Mine was heavily worked from 1895 to 1918, then operated as a unit with the Morgan and the Calaveras from 1918 to 1926 and from 1933 to 1942 when operations ceased due to a mill fire. Shortly thereafter, all California gold mines were closed by executive order. The Morgan and Calaveras, along with the Finnegan, Reserve, and Stanislaus came to be known simply as the Carson Hill Mines and, as a unit, this group produced over $26 million in gold.

The Carson Hill mine became one of the few early California Mines to remain active into the modern era when it was reopened as an open pit mine in 1986.

44
The Producers
Conclusion

 HILE not every well-known gold mine was a great producer, every great producer became well-known. Calaveras County's two most productive gold districts, Carson Hill and Angels, received world renown from the earliest years of the Gold Rush until most of the mines shut down at the beginning of World War I. Other districts, such as Blue Mountain and Paloma, have remained relatively unheralded despite the fact that they made notable contributions to the $2.5 billion in gold California has produced. Another significant producer was the Royal Mine, Hodson District.

The Hodson District — The town of Hodson once stood on Johnny Creek at the south end of Salt Spring Valley. Hodson was truly a "mining town", for it was built in the late 1890s by the management of the Royal Mine to accommodate its workers. (J. T. Hodson, of London, was the mine's primary financial backer.) During the copper boom of the 1860s, the region was called the Madam Felix Copper Mining District in honor of one of the valley's most prominent citizens. From the 1880s to the 1890s, the Hodson area was called Pine Log.

While some mining of placer gold took place during the early years, the first extensive lode mining in this area was done by Pine Log Gold Mining around 1878. The Royal Mining Company, begun in 1883, was absorbed by Pine Log Gold around 1889 and reorganized as the Royal Consolidated Mining Company in 1890. Hodson's representative, J. C. Kemp Van Ee, bought out the partnership in 1897. By the turn of the century, the Royal's shaft was approaching 1000 feet and a 40 stamp mill was in full operation.

The Royal Mine had its heyday during 1902 and 1903, then began to run into processing difficulties as well as employee and financial problems in 1903 and 1904. Its magnificent 120 stamp mill operated for only two years. A major lawsuit caused suspension of operations in 1905 and the mine remained inactive until it was purchased by new investors in 1914. Over the next 40 years, the Royal would change hands numerous times, until all major activity was finally silenced by Executive Order in 1942. During its relatively short period of operation, the Royal Mine produced more than $5 million in gold.

Other mines of the Hodson District included the Butcher Shop, Empire, Skyrocket, Gold Knoll, Gold Metal, Pine Log, Wilber Womble, and a million dollar producer called the Mountain King.

Jenny Lind District — While no one mine of this district was especially notable, the mines were numerous and consistent. Early placer diggings along Rich Gulch and North Gulch, south of the Calaveras River, were quite successful and later the area around Jenny Lind was extensively hydraulicked. Major dredging operations, established around the turn of the century, account for a large portion of this district's total gold production.

Mokelumne Hill District — This district encompassed a wide area, containing a variety of types of mines. The Mokelumne River and its tributary gulches were placer mined very early in the Gold Rush. The knolls around Mokelumne Hill were mined by pocket and coyote methods with great success throughout the 1850s and large amounts of gold were recovered by drift mining and hydraulic operations along nearby Chili Gulch and Old Woman Gulch into the latter part of the century.

From the 1880s until the turn of the century, the Quaker City and Boston quartz mines of this district both produced in excess of $1 million in gold. Other quartz mines in the area included the Easy Bird, Hamby, Lamphear, and Nuner.

Mountain Ranch District — Relatively small in size, the district encompassed the towns of Mountain Ranch, El Dorado, and Cave City and contained only one notable producer, the Gaston Hill quartz mine. Significant early placers were mined out by 1860.

Paloma District — A prominent quartz ledge was located in this district in the early 1850s and an incline shaft was sunk as early as 1853. Two early quartz mines, the Alexander and the Paloma, were later purchased by California Senator William Gwin and this combined operation was incorporated as the Gwin Mining Company in 1872.

The main shaft of the Gwin Mine reached the 1500 foot level in 1879, however, work at that depth was discontinued due to uncontrollable water seepage. By the early 1880s, it appeared that most of the worthwhile ore had been removed and mining operations were discontinued. The Gwin was reopened in 1894 by F. F. Thomas, who had success-

Gwin Mine in the Lower Rich Gulch before the steel headframe was installed. (Calaveras County Historical Society)

fully reestablished the Kennedy Mine operation at Jackson a few years earlier. Despite the relatively low grade of the ore, Thomas was able to make the mine one of the most profitable in the Mother Lode and had taken the main shaft to 2800 feet by 1908. In that year, the mine was closed by worried investors. The total gold production of the Gwin Mine was nearly $7 million.

Railroad Flat District — The numerous short quartz veins of this district did not extend to any depth, but were quite rich in some areas. The Fine Gold and the Sanderson were the two most productive lode mines, bringing out $200,000 and $100,000 respectively. Other notable quartz mines of the district were the Bald Eagle, Clary, Jeff Davis, Kaiser Wilhelm, Mohawk, Old Gray, Petticoat, Poe, Prussian Hill, Summit, and Swiss.

Rich Gulch District — This district lay adjacent to the West Point and Railroad Flat districts and included the town of Jesus Maria. Quartz veins throughout this part of the county were quite shallow and lode mines were usually short lived. Although the rich deposits were quickly used up, the

Quartz Glen mine was able to extract in excess of $1/4 million during its operation.

San Andreas District — This large district may have included several thousand placer mines during the early years, and was mined by all methods during the 19th century. Placer mining took place along the Calaveras River, its forks, and numerous tributary creeks and gulches. The area was home to many quartz mines, including the Commadore, Etna, Everlasting, Fellowcraft, Ford, Gottschalk, Golden Hill, Helen, Holland, Kate Hageman, Lookout Mountain, Mester, Pioneer Chief, Rathgeb, and Thorpe; but only the Union was a major producer.

Sheep Ranch District — (For details of the major mines of this district, see Chapter 40.) The major producer of this district was the Sheepranch Mine, which extracted over $7 million in gold from 1868 to 1942. The Washington Mine brought out over a half million dollars, and the Mar John, $350,000+. The Right Bower and Sonoma were also significant producers.

Vallecito District — Most of the gold produced by this district was taken from the placer deposits

The Royal Mine hoist house and crusher.
(Calaveras County Historical Society)

of Coyote Creek and its tributary gulches during the early years of the gold rush. Following the typical placer-mining progression, the district was mined by hydraulicking through the 1880s and by dredging after the turn of the century.

West Point District — The area around the town of West Point gave rise to an unusually high concentration of lode mines and quartz mills during the 1860s and '70s. As noted in the Railroad Flat and Rich Gulch districts, the gold bearing veins were rich, but short and shallow. The number of individual mine shafts sunk in this district, which includes a portion of Amador County, probably exceeds five hundred.

The most productive mine of this group, the Champion, was located in Calaveras County and yielded over a half million dollars. Other major producers included the Blackstone, Keltz, Lockwood, Woodhouse, and Yellow Aster.

At the beginning of World War II, President Roosevelt signed what is now probably the most widely remembered Executive Order ever issued. . . L208. It said, quite simply, that gold was not important to the war effort and that all gold mines were to be shut down until further notice. During the shutdown, deep rock mines (the most productive mines) filled up with water which weakened the walls and ceilings of the shafts and drifts causing cave-ins and other problems. After the war, the few mining companies who attempted to reopen found that it just wasn't worth the time and expense. The Gold Rush was really over.

During the past half century, many attempts have been made to prove that gold mining in California can once again be a profitable enterprise. Most have failed -- others are still trying. With modern technology and the spirit of the old 49er, these modern argonauts hope that soon there will be a new rush for gold -- between the rivers.

45
Giants Along the High Trail
Part One

N 1852, during the height of the Gold Rush, the Union Water Company hired a large number of men to construct a water ditch from high elevations of the Stanislaus River to Angels Creek, thereby providing a continuous and abundant water supply for the mines at Murphys and other camps further down the mountain. These men included engineers to plan and carry out the project; masons to construct the dam; carpenters to build flumes; ditch diggers; and at least one professional hunter, Augustus T. Dowd, who supplied these workers with fresh meat. Late one spring afternoon, Dowd returned to camp and excitedly told the others of a great "find" he had made. It wasn't gold, or even a large herd of deer. . . . .it was a tree. Certainly not an ordinary tree, but a tree that Dowd believed must surely be the largest of its kind in the world.

Dowd's description of the great tree was so impressive that no one believed it. In fact, the workers decided that the hunter was quite probably trying to coax them into the woods for some sort of practical joke and they would have nothing of it. His credibility spoiled, Dowd later devised a plan to lure them to the spot by convincing them that he had killed a large bear and needed as much help as possible to carry the carcass back to camp. Unwittingly, this small band of construction workers were about to be given the first guided tour of the Calaveras Big Tree.

Augustus Dowd was probably not the first white man to see Calaveras County's giant sequoias, but the nature and circumstances of his encounter were such that he has been given the "honorary" title of discoverer of the Big Tree. Union Water Company President, William Hanford, was most certainly the first "developer" of this now famous grove, although the legacy he left is far less noble. In 1853, Hanford had a large section of bark stripped from Dowd's giant tree (now called the Discovery Tree) and sent it to the Eastern States as a touring display. The tree itself was then felled using a type of large hand drill called a "pump auger." Numerous holes were bored into the trunk around its grand circumference, and the connecting wood was chipped away with chisels until, after nearly one month of work,

the great titan finally crashed to the forest floor. (In 1854, a second tree, called the "Mother of the Forest," was also stripped of its bark to make a display that was sent to the Crystal Palace Exhibition in London. Without its protective covering the tree eventually died.)

Even in a time when wide-spread concerns for "conservation" and "natural preservation" were one hundred years distant, the felling of the great sequoia was answered by a loud cry of anger from at least one early Californian, John Muir, who wrote a commentary titled, "The Vandals Then Danced Upon the Stump."

And dance they did. . . . for the remainder of that century and a portion of the next! By the winter of 1853, the huge stump had been planed smooth and the two story Mammoth Tree Hotel was standing nearby. A bar and bowling alley was also constructed, using the long trunk of the Discovery Tree as a base. A section of the trunk was left between the stump and the bowling alley for display purposes (called a "Chip off the Block"), and a stairway was constructed so that tourists could climb to the top.

In the years that followed, the Big Tree Grove became a getaway and tourist attraction of national, and even world-wide renown. Emigrants passing over the Sierra Mountains took great pride in mentioning in their journals that they had stopped and "danced on the Big Stump," and members of San Francisco society who had not yet made the pilgrimage to the Big Tree Grove were considered quite out of vogue. The *San Andreas Independent* reported on a Grand Ball held at the resort in May of 1857, stating that a spring floor had been laid down between the hotel and the stump, and that the stump had been covered with an "arbor" of cedar boughs for the protection of both it and the dancers. In May of '58, the *Independent* had high praise for the popular retreat:

As a fashionable resort, the Hotel is equal to any in the state, and parties visiting the grove can go assured that everything necessary for health or recreation is provided in a liberal manner.

Of course, the construction of such a large and elaborate enterprise required the clearing of many additional trees, as evidence the numerous stumps

Mammoth Grove Hotel, Calaveras Big Trees
(Calaveras County Illustrated and Described, 1885)

ELLIOTT LITH. OAKLAND.

visible in early drawings and lithographs of the grove. (It is amazing to see how well this area -- now called the North Grove -- has recovered from that early desecration.)

The entry to the grove was marked by two large sequoias called the "Guardsmen" (later called the "Sentinels") between which the main road ran. In 1860, Sperry and Perry owners of the hotel in Murphys, had taken over the grove, and in 1861 they constructed a new, larger Mammoth Grove Hotel. They also replaced the cedar bough structure which covered the "Big Stump" with a more permanent, domed pavilion. The surface of the stump, measuring more than 25 feet in diameter, provided a large and very solid dance floor. Calaveras pioneer C. B. Demarest claimed that "thirty-two couples once danced a cotillion (upon the stump), still leaving room enough for the fiddler."

During the winter of 1862-63, the Big Tree area was hit by heavy storms and the bar and bowling alley which had been built over the trunk of the Discovery Tree was crushed by the weight of the snow. The Big Stump Pavilion would meet the same fate nearly three quarters of a century later, during the storms of 1934. The Mammoth Grove Hotel survived until 1943, when it was partially destroyed by fire. (Fire also damaged the remains of the Discovery Tree, removing all evidence of its use as a bowling alley.)

As roads and transportation improved during the latter half of the 19th century, the Big Trees became even more popular. Routes to the resort were outlined in the publication, *Calaveras County Illustrated and Described, 1885.*

Tourists, to visit these trees, leaving San Francisco, can take the Central Pacific Railroad to Stockton, and the Copperopolis Railroad to Milton, or the new narrow gauge railroad which connects with the Central at Lodi, thence to Valley Springs and San Andreas. Connection is made on either route with Matteson's daily line of stages to the Big Trees. A daily coach leaves the Big Trees for Milton, connecting at Murphys with a daily line to Yosemite Valley via Hutchings' new route, being the shortest and best.

The road to Big Trees and beyond changed several times during the 19th century. The original trail which passed through this area was a southern "loop" of the Emigrant Trail (also called the Carson Canyon Route), which generally followed the path of what is now Highway 88 in Alpine and Amador

Todays visitors are as inspired by the big trees as those who first saw them 100 years ago.

(It should be noted that while many historians have tried to delineate the exact locations of the early trails mentioned above, such attempts are merely educated guesses. Truly accurate maps of this area were not produced until the late 1850s and descriptions taken from emigrant journals are often vague. Sections of early trails which were well marked became worn by frequent travel, while in other places the traveler simply chose the path of least resistance that took him in the right direction. Accordingly, trails constantly changed as easier routes were discovered and settlements were established. This is highly evident within the Big Trees Park itself, where almost none of the modern roads follow the path of the early 19th century trails.)

Ironically, it was not the Gold Rush of California or the discovery of the Big Tree that motivated the construction of an "improved" road along the Ebbett's Pass route -- it was the discovery of silver in Nevada. (Today's Ebbitts Pass was originally called Silver Pass, and was discovered in 1861.) In 1862, the Big Tree and Carson Valley Turnpike Company was incorporated for the purpose of constructing a toll road from Big Tree Grove to the Nevada border, by which supplies could be transported from California to the silver mines. The omnipresent Sperry and Perry were major stockholders in the state-authorized venture, such a road being highly beneficial to their "hostelry" interests at both Murphys and Big Tree Grove.

One can only imagine the hardships faced by early engineers in the construction of such a road through the rugged Sierra Mountains. The original contract, which called for the road to be completed within two years, had to be extended for two additional years in 1864, and the Turnpike Company was ready to bow out. The project was finished by Harvey Blood and J. Curtis. Blood operated the turnpike until 1911, when it became the "Alpine Highway," part of the free state highway system.

Counties to near today's Silver Basin Ski Area, then went northwest to Placerville. The southern loop began around Markleeville, in Alpine County, and generally followed the route of today's Highway 88 through Hope Valley to Blue Lakes and Hermit Valley to Highway 4 and down the mountain, with one segment turning northwest to West Point and another continuing into the Central Valley.

46
Giants Along the High Trail
Conclusion

ODAY'S tourist visits Calaveras County primarily because of its Gold Rush history. They flock to see the historic old mines and buildings and they brave the rough, winding back roads in search of ghost towns and historical markers. But even in Gold Rush times, the county had one of California's first major tourist draws -- the Big Tree Grove. During the early part of the century, visitors came by stage or by horseback. From the 1870s they came by train to Milton or Wallace, then caught Matteson's Big Tree Stage to the grove.

It was, of course, the giant sequoias that were the primary attraction, however, the Big Tree resort offered far more than just a hotel in the pines, as this contemporary description reveals:

There is good hunting ground in the vicinity, mountain quail are abundant nearby, and on the Stanislaus, three miles distant, grouse and deer abound. The San Antonio contains trout of fine size. Delightful horseback or buggy rides conduct the visitor to many points of scenery or objects of curiosity, among which, besides the falls of San Antonio, may be mentioned the Basaltic Cliffs of the North Fork of the Stanislaus River, and the cave at Cave City fifteen miles to the west, and the Natural Bridges near Vallecito.

Ironically, Calaveras County's only major route across the Sierra Mountains, a branch of the Emigrant Trail, ran past the grove as well, making the Big Tree Road one of the most traveled routes in the Mother Lode and giving rise to numerous small villages and "road houses" catering to tourist and traveler. The town which perhaps benefitted most from Big Tree traffic was Murphys.

While Murphys was born of -- and nourished by its gold mines, the town's commercial establishments were quick to take advantage of their fortuitous location on the road to Big Tree Grove. James Sperry and John Perry, owners of the Mammoth Grove Hotel also conveniently owned the Murphys Hotel as well; and T.J. Matteson, who provided the primary conveyance to the grove for over forty years, was headquartered in Murphys.

Harvey Blood, who figured significantly in the construction and operation of the Big Tree - Carson Valley Turnpike, purchased the Murphy's Hotel in the 1880s, then sold it to Elizabeth Mitchler in the latter part of that decade. The Mitchler Hotel became a noted historical landmark and tourist stop, and the old hotel registers contained the names of famous early Big Tree travelers.

About mid-century the Avery family purchased a parcel of land with a little four-room house halfway between Murphys and Big Tree. With a steady flow of travelers passing up and down the Big Tree Road, it wasn't long before additions had been made to the old homestead, and a roadhouse, appropriately called the "Halfway House," was in full operation. During the 1880s, a second story was added to the hotel, which by then was surrounded by corrals, barns, stables, a store, a dance hall, and a Post Office for the town of "Avery."

Travel to the Big Tree Grove by stage or wagon was slow and tedious, even on the improved roads of the late 19th and early 20th century and the facilities at Avery were a welcome sight for weary travelers. After the introduction of the automobile, however, many towns like Avery began to see a marked decrease in business. The Avery Hotel was bypassed by Highway 4 and when the town was mostly destroyed by fires in 1946 and '47, the buildings were never replaced.

Between Avery and Big Tree Grove were two large ranches, the Dunbar and the Moran. These provided meat, vegetables, and fruit (primarily apples) to nearby resorts from the late 1800s into the 20th century. This area would later become the location of one of Calaveras County's newest towns, named for its founders, Bob and Bernice Arnold. The town of Arnold began in the 1930s as a bar, restaurant, and three cabins. Today it is one of the county's fastest growing communities, due in great part to its close proximity to Calaveras Big Trees, Mt. Reba, and the Bear Valley Ski Area.

East of the Big Tree Grove, in the 1850s, there was a small sheep ranch with a cold running spring at which many of the early emigrants took refreshment after their long and rugged Sierra crossing. The ranch was purchased by Scotsman John Gardner around 1852 and it wasn't long before he too was involved in a profitable roadhouse business. A hotel was built at the Cold Springs Ranch (also

Blood's Station toll gate, 1914.
(Calaveras Historical Society)

Avery Hotel - 1930s
(Calaveras Historical Society)

called Gardners Station) in the early 1860s, probably about the time that construction began on the turnpike. When the toll road finally went into operation, Gardner's hotel served as toll house for the western gate.

By the turn of the century, Gardner's Station had grown to considerable size, with a general store and other commercial buildings. A post office was established in 1902, but as was often the case, the Post Office Department didn't like the town's given name, so Gardner submitted the name "Dorrington," in honor of his wife, Mary Rebekah Dorrington Gardner. Mary made the arduous journey across Panama alone, in 1851, to join her husband in the California gold fields.

About 15 miles northeast of Dorrington, in the 1870s, the Gann ranching family set up a mountain grazing range along the Big Tree Turnpike. The property was homesteaded by Charlie Gann in the early 1900s and this area, once called Gann's Station, is now simply called Ganns. A roadhouse at nearby William's Springs serviced turnpike travelers. Also nearby was Poison Springs, named for an incident involving the demise of an entire herd of sheep, possibly "done in" by angry cattle ranchers who wanted them off their range.

The community now called Tamarack did not come into existence until 1936, although the valley was popular with both emigrants and Native Americans. During those early days it was called "Onion Valley" because of the large crop of wild onions found growing on the flat. Like many of the meadows along the turnpike, this valley became a summer grazing range for foothill ranchers, starting in the 1860s. The valley was homesteaded by David Filippini in the 1880s, then passed through several

hands until William Hutchins opened a store there in the 1930s. It was Hutchins who named the place "Tamarack" for the tall pines native to this section of the high Sierras.

Alpine County, Calaveras' Sierra neighbor, lies just east of Tamarack and was organized in 1864 from parts of Amador, Calaveras, Tuolumne, El Dorado, and Mono counties. Its seat of government in those early years was the bustling silver mining camp of Silver City (formerly Kongsber). After the silver mines began to play out, Silver City all but disappeared from the map, and the county seat was moved to Markleeville.

Blood's Station was the eastern toll gate for the Calaveras County section of the turnpike, operated by Harvey Blood into the 20th century (see previous chapter). Mount Reba is named for Blood's daughter, whom legend says endeared herself to the government surveyors who mapped the area by bringing them "purloined" pies. Today, of course, Bear Valley and Mt. Reba are popular ski resorts.

While today's Highway 4 does not exactly follow the old Big Tree - Carson Valley road, the remains of early settlements and even part of the old road itself are accessible, including, of course, the giant sequoias of Calaveras Big Tree. The grove was deeded to the state of California in 1931 and became part of the State Park system. After nearly three quarters of a century of protective management, most of the damage done by early developers has been reclaimed while still allowing public access to the park's history and beauty. Today, just as they did in gold rush times, tourists flock to the Mammoth Grove to picnic and play in the mountain air and stare in wonder at the giants along the high trail – between the rivers.

47
All the World in
a Single Room

They came in their usual desultory fashion – the fashion of country school-children the world over -- irregular, spasmodically, and always as if accidentally . . . . appearing from ditches, behind trunks, and between fence rails; cropping up in unexpected places along the road after vague and purposeless detours -- seemingly going anywhere and everywhere but to school!

from *Cressy*, by Bret Harte

RIOR to the Gold Rush, the few children living in California were either educated through the missions or by private tutors, or they received no formal education at all. At the end of the 1840s, two great events had left the new republic in a great degree of turmoil and confusion -- the signing of the Treaty of Guadalupe Hidalgo transferred ownership from Mexico to the United States, and gold was discovered at Sutter's Mill. Therefore, when the first California legislature met in the winter of '49, education was far down their list of concerns and for the most part they simply "sloughed" it off to churches and local governments.

During the early part of the 1850s, women and children began arriving to join husbands and fathers in the gold fields, first by the hundreds, then by the thousands. As the "feminine presence" turned rowdy gold camps into "cultured" towns and rickety leantos into houses and homes, organized education became a logical concern.

Because, at this time, there were no regulations requiring any type of certification, anyone who had more than a basic education and the inclination to instruct could be a teacher. Since most towns had at least one church and since it was only used on Sundays, that building would often become the school house with the parson or his wife frequently taking the additional role as teacher. The first school in Calaveras County was very likely located in the Methodist Church of Fort John, in what is now Amador County.

According to late historian Coke Wood, a school was organized in the Methodist church-tent in Mokelumne Hill in 1852. The minister's wife, Mrs. Isaac Fish taught five children, three hours a day, for the rather hefty sum (for the time period) of seventy-five dollars a month. Until 1853, all of Calaveras County's schools were private schools and the teacher's salary was "negotiated" with individual parents or the community as a whole. Teachers who taught in richer camps could, of course, negotiate top wages. On the average though, few received more than $3 or $4 dollars per student, per month. This meant that the teacher also had to be a good salesperson — able to convince the miners and ranchers that providing a formal education for their children was more important than having them work in the mines or fields.

Although there is no clear record when the first "public" schools were opened in Calaveras County, by the time the County Board of Supervisors first met in 1855 public schools were in operation at Angels Camp, Cave City, Mokelumne Hill, Murphys, and San Andreas. Between 1855 and 1859, additional districts were organized for Chili Gulch, Douglas Flat, Middle Bar, Pleasant Springs, San Antonio, Vallecito, and Jesus Maria, giving the county a total of twelve districts under the direction of the first elected Superintendent of Schools, Robert Thompson.

In his report of November 1861, the dedicated Thompson chastised one of his districts for failing to follow rules that allowed them to draw public funds:

The census returns from Cave City shows that they have 48 children for which they would have been entitled to draw, if the teachers had made a report. This makes the second year that the Cave City District has lost its share of the school fund, through the neglect of its teachers.

The school fund was constructed from several sources, including private subscription, state funds, and a tax of 2½ cents on every $100 of property within the county. In 1861, the cost of operating Calaveras County schools for one year was just over $13,000, of which $4000 went to build a new school house in Murphys.

By the turn of the century, Calaveras County had fifty-seven districts with a total enrollment of nearly 2500 students. Over 50 individual school houses were in use, mostly the one-room type typical of the period.

In most small town schools of the 19th century, students from 8 grades were taught by a single teacher in the same room. Those working on the

One of the county's more impressive early schools was this two-story building in Copperopolis. (Calaveras Historical Society)

same level would be seated in the same general area of the room and while the teacher gave individual instruction to that group, the other grades were involved in written assignments or study.

(This writer feels fortunate to have spent the first three of his sixteen academic years in just such a school, one of the last of its kind in the state of Missouri. Despite what one might assume, my fellow classmates and I probably retained more from those lessons than from any we later received from five separate "specialized" teachers in "modern" multi-room schools. OHM)

The subjects taught were basic and general: reading, penmanship, English, arithmetic, science, history, and geography. For upper grades, the curriculum might have been expanded to "specifics" such as biology, chemistry, American history, literature, etc. The school day generally ran from 8:30 A.M. to 3:30 P.M. All grades took "recess" for 30 minutes mid-morning and another half-hour was allowed for lunch, which everyone brought from home in a bag or box. The restrooms were "out houses" -- one for the boys and one for the girls. Drinking water came from a deep well or nearby spring, and was usually "fetched" at the beginning of each day by the older boys.

In most cases, and as one might expect with such a large and varied classroom, the teacher ruled with an iron fist. A mild punishment would usually consist of some sort of "embarrassment", such as having the child stand in front of the class or sit in a corner for a specified time. "Corporal" punishment was common for severe disciplinary problems -- a wooden paddle, ruler, cane, or switch being applied with force and frequency to fit the offense. (For the most part, the child received far less severe punishment from the teacher than he or she would have gotten at home for the same misdeed.) Students kept after school usually had some hard explaining to do when they came home late, leading to some highly creative but seldom believable tall tales.

For children of a small Mother Lode community, many of whom had never ventured further than the next town, the school house was their one connection to the wide world which lay beyond. They learned of the trains and ships that could carry them to far-off lands where the people were strangely different from themselves. They learned of the latest inventions -- machines that could do the work of several men or make back-breaking chores as simple as turning a crank. And they learned that with education and dedication, they could be

The Petersburg School was later moved to North Branch. (Calaveras Historical Society)

This little one room schoolhouse at Esmeralda was typical of Gold Rush schools. Note the single male student - his friends were probably helping in the mines or with farm work. (Calaveras Historical Society)

anything they wanted to be. From the one-room school houses of Calaveras County came many of the men and women who would shape the future of the young state of California.

With the twentieth century came the slow demise of the one-room school. Many of Calaveras' fifty-plus districts were consolidated, the schools were enlarged, and the various grades placed in separate rooms. In 1904, the Calaveras Union High School District was approved by the voters, providing for the construction of the first school for grades nine through twelve. Both San Andreas and Angels Camp wanted the school built in their respective towns and when it was finally located in the former place, the latter decided to form their own district. Calaveras Union High School began classes at San Andreas in September, 1905. Bret Harte High School opened in Angels Camp that same fall.

Some might say that today's elementary and high school students bear absolutely no resemblance to their counterparts of a century ago. Perhaps in appearance and musical tastes they are correct. But boys are still interested in sports and mischief and girls -- and girls are still interested in romance and clothes and boys -- and for the most part, none of them are too terribly interested in going to school, although they have learned to accept it as a part of life. And whether they realize it or not, while the schools may be bigger and the rooms may be many, today's student, just like those of Gold Rush California, have the chance to see the world in a single room -- between the rivers.

151

Bibliography

Calaveras County Specific

- Calaveras County Information Directory. San Andreas, California: Calaveras County Chamber of Commerce, 1979.
- Costello, Julia G. *Historical and Archeological Research at the Calaveras Big Trees Cottage Area.* California Department of Parks and Recreation, 1968.
- ——————. *Melones: A Story of a Stanislaus River Town.* San Andreas, California: Calaveras Heritage Council, 1986.
- Elliott, W. W. *Calaveras County Illustrated and Described 1885.* Oakland, California: W. W. Elliott & Co.
- *Las Calaveras: Quarterly Bulletin of the Calaveras County Historical Society.* Vols 1 - 40, 1952-1991; San Andreas, CA.
- Long, Ernest A. (editor). *Trips to the Mines: Calaveras County 1857-1859.* San Andreas, California: Calaveras Heritage Council, 1976.
- Stone, Rhoda & Charles A. *The Tools are On the Bar: The History of Copperopolis, Calaveras County, California.* Rhoda & Charles Stone, 1991.
- Wood, Richard Coke. *Calaveras, the Land of Skulls.* Sonora California: Mother Lode Press, 1955.
- ——————. *Murphys, Queen of the Sierra.* Angels Camp, California: Calaveras Californian, 1948.
- ——————. *Big Tree - Carson Valley Turnpike Ebbetts Pass and Highway Four.* Murphys, California: Old Timers Museum, 1968, 1985.

Calaveras Related

- *A History of Tuolumne County.* San Francisco: B. F. Alley, 1882. Reprint 1983.
- Cenotto, Larry. *Logan's Alley.* 2 Vols. Jackson, California: Cenotto Publications, 1988.
- Mason, J. D. *History of Amador County California.* Oakland, California: Thompson & West, 1881
- Stoddart, Thomas Robertson. *Annals of Tuolumne County.* Edited by Carlo M. De Farrari. Fresno, California: Valley Publishers, 1977.

California Specific

- Lavender, David. *California: Land of New Beginnings.* San Francisco: Harper & Row, 1972.
- Nelson, Maidee Thomas. *California Land of Promise.* Caldwell, Idaho: Caxton Printers, 1962.
- Rolle, Andrew F. *California: A History.* New York: Thomas Y. Crowell Company, 1963.

Diaries and Other 19th Century Works

- Bancroft, Hubert H. *History of California.* 7 vols. San Francisco: History Co., 1888. Reprint. Santa Barbara: Wallace Hebbard, 1963.
- Borthwick, J. D. *Three Years in California.* Edinburgh: William Blackford & Sons, 1857. Reprint. Oakland, California: Biobooks, 1948.

- Bruff, J. Goldsborough. *Gold Rush: The Journals, Drawings, and Other Papers of J. Goldsborough Bruff, April 2, 1849 - July 20, 1851.* Edited by Georgia Willis Read and Ruth Gaines. New York: Columbia University Press, 1949.
- Colton, Walter. *Three Years in California.* New York: A. S. Barnes & Co., 1850. Reprint. Oakland, California: Biobooks, 1948.
- Doble, John. *Journal and Letters from the Mines.* Denver, Colorado: Old West Publishing Co., 1962.
- Gerstacker, Friederich. *Journal of a Journey Round the World.* New York: Harper, 1853.
- *Harper's New Monthly Magazine.* Vols. 1 - 31, New York: Harper & Bros., 1851-1865.
- Robinson, Fayette. *California and its Gold Regions.* New York: Stringer & Townsend, 1849. Reprint. New York: Promontory Press, 1974.
- Street, Franklin. *California in 1850 Compared with What it Was in 1849, with a Glimpse at its Future Destiny.* Cincinnati: Ben Franklin Books, 1851. Reprint. Ne York: Promontory Press, 1974.
- Taylor, Bayard. *El Dorado.* New York: Putnam, 1865. Various reprints.

Gold Rush Specific

- Gudde, Erwin G. *California Gold Camps.* Berkeley, California: Univ. of Ca. Press, 1975.
- Holliday, J. S. *The World Rushed In.* New York: Simon & Schuster, 1981.
- Jackson, Joseph Henry. *Anybody's Gold.* New York: D. Appleton-Century, 1941.
- Johnson, William Weber. *The Forty Niners.* Alexandria, Virginia: Time-Life Books, 1974.
- Levy, JoAnn. *They Saw the Elephant: Women in the California Gold Rush.* Hamden, Connecticut: Archon, 1990.

Gold Rush Related

- Clemens, Samuel L. (a.k.a. Mark Twain) *Roughing It.* Hartford, Connecticut: American Publishing Co., 1872. Various Reprints.
- Emanuels, Roger. *California Indians: An Illustrated Guide.* Walnut Crk., California: Diablo Bks. 1990.
- Gagey, Edmond. *The San Francisco Stage.* New York: Columbia Univ. Press, 1950.
- Clark, William B. *Gold Districts of California.* CDMG Bulletin 193. Sacramento, California: California Division of Mines and Geology, 1963. Revised 1980.
- Groh, George W. *Gold Fever.* New York: Morrow & Co., 1966.
- Harlow, Alvin F. *Bret Harte of the Old West.* New York: Julian Messner, 1943.
- Heizer, Robert F. and Whipple, M. A. *The California Indians.* Berkeley, California: Univ. of Cal. Press, 1971.
- Jackson, Joseph Henry. *Bad Company.* New York: Harcourt, Brace, & Co., 1939.
- Kroeber, Alfred L. *Handbook of the Indians of California.* Washington, D.C.: Smithsonian, 1925.
- Rourke, Constance. *Troupers of the Gold Coast.* New York: Harcourt, Brace, & Co., 1928.
- Vestal, Stanley. *Kit Carson: Happy Warrior of the Old West.* New York: Haughton Mifflin, 1928.
- Winther, Oscar Osburn. *Via Western Express & Stagecoach.* Stanford University, California: Stanford Univ. Press, 1945.

Index

Abbeys Ferry, 86
Adams & Co., 42, 43-44
Agostini and Thompson Store, 130
Alabama Gulch, 48-50
Alabama Hill, 50
Alabama House, 102-103
Albany Flat, 106-108
Alcalde, 28-30
Algiers, 115-118
Alpine Highway, 144
Alta California newspaper, 99
Alta Mine, 136
Altaville, 109
Alto Mining District, 136
Amalgamation, 95-98
American Dredging Company, 136-138
American Hotel, 102
American River, 1
Anderson's Saloon and Hall, 129
Angel, George, 3, 106
Angel, Henry, at Angels Camp, 3, 106
Angels Camp, 106-109, 111
Angels Camp Mining District, 136-138
Angels Hotel: and Mark Twain, 25-27, 111
Angels Mine, 136-138
Angier, Dr. D. L., 48-50
Antelope Trail, 91-94, 106-108
Apautawilu (Indian Village), 50
Appelamminy River, 1, 84-86
Arnold, 145-147
Arrastra, 95-98
Avery, 145-147
Bald Hill, 109
Baldwin, Drury: assemblyman, 6
Bar: defined, 69, 75
Bear Mountain, 68
Bear Valley, 147
Bella Union saloon and gambling hall, 102-105
Ben Coon, 27
Benicia: state capital at, 4-6
Beritzhoff, Alexander, 130-132
Bidwell, John, 37
Bidwell-Bartleson Party: 1-3;
    on Stanislaus River, 84-86
Big Bar, 119-122
Big Tree and Carson Valley Turnpike, 144-147
Big Tree Grove: 142-147; stage to, 126
Bigler, Gov. John:
    organizes California Rangers, 16
Black Bart (aka Charles Boles, aka Black Bart), 18,
19-21, tried at San Andreas, 105
Blood, Harvey, 144
Bloods Station, 147
Blue Mountain City, 136-138
Blue Mountain Mining District, 136-138
Boles, Charles-see Black Bart
Bolton, Charles-see Black Bart
Borthwick, J.D.: describes ferry crossing, 84-86
Boston Bar, 63-65

Botellier, Joaquin, 16
Boulder Ledge, 108
Bouvard, Father: and St. Andrews Church, 102
Brannan, Samuel:
    publisher *California Star* newspaper, 102
Bret Harte High School, 150
Brown, George and Alfred, 115-118
Brown's Express, 115-118
Brownsville, 115-118
Buhach insecticide, 57-59
Burnett, Gov. Peter H., 4
Buster, Dan, 133-135
Butterfield & Co., 44
Butterfield Overland Express (Stage), 44
Calaveras Big Trees, see Big Tree Grove
Calaveras Cement Company, 130
Calaveras Chronicle newspaper, 99-102
Calaveras County: doctors, 112-114;
    county seats, 4-6;
    county seat at San Andreas, 102-105;
    county seat at Mokelumne Hill, 119-122
Calaveras, Indians, 7-12
Calaveras, origin of name 63
Calaveras River, 1
Calaveras River, 63-65
Calaveras Skull, 109-111
Calaveras Union High School District, 150
Calaveritas Mining District, 136-138
Calaveritas: town, river, and creek, 130
California Indians, 7-12
California Rangers, 16
California Star newspaper, 99
California: independence, 4; state capitals, 4
Californian newspaper: and Bret Hart, 22-24;
    and Samuel Clemens, 25, 27;
    established, 99
Camanche Dam and Lake, 59
Camanche Mining District, 136-138
Camanche or Camanche Camp, 57-59
Camp Store, 45-47
Campo Seco Mining District, 136-138
Campo Seco: 51-53; raids on Mexicans at, 68
Canavero and Segale: saloon and store, 133
Carmen City, 94
Carrillo, Joaquin, 16, 18
Carson Creek Consolidated Mining Co., 95
Carson Hill, 87-90
Carson Hill Mining District, 138
Carson, James, 3, 106;
    describes Angels Camp, 106-108;
    describes Murphys, 115-118
Carson, Kit, 37-39;
    alleged connection with West Point, 60
Carson Pass, 36-37
Catts Camp, 57
Cave City, 133-135
Caves: at Cave City, 133-135; Moaning Cave, 118
Central Ferry, 86
Central Hill Mining District, 115-118

Central Trail, 34
Central Valley, 1
Chabot, Anthony 57-59
Chagres, Panama, 31-33
Chase's Diggings (Chase Claim), 133
Chavanne, Andre, 133-135
Chavanne Mine, 127-129
Chaw'se (grinding rocks),
    described by Doble, 12
Chee Chee Flat, 129
Cherokee Mine, 109
Chicken Ladder, 106-108
Chilean War, 119-122
Chili Gulch, 119-122, 139
Chinese Camp, 13-15
Chinese Walls, mis-identified, 79
Chinese Wars (Tong Wars), 13-15
Chinese: at Campo Seco, 51-53;
    in the Gold Rush, 13
Chinn's Store, 66
Cholera, 112
Christmas in camp, 28
Clark Ditch, 62
Clemens, Samuel (Mark Twain):
    at Angels Hotel, 111; on journalism, 99
Cold Springs Ranch (Gardner's Station), 145-147
Colton, Rev. Walter:
    publisher *Californian* newspaper, 99
Complex ores, 98
Consolidated Mining Company, 73-75
Contra Costa Water Company (CCWC), 59
Coon, Ben or Ross, 111
Copper Cañon, 76
Copper mining, 76-79;
    shipping ore, 80: at Campo Seco, 51-53
Copperopolis, 76-79, railroad to, 80-83
Copperopolis Hotel, 79
Coronel, Don Antonio, 3
Costa, Luigi: store at Calaveritas, 130
Cosumnes River, 1
Coyote mining, 73
Cradle, see Rocker
Crime in gold camps, 13-15
Cuneo, Frank, 133
Curtis, J., 144
D. L. Angier, 6
Davis-Winter Ledge, 108
Davis-Winter Ledge, 136
de Arrillaga, Gov. Jose', 84
DeCourcey, A.:
    Calaveras Chronicle editor, 99-102
Demarest, Cornelius: describes Altaville, 109
DeMartini Ranch, 65
Den, Dr. Richard Somerset, 114
Diamond Bar, 79
Diegueno Indians, 7-9
Diggings (diggin's or digs): origin of term, 69
Discovery Tree, 142
Diseases of miners, 114

Ditches, Union, 115-118
Ditches: Clark, 62; origin of, 72;
    Silver Ditch, Union Ditch,
    Table Mountain Ditch, 102;
    origin of, 69-72; Union Ditch, 115-118
Doble, John: at Pleasant Springs, 6;
    mentions women in camp, 54-56;
    and Pleasant Springs Indians, 12, 50
Dogtown, 132
Dolores River, 1
Donner Party, 37-39
Dorrington (Gardners Station), 145-147
Doten, Alfred: in Jenny Lind area, 130-132
Double Springs: second county seat, 4-6
Douglas Flat, 118
Douglas Hill (Showalter Hill), 102
Dowd, Augustus T., 142
Dredging: in Camanche District, 136-138
Drift mining, 73-75
Dry Diggin's, 66
Duck Bar, 133-135
Dueling, 105
Dunbar Ranch, 145-147
Duran, Father Narciso:
    and origin of name Mokelumne, 119
E. P. Jones: pub. California Star, 99
Eagle Hotel, 129
East Bay Municipal Utilities District
    (East Bay MUD), 57-59
Ebbetts Pass, 144
Echeandia, Governor of California, 1-3
El Dorado, 127
El Rio Guadalupe, 84
Emigrant Trail, 34-39, 142-144
Emigrants: methods of travel, 31-33
Entertainment: in the mining camps, 47, 56
Eproson, Robert, 53
Esmeralda (Indian Creek), 133-135
Estanislao, 84-86
Etna Mine, 109
Executive Order L208, 141
Express companies, 40-44; Brown's Express, 118
Farnham, Eliza, 54
Feather River, 1
Felix, Sylvester & Josephine, 91-94
Felix, town of, 94
Ferries, 86-90
Finnegan, James, 95
Fires: Angels Camp, 106-108; Copperopolis, 79;
    Milton, 83; Murphys, 118;
    San Andreas, 102-105; Vallectio, 102-105
Foreman, David, 130-132
Foreman's Ranch, 130-132
Forks in the Road (Altaville), 106-108, 109
Fort John, Amador County, 148
Forty-niner Trail, 34-39
Fourth Crossing, 130-132
Fremont, John C.: describes Mokelumne River,
    193; maps Calaveras River, 63;

names Stanislaus River, 84-86;
  crosses Sierra Mountains, 37
French Camp, San Joaquin County, 86
French Hill, 119-122
French, J. M., 87-90
French War: at Mok Hill, 122;
  at San Andreas, 102
Fricot City, 135
Fricot, Desire, 135
Furguson, A. P., 127-129
Gamblers, 15, 45-47
Gann Ranch and Station, 147
Gardner's Station (Dorrington), 145-147
Gaston Hill Mine, 139
Gatewood, William J., 105
Gerstaecker, Friedreich: at Murphys, 115-118
Gilbert, Eliza (aka Lola Montez), 56
Gillis, Jim, 111
Glencoe, 60
Gold Camps: life in 25-30, provisions for, 45
Gold Hill, 102
Gold Hill House, 102-105;
  as first county hospital, 114
Gold: origins, 69-72;
  prior to the Gold Rush, 69;
  where found, 73
Golden Era newspaper, 24
Goodwyn, Dr. Peterson, 105
Gopher Ridge, 91; copper mines, 76
Gorgona, Panama, 31-33
Grasshopper City, see Telegraph City
Greasertown, 63-35; raids on Mexicans at, 68
Greely, Horace, stage ride of, 126
Green & Vogan Stage lines, 123-126
Ground sluicing, 73
Grunsky, Charles, 6, 48-50
Guadalupe Hidalgo, Treaty of, 4
Guadelupe River, 1
Gum Tree Claim, 22-24
Gwin Mine, 139
Gwin, William, 139-141
Haggin, Ben Ali, 127-129
Halfway House, 145
Hamilton, H., *Calaveras Chronicle* editor, 99-102
Hance, John, 95
Hanford, William, 142
Hangtown (Placerville), 3
Happy Valley, 119-122
Hard rock mining, 73-75
Harte, Bret (aka Francis B. Hart), 22-24;
  arrival on Stanislaus, 84;
  on school children, 148;
  "To the Pliocene Skull", 111
Hearst, George, 127-129
Heckendorn Mine, 136-138
Hill, Myron, 106
Hodson, 94, 139

Hodson Mining District, 139
Hoerchner, Dr. Adolph H., 48-50; 114
Hog Hill, 76, 79
Hog Pen Mine, 109
Hogan Dam, 63-65
Holden, Erastus, S., 79, 80-83
Holman, Constable S. D., 57
Hughes, Hiram, 76-79
Hughes, William Napoleon Bonaparte, 76
Humbolt River, 36
Humbolt Sink, 37
Hung'e (roundhouse), 12
Hutchins, William, 147
Hydraulic mining, 73-75
Independence, 62
Independence Rock, 36
Indian Creek, 133
Indian Gulch 60
Indians, 7-12; cave burial, 135;
  Estanislao, 84-86
Irvine, William: and Morgan Mine, 138
Jackass Hill, 25-27, 111
Jackey Camp, 127
Jackson, as Calaveras County seat, 6
James Bar, 68
Jeffrey, William, 87
Jenny Bar, 66-68
Jenny Lind, 65; 66-68
Jenny Lind Mining District, 139
Jim Smiley and His Jumping Frog, 25-27
Joaquins, the five, 16
Johnston, Wade:
  describes Upper Calaveritas, 130
Jones, Dr. William, 109-111
Jumping Frog Jubilee, 111
Jumping Frog of Calaveras County, 25-27
Jupiter Gravel Mining and Water Co., 130-132
Keefer, Willaim A.: disappearance of, 132
Keen, Richard Augustus:
  relates "Nigger Hill" story, 119-122
Kentucky House, 102-105
Keystone Mine, 109
Kings River, 1
Kohlberg, 48
Kongsberg (Silver City), 147
La Grange, 22-24, school house, 24
La Riviere, 130-132
Lancha Plana, 59
Las Llagas River, 1
Lasquisimes, see Stanislaus River
Latham, Milton, 80-83
Latimer's, 63-65
Laughlin, Edward, 79
Le Pasión River, 1
Leoni, Giacamo, 65
Les Fourcades, 119-122
Lightner Mine, 136
Limerick Camp, see Camanche

Lind, Dr. John Y., 65-68
Lind, Jenny, 66
Liquor in the mines, 47
Littlejohn Creek, 91-94
Lode Mining, 95-98
Lode: defined, 75; described, 69;
  technical description, 75
Long Tom, 72
Lotta Crabtree, 56
Love, Capt. Harry, 16
Lower Calaveritas, 130
Madam Felix Copper Mining
  District, 91-94, 139
Madison Mine, 98
Magnolia Saloon, 118
Maidu Indians, 7
Mail to the mines, 40-44
Mammoth Tree Hotel, 142
Mark Twain (aka Samuel Clemens), 25-27
Markleeville, 147
Marshall, Ben: and Joaquin Murietta, 16;
  ranch on Marshall's Trail, 91
Marshall, James, 3: test for gold, 54
Matson, Jim, 109-111
Matteson, Edward, and hydraulic mining, 73
Matteson, T. J., stage line 126
Matteson's Big Tree Stage, 145
McCarty, Thomas, 91
McKeon, John, 127
McLean, George, 87
McLeans Ferry, 86-87
Me-wuk (Miwok) Indians, 7-12;
  and Mokelumne River, 119;
  at Murphys, 115;
  at Apautawilu (Pleasant Springs), 50
Melones, 3, 87-90; mines, 87, 138
Melones & Stanislaus Gold, Silver,
  & Copper Mining Company, 90
Melones Dam and Reservoir, 90
Meloneys, see Melones
Merced River, 1
Metropolitan Hotel, 105
Mexicans; at Campo Seco, 51-53;
  in the Gold Rush, 13
Middle Bar, 1-3;
Milton, 80-83
Miners, lifestyles, 25-30
Mines, 136-141; at San Andreas, 105;
  of San Antone, 133; Altaville, 109;
  San Andreas, 108, 109-111;
  West Point area, 60-62; Oro y Plata, 115-118;
  districts, 136-141;
  of Sheep Ranch, 129;
  quartz gold, 95-98
Mines, Morgan, 87-90
Mining, 69-75, glossary of terms, 75
Mining Districts, 136-141
Mining Methods, 69-75
Missouri Gulch, 115-118

Mitchler Hotel (Murphys Hotel), 145
Moaning Cave, 118
Modoc Indians, 12
Mokelumne Hill & Campo Seco Canal, 53, 57
Mokelumne Hill, 119-122; Mining District, 139;
  third county seat at, 4-6;
  first school at, 148
Mokelumne River, 1; camps of the, 57-59;
  origin of name, 119; Middle Fork, 60;
  South Fork, 60
Monk, Henry, 126
Montez, Lola, 54-56
Moonlight Flat, 105
Moraga, Gabriel, 1; and Yokut Indians, 9;
  explores the Stanislaus, 84;
  discovers the Calaveras River, 63
Moran Ranch, 145,
Morgan, A., 95
Morgan Mine, 87-90, 95, 136-138
Mormon Trail, 34-36
Morse, Harry, 18
Mosquito Gulch, 60
Mother Lode: defined, 1, 69, 75
Mother of the Forest, 142
Mount Reba, 147
Mountain King Mine, 139
Mountain Ranch, 127
Mountain Ranch Mining District, 139
Muir, John, on Big Tree Grove, 142
Munoa, Manuel, 65
Muñoz, Father Pedro, diaries of, 84
Murietta, Joaquin, 16-18; in Murphys, 118;
  at Yaqui Camp, 105
Murphy, John and Daniel, 3, 106;
  and town of Murphys, 115
Murphys, 115-118; and Big Tree Road, 145
Napoleon City, 79
Napoleon Mine, 76-79
New Diggings, 91-94
New Hogan Reservoir,
  effects on Calaveras camps, 63-65
Newspapers, 99-102
Nigger Hill, 119-122
North American House, 66, 68
North Branch, 63-65
North Gulch, 66
O'Byrnes Ferry, 86
O'Neil Creek, 130
Ocomorenia, Joaquin, 16
Old Gulch, 130
Old Spanish Trail, 34
Old Woman Gulch, 139
Onion Valley, 147
Oregon Gulch, 51
Oregon Trail, 34
Owlsberg, 115-118
Pacific Railroad Bill of 1862, 80
Paloma Mining District, 139
Panama City, 31-33

Panama, crossing 31-33
Panning: equipment, 69, methods, 69
Pardee Dam: effects on Campo Seco, 51-53
Pardee Reservoir, 59
Parkhurst, Charlie, 60-62
Parrots Ferry, 86
Pay dirt: defined 69-72
Peach Orchard, 91
Pellet, Sarah, 54
Penn Mine, 136-138
Penn Mining Company, 51-53
Pennsylvania Gulch, 115-118
Perez, Benito, 3
Perry's Store, 66
Petersburg, 63
Physicians, 112-114
Pike, Jacob, 94
Pine Log Mining, 139
Pioneer Cemetery, 63
Pioneer Hotel, 129
Pioneer Road (Stockton Road), 106
Piper, Philip F., 102
Pit, hydraulic, 73
Placer gold: defined, 69, 73, 75
Placer Times newspaper, 99
Pleasant Springs, 112;
    confusion with Pleasant Valley, 6;
Pleasant Valley, 63, 66;
    proclaimed first county seat, 4-6
Poison Springs, 147
Polk, President James K.:
    mentions California gold, 10
Pope, Capt. Robert, 102
Poverty Bar, 57
Prostitution, 15, 54-56
Provisions, 45-47
Quail Hill, 76
Quartz gold: defined, 73;
    early mining of, 73-75:
    mining methods, 95-98
Railroad Flat, 62
Railroad Flat Mining District, 139-141
Railroads: early history of 80;
    in Calaveras County, 80-83
Rasberry, Bennager, 106-108
Red House Ranch, 91-94
Reddick, William: at Fourth Crossing, 130-132
Reed & McCarty discover copper, 76
Reeds Turnpike, 76-79
Reserve Mine, 136-138
Reynolds & Co., 40
Reynolds Ferry, 86
Rich Gulch Mining District, 139-141
Rich Gulch: on Calaveras River, 139; Upper, 48;
    near San Antonio, 133;
    in many locations, 119; Lower, 48;
    near Jenny Lind, 66

Riffles, 69-72
Rio le Pasión, 1
Rivers: American, 1; Appelamminy, 1;
    Calaveras, 1; Calaveras, 63-65;
    Cosumnes, 1; Dolores, 1; Feather, 1;
    Guadelupe, 1; Humbolt, 36; Kings, 1;
    Las Llagas, 1; Le Pasión, 1; Merced, 1;
    Mokelumne, 1; San Francisco, 1;
    Stanislaus, 1, 84-86; Tuolumne, 1
Robinson, John, 51-53
Robinsons Ferry, 86-90;
    visited by Bret Harte, 22-24
Rock Creek, 91-94
Rock Creek Grove, 80-83
Rock walls at Telegraph City, 79
Rocker (cradle), 69-72
Romaggi family; home at Albany Flat, 106
Roosevelt, President Franklin D.:
    executive order L208, 141
Roundhouse, 10-12
Routes to California, 31-39
Royal Consolidated Mining, 139
Royal Mine, 94, 139
Sacramento: made state capital, 4
Salt Lake City, 34-36
Salt Spring Valley, 91-94
Samuel Clemens (aka Mark Twain), 25-27
San Andreas, 102-105; awarded county seat 4-6
San Andreas Independent newspaper, 102
San Andreas Mining District, 139-141
San Antonio Camp (San Antone), 133
San Antonio Creek, 130-133
San Domingo, 133
San Domingo Creek, 130-132
San Francisco River, 1
San Jose: first state capital, 4
Sandias, 87-90
Sante Fe Trail, 34
Schools, 148-150; Salt Spring Valley, 91-94
Scribner, John and Philip, 106
Second Crossing, 63, 130
Sentinels (Guardsmen), 142
Serra, Father Junipero, 7
Sheep Ranch (Sheepranch), 127
Sheep Ranch Mining District, 139-141
Sheepranch Mine, 127-129
Sierra Mountains: crossing 37-39
Sierra Railway, 83
Silver City (Kongsberg), 145-147
Silver Ditch, 102
Skull Cave, 133-135
Slab Ranch, 106-108
Slickens, 73-75; defined 75
Sluice Box, 69-72
Slumgullion, 87
Smith, Jedediah Strong, 1;
    on Stanislaus River, 84-86
Smith, Tom, 127-129

Soap Gulch, 60
Sonora Herald newspaper, 99-102
South Gulch, 63
Sperry and Perry, 142; hotel 115-118
St. Joseph Lead Company, 129
St. Joseph, Missouri, 34
Stagecoaches, 123-126
Stamp Mill, 95-98
Stanislaus River, 1, 84-86
Stevenot family, 90
Stevenot, Gabriel, and Reserve Mine, 136-138
Stevenson, Col. Jonathan, 51;
    members of regiment in Calaveras, 106;
    on Stanislaus River, 84-86
Stockton, founded as Tuleberg, 84-86
Stockton Hill, 119-122
Stockton Road (Pioneer Road), 68, 106-108
Stockton-Copperopolis Railroad, 79-83
Stores, storekeepers, and provisions, 28-30, 45-47
Stoutenburg (or Stoutenberg), 115
Sublette Route, 34-36
Sullivan, John, 127
Sundays in camp, 28
Sutter Creek, Amador County, 3
Sutter, Johann (aka John Sutter), 3
Sutter's Fort, 3
Sweetwater Creek, 34-36
Table Mountain, 65
Tailings, 95-98
Tamarack, 145-147
Taylors Bar, 65
Telegraph City, 76-79
Territorial Enterprise newspaper, 25
Tertiary, defined, 69-73, 75; gold in, 73-75;
    drift mining, 73
Tevis, Lloyd, 127-129
Thanksgiving in camp, 28
Third Crossing, 102-105, 130-132
Thomas, F. F., 139-141
Thompson, Superintendent Robert, 148
Thorn, Sheriff Ben: at Wallace shootout, 57
Three Card Monte, 45-47
Three Fingered Jack, 16
Tobin, Capt., 48
Todd, Alexander, 40-42
Tong Wars, 13-15
Tongs, Chinese, 13-15
Tornado Hotel, 80-83
Tower, Jacob, 91-94
Transportation: early forms of, 80;
    railroads, 80-83; early trails, 123;
    stage service, 123-126
Trappers, early French at Mok Hill, 119
Treaty of Guadalupe Hidalgo, 4
Tremont House, 66-68
Truckee Pass, 36
Tulare Lake, 91-94
Tule Lake, 91-94
Tuleberg, 84-86

Tuolumne River, 1
Tuolumne: village named by Moraga, 84
Twain, Mark, see Clemens, Samuel
Union Copper Mine, 76-79
Union Gold Mine, 102-105, 139-141
Union Water Company, 142; ditch, 115-118
Upper Calaveritas, 130
Utica Mine, 136
Valenzuela, Joaquin, 16
Vallecito (Murphy's Old Diggins), 115
Vallecito Mining District, 141
Vallejo, Gen. Mariano, 4
Vallejo: state capital, 4
Valley Springs, 83
Van Ee, J. C. Kemp, 139
Victor Mine, 109
Volcano: connection with West Point, 60-62
Wallace, 57, 83
Wallace, W. A., 127-129
Weaverville, 13-15
Weber, Capt. Charles M., 3;
    establishes Tuleberg (Stockton), 84-86;
    ranch, 119, mining expedition, 119
Wells Fargo, 42-44; and Black Bart, 19-21
West Point, 60-62
West Point Mining District, 141
Wheeler, Simon, 111
White House Ranch, 91
Williams Springs, 145-147
Wimmer, Elizabeth, 54
Wingdam (Wingdam Stage), 118
Winter Brothers, 75
Winters Bar, 57, 68
Wintertown (Altaville), 109
Women: in the Gold Rush, 54-56
Wood, Harvey, 87-90
Workman, William, 130
Yaqui Camp, 130
Yellow Bird, 16
Yokut Indians, 7-9
Zwinge, Joseph: prop. American Hotel, 102